REINVENTING
ADULT JEWISH
LEARNING

REINVENTING ADULT JEWISH LEARNING

BETSY DOLGIN KATZ

KTAV Publishing House, Inc.

KTAV Publishing House, Inc.
888 Newark Avenue, Suite 119
Jersey City, NJ 07306
Email: *bernie@ktav.com*
www.ktav.com
(201) 963-9524
fax: (201) 963-0102

Library of Congress Cataloging-in-Publication Data

Katz, Betsy Dolgin
Reinventing adult Jewish learning / Betsy Dolgin Katz.
    p. cm.
Includes bibliographical references.
ISBN 978-1-60280-207-0
1. Katz, Betsy Dolgin--Career in Jewish education. 2. Jewish educators--
United States. 3. Jewish religious education of adults--United States. 4.
Judaism--Study and teaching (Continuing education)--United States. I. Title.
BM102.K36A3 2012   2012006813
296.6'8--dc23

Dedicated to **Florence Zacks Melton** who
provided the design and inspiration for the
reinvention of adult Jewish learning. — B.D.K.

Contents

Introduction

Like so many significant occurrences in life, writing this book began very simply. I received a phone call from the chairman of a task force whose goal was to select the first group of Avi Chai Foundation Fellows. I was asked if I would be interested in writing a proposal for a book about my experiences in Jewish education, a professional memoir. Believing that others could benefit from reading about my decades as an educator in the Jewish community, Avi Chai offered me an opportunity to pass along the lessons learned in my generation to the next. It was to be a personal story—not research; a record of experiences and observations—not investigations. The mission of the Avi Chai Foundation, which had been created and endowed by Zalman Bernstein, is perpetuation of Jews, Jewish literacy, and Judaism and ensuring the centrality of the State of Israel to the Jewish people. Jewish learning for adults in all varieties of settings advances these goals.

In reflecting on my career, I saw my work in the context of events that shaped the American Jewish community. An incredible combination of history, experiences, and teachers influenced me. My professional journey was shaped by political and social forces at work around me. Looking around my office cluttered with papers, articles, workshops, and books, I understood that my career was guided by a continuous, intense desire to learn, to teach, to write, and to share knowledge with other professionals. I chose not to enter academia but rather to bring the research and scholarship I could acquire to the practice of adult Jewish learning. An opportunity to write about it was a natural extension of this process.

I can confidently say that I am the only Jewish educator in history born in Fairbury, population: 2,500. It is a rural community in central Illinois known best for Honegger's Feed Mill, the annual Livingston County Fair, and its consolidated country school system. Fairbury's Jewish population never topped thirteen. In spite (or maybe because) of that, I never took my Judaism and our Jewish identity for granted. I knew I was Jewish and grew up eagerly learning about it.

From the time I was very young, my father transformed our "playroom" into a "Sunday school" where he taught my two sisters and me about Jewish holidays, history, and Hebrew from books sent by our concerned aunts who lived in Chicago, one hundred miles away. Our mother taught us how to create a *kosher* Shabbat-observant home under the most challenging circumstances. We had home schooling before there was a name for what we were doing.

Another inspiration was my grandmother, Dinah Shulman Pershin, who arrived in America from Russia in 1910 at the age of seventeen. She lacked any formal education, but anticipating coming to America, she asked a wealthy, educated woman in her *shtetl* to teach her English in exchange for cleaning chicken coops and the indoor area where chickens were herded on cold Russian nights. The lessons provided her with enough English to navigate the maze of experiences that awaited her in America. My grandmother died at one hundred and four, but her stories, her life, and her values remain with me.

One subtle, perhaps unintended lesson on the value of Jewish learning I was taught while helping Grandma and my mother prepare the house for *Pesach*. The story was about how she and her four brothers and sisters helped ready their one-room home for Passover. Grandma Dinah had three very important responsibilities. One was getting on her hands and knees and using a large spoon she would scrape an assigned section of the dirt floor of their one-room home, searching for *hametz*, "crumbs," that may have fallen and been pressed into the ground. Another responsibility was to *kasher* their few dishes and utensils for the holiday. Walking to the stream on the edge of the village and immersing dishes and utensils in the water sometimes required chopping a hole in the ice. Then, after three days, she would return to the stream and, when necessary, chop the items free from new ice which had formed. Grandma's third responsibility—her favorite—touched me most deeply. She would wait for a windy day and then take books from a small corner cupboard and lay them on an old blanket in front of their house. When all the books were spread open on the cloth, she would watch the wind blow through their pages removing the *hametz* that may have fallen in their crevices as her father and brothers were studying.

A one-room house with a dirt floor. Pots soaking in the stream. Books. No matter how poor or unadorned life was, books were a valued possession. When I was a child, I, too, would look for crumbs that might have fallen in my books. As I grew older, the story of the books reminded me of the significance of learning for Jews in every generation.

In fact, it was Mrs. Danforth who linked my enthusiasm for books with teaching. She was the second-grade teacher at Isaac Walton Elementary School in Fairbury. She was never my teacher but, when I was in sixth grade, she had to leave school early one day. My friend Marsha and I were asked to take charge of Mrs. Danforth's class; her son, a soldier during the Korean War, was unexpectedly coming through Fairbury for a brief visit. Mrs. Danforth gave us careful instructions: Tell the students to draw pictures to illustrate the story you will be reading them. You can play the records on the table while they draw and color. Walk up and down the rows while they are working and talk with them about what they are doing. Our sixth-grade teacher was right across the hall in case we needed him.

That night I wrote in my diary:

Dear Diary,
Today I taught school. Mrs. Danforth had to go home early. Marsha and I stayed with the class. We drew pictures, played records, and read stories. It was great!

That was it. I never looked back. I wanted to be a teacher.

When we lived briefly in Great Neck, NY, my formal Jewish learning began. I attended Hebrew High School at Temple Israel. My parents had prepared me well so I soon felt part of the community. The Conservative movement's Leaders Training Fellowship offered challenging study based on materials prepared by Chaim Potok and Joel Kramer. It led to my taking a leadership role in United Synagogue Youth, whose programs centered on informal learning and socializing. Through all these activities, I was influenced and supported by my Hebrew high school teacher, USY director, and leader of the Shabbat Youth Service, possibly because they were the same person— Harold Malitzky. Harold affected how I thought, prayed, and played. As I would realize later, connecting to Judaism happens most readily when there are multiple experiences within a close community. Classes, prayer, social activities, camping, travel, and the arts brought me into a warm and fascinating world and launched my journey toward becoming a Jewish educator.

Camp Ramah in Wisconsin strengthened my commitments to learning and to that community. There, my passion for Jewish text study and for the State of Israel originated. I studied my first page of Talmud with Rabbi Seymour Fox, *Tanach* with Rabbi Yohanan Muffs, and the philosophy of Abraham Joshua Heschel with Rabbi Louis Newman. There I met, in order of importance, my husband Michael and Samuel Mendel Melton. The summer of 1964 summed it up: Michael and I were married in June, spent our honeymoon as counselors with sixty Ramah high school students in Israel, and returned to the United States to attend graduate school at Ohio State University in Columbus. I was hired as assistant principal at Tifereth Israel in Columbus, a synagogue school testing a new Melton Bible curriculum. There I taught my first adult education class. I was mentored and inspired by Dr. Saul Wachs who directed the educational program.

My work in synagogues continued when we moved to Chicago and I became the assistant principal at North Suburban Synagogue Beth El. Choosing that position in spite of a Master of Arts degree in English literature and a job offer from a public high school, was a turning point in my life. "There are many people who can teach English," my father said at the time, "but few who can contribute to Jewish education." Although my formal education had prepared me to be an English teacher, my experiences had prepared me to be a Jewish educator. Under the tutelage of Dr. Louis Katzoff, I learned how to run a school with over 1,000 students and became more adept and committed to teaching texts to children and adults. At that time, I also learned from Shrage Arian, a member of Beth El Congregation and the Superintendent of Chicago's Board of Jewish Education. Shrage was once asked, "If you had only five minutes to teach Torah, what would you do?" After only a brief hesitation, Shrage answered, "I would pick up the Torah and dance with it!"

While raising my family, I remained connected to Jewish education, specifically to teaching my peers. Parent Effectiveness Training (PET) was popular in those days so Fran Alpert, a close friend and public school teacher, and I began teaching JET (Jewish Effectiveness Training) which provided women with knowledge of Judaism and the skills to bring Jewish activities and observance into their homes. Fran and I planned to create a women's learning center. For funding, we turned to Dolores Kohl, an educator and a philanthropist. Dolores had a higher priority and convinced us to change direction. We helped her create the Kohl Jewish Teacher Center where I began my work in teacher education.

My experiences at the Kohl Jewish Teacher Center followed by sixteen years at the Board of Jewish Education and the Community Foundation for Jewish Education in Chicago prepared me for what came next: more than two decades as the North American Director and an adult educator with the Florence Melton Adult Mini-School (FMAMS). Florence Melton was a prophet. When the Hebrew University's Melton Centre created the curriculum for the Florence Melton Adult Mini-School in the early 1980s, it was anticipating a time when fighting assimilation in North America through adult Jewish literacy education would be a priority. By the time communities around the country were seeking to assure Jewish continuity through learning, the Mini-School had already been tested, adapted, and proven successful. This two-year school for Jewish adults spread rapidly around the country. By now it has educated 30,000 individuals in over one hundred communities around the world.

My experiences in Jewish education and, specifically, in adult Jewish learning began at a time when adult learning was expanding and taking on a distinctive American identity. Earlier, American Jews had recognized their responsibility for ensuring the future of Judaism. With the destruction of Eastern European Jewry and the end of that center of learning and culture, the world's largest surviving center of Jewish population took on the task of inspiring and educating another generation. A brief overview of the history of Jewish learning in America and the evolution of this new context for adult learning can be found in the opening section of this book. This set the stage for the work I was to pursue.

In 1975, when Ktav published Dr. Israel M. Goldman's *Lifelong Learning Among Jews: Adult Education in Judaism from Biblical Times to the Twentieth Century* and addressed the state of adult Jewish learning in the United States, the author recognized the contributions to adult Jewish learning made by individual rabbis, the seminaries of three major branches of Judaism and their constituencies, local boards of Jewish education, Hebrew colleges, and B'nai B'rith. He considered adult learning to be "a major activity in American Jewry."

My career extends from the last period of adult Jewish education Goldman describes. There have been major shifts in the Jewish community since that time including where and how adults learn and what they learn. Although changes continue to occur, lessons learned during the last four decades remain useful—in the same way that wisdom from prior generations strengthened my work. A purpose of this book is to communicate some of those lessons.

Diversity in the American Jewish community has increased exponentially. Adult learning has had to reinvent itself to remain attractive and relevant. America offers Jews almost limitless religious freedom, allowing individuals to construct personal versions of Judaism. At one extreme are those who assimilate. On the other hand, there are many who seek Jewish knowledge in order to take responsibility for their Jewish life and that of their children and grandchildren. Within one person's lifetime, "Jewish life" changes constantly. When following existing models does not work as it has in the past, Jewish learning allows adults to discover or create their own pathways within the broad Jewish community.

The last four decades have witnessed adaptations of existing institutions and the creation of new programs and institutions to serve Jewish adults. In examining the innovations, I focus on four major settings that responded to the increasing diversity: synagogues, nationwide education efforts, teacher education centers, and Israel education. In addition, I describe innovative programs in federations, retreat settings, and Jewish community centers. The pages that follow comprise my professional memoir. It contains accounts of challenges, successes, failures, and the lessons learned from them. There remain unanswered questions and unfulfilled needs that are raised throughout the book—particularly in the final chapter.

Sections of chapters called "Other Voices" are written by educators and community leaders with whom I worked. Their experiences illustrate and expand lessons learned. Their stories and commentaries add color, variety, and depth to my accounts of adult learning.

This is a book for leaders committed to learning, members of institutions who plan adult programs, academics and their students, professionals who work with adults in formal and informal education settings, and students who learn in continuing education classes. It is hoped that the models and lessons will inspire, inform, and support their vital role in sustaining and enriching American Jewish life.

Acknowledgements

Before I began writing *Reinventing Adult Jewish Learning*, I was under the impression that writing a professional memoir was simply a matter of remembering and documenting. Writing this book became so much more. Although initially invisible to me, historical and social forces, educational advancements and retreats, fortunate choices and fortuitous accidents shaped my professional life. Most remarkable are the family, friends, and colleagues who have been indispensible teachers, models, guides, and inspiration throughout my career.

I could not have written this book without the love of Judaism and Jewish learning instilled by my parents, Seymour, *z"l*, and Saralie Dolgin, *z"l*. I also could not have written this book without the initiative and support of the Avi Chai Foundation these past three years. In between these points were my rabbis and teachers Rabbi Alan Bregman, *z"l*; Dr. Barry Chazan; Rabbi Burton Cohen; Alan Hoffmann; Dr. Louis Katzoff, *z"l*; Dolores Kohl; Rabbi Vernon Kurtz; Harold Malitzky, *z"l*; Dr. Jonathan Sarna; Rabbi Samuel Schaffler, *z"l*; Dr. Saul Wachs; Gordon Zacks; and Florence Zacks Melton, *z"l*.

At my side were colleagues, who not only taught, led, and inspired me along the journey but who are the twenty-four individuals who lent their "Voices" to this narrative describing, from their perspective, the reinvention of adult Jewish learning.

Thank you to Rabbi Karen Kedar who answered the questions of a novice writer, modeled good writing discipline, and connected me to Arthur Maggida, the person who not only edited my work but taught me how to write. And to Seymour Rossel—how grateful I am that our paths crossed once again—you saw the need for this book and supported me enthusiastically through its completion.

My gratitude extends to students at Spertus Insitute, Gratz College, Chicago Board of Jewish Education, and the Community Foundation for Jewish Education who continue to teach me and influence my writing.

Thank you to my friends who stuck with me in spite of my obsession, who cheered me on when I was frustrated and hugged me when I reached a milestone. Thank you to those friends who provided guidance—whether it related to law, writing, education or publishing.

I am grateful to my children and grandchildren, Allen and Jill Katz, Jacob and Shira; Hannah Katz and Craig Kornbluth, Dina, Rachel and Evan—and to my sisters Erica Dolgin and Miriam Kohn. You kept up my spirits and my focus on the ultimate goal. This book is part of a legacy—not only a physical object and a record of where and why I loved my work—but I hope you also find in it a spiritual legacy reflecting what is beautiful, enriching, and meaningful in Judaism and the Jewish community.

Michael, I could not have done this without your love, your encouragement, and your support. Whether it was a kiss, a celebration of an accomplishment with a homemade gourmet dinner, a precise proofreading of a chapter, or a computer adjustment, you were there for me. You bless me on Friday night, but you are my blessing.

As we recite when completing a tractate of the Talmud—or a Melton course—I close with the words "May it be Your will, my God, that as You have helped me to complete this portion of my studies, that You will continue to help me begin new areas of learning—to teach and to learn ...."

Background
The World
We Entered

The secret to success in life is to be ready for opportunity when it comes. — Benjamin Disraeli

Chapter I

Surviving Catastrophe

American Jews are realizing that they have been spared for a sacred task—to preserve Judaism and its cultural, social and moral values.
— American Jewish Yearbook, 1941

Adult Jewish learning developed and eventually thrived in North America out of necessity. As a result of the destruction of the Eastern European Jewish community, America became a reluctant host to the largest Jewish community in the world. Despite all that occurred in World War II and the difficulties entering American society, many Jews devoted themselves to expanding Jewish education and culture. To some, being Jewish was a form of resistance, a way to rise above the horrors of the Holocaust and continue as Jews in the name of those who had perished. To others, learning became a way to recapture what was positive and revitalizing in Judaism. Leaders established organizations for Christian-Jewish dialogue and for Jewish advocacy. They founded day schools, camps, and new synagogues. Jewish community centers helped integrate refugees and immigrants into American society and then redesigned themselves into centers for the entire community. In spite of the pressures they perceived to become "American," many Jews helped resettle and support European Jews in the struggling Jewish community in Palestine.

Other Voices

Dr. Eliot Lefkowitz, education consultant at Am Yisrael congregation, Northfield, Illinois and adjunct professor at Spertus Institute of Jewish Studies and Loyola University of Chicago

We have an awesome responsibility, not only to bear witness to the *Shoah* but also to perpetuate the traditions the Nazis sought so brutally to destroy. Among these was the idea that lifelong Jewish learning would lead to a life infused with Jewish values, Jewish identity and a Jewish belief system. Through lifelong Jewish learning, we engage in an ongoing dialogue with Jewish sages. Those lost in the *Shoah* had engaged in a similar dialogue. Through lifelong Jewish learning, we confront fundamental questions about God and about human beings. Those lost in the *Shoah* had confronted similar questions. And through lifelong Jewish learning, we engage with classical Jewish texts. Those lost in the *Shoah* had engaged with those texts.

Lifelong Jewish learning seeks to make Judaism relevant to our lives. It helps us realize that Judaism enriches not only our minds but also our souls. We come to understand that study leads to moral and ethical action: those lost in the *Shoah* had a similar understanding. We hear the voice of God, the same voice heard by those lost in the *Shoah*. Adult Jewish education links us with those who perished. It not only honors the dead but also witnesses to the fact that the Jews are an eternal people whose core value is *Talmud Torah k'neged kulam*, "The study of Torah exceeds all."

Jewish intellectuals became spokesmen—they were primarily men—of a generation of prominent authors and journalists read by non-Jews as well as Jews. As Elliot E. Cohen, the founding editor of *Commentary* magazine, wrote in the first issue in 1975,

We have faith that out of the opportunities of our experience here, there will evolve new patterns of living, new modes of thought, which will harmonize heritage and country into a true sense of at-home-ness in the modern world. Surely, we who have survived catastrophe can survive freedom, too.

The founding of the State of Israel in 1948 immeasurably affected the identity of millions of Jews around the world. The pride in Israel's birth and its heroic defense against seemingly impossible odds were reflected in the growth of synagogue membership, the strengthening of Jewish organizations and the expansion of Jewish philanthropy. Jewish self-esteem was also bolstered when Will Herberg's *Protestant, Catholic and Jew* was published—the book title put 3 percent of the population on equal standing with other religious groups in America.

We affiliated with Jewish organizations, yet we still desired to blend in. We wanted to be Jewish, but not *too* Jewish. Synagogues reflected that paradox. In the late 1940s and 1950s, Reform and Conservative synagogues thrived. Reconstructionist Judaism, which had been created in America in the 1920s under the leadership of Mordecai Kaplan, grew along with these other denominations. Jews' upward mobility was reflected by so many moving to the suburbs. Building synagogues and paying dues became an expression of Jewish identity. Jonathan Sarna writes in *American Judaism* (2004), 60 percent of America's Jews were affiliated with synagogues by the 1950s, "a figure never exceeded and the only time in the twentieth century that more than half of America's Jews were synagogue members."

Synagogues provided a place to celebrate being Jewish and to identify as a Jew. Whether it was for holidays or Shabbat, weddings, *b'nai mitzvah*, births, or deaths, Jews gathered for community and rituals at key moments of their lives. In place of the home as the source of Jewish learning and identity, Hebrew schools and Sunday schools were given responsibility for the next generation. Unfortunately, parents sent children to learn, but few parents were interested in deepening their own knowledge and identity. In effect, synagogues were constructed with revolving doors: families entered so children could prepare for confirmation and *b'nai mitzvah* and exited soon after the ceremony and the party. With adult learning a low priority among Conservative and Reform Jews, the lack of education was reflected in weakening commitment to Jewish values and rituals: by the 1980s, 75 percent of U.S. Jews did not keep *kosher*, 40 percent did not fast on Yom Kippur, 90 percent did not attend services once a month or more.

On the other hand, there was a renewed interest in Orthodoxy. In spite of concerns whether a vibrant Orthodox community could be established in America, Eastern European leaders had come here after the war, seeking a secure haven. Joining a small but strong Orthodox community, they established *yeshivot*, *kollelim*, and *shuls*—a rebuke to everything that the Nazis had tried to destroy. In *Jew vs Jew: Struggle for the Soul of American Jewry* (2000), Samuel Freedman writes:

> Fewer than a hundred thousand Orthodox Jews entered the United States in the generation after the war, and yet their effects were profound .... [F]or the first time in modern American history, the secular humanist impulse of American Jewry, as expressed most powerfully by *Yiddishkeit*, faced the challenge of a vibrant, charismatic, and almost completely antithetical belief system with institutions and folkways of its own.

As Reform and Conservative Jews were exiting cities for the suburbs, allegiance to complete Shabbat observance required Orthodox Jews to remain within walking distance of their synagogue. There was a mistaken impression that, with the destruction of European Jewry, the Orthodox movement had lost its heart and soul. In addition, it was feared that by remaining within its urban conclaves while so many other Jews moved to the suburbs, Orthodoxy would eventually lose contact with the greater Jewish community from which it could attract new members. American Jewry underestimated the resilience and the will of the Orthodox, especially when challenged to preserve the vitality of Jewish life in America.

American Jews responded with extraordinary support for Israel during the 1967 Six-Day War. In this moment of peril for the Jewish State, Jews set aside fears of asserting their Jewish identity: Israel's survival was paramount. The encounter reminded Jews of their vulnerability and the need to support each other. It engendered pride in being Jewish and, again, overcoming threatened destruction. I remember my feelings at the end of those six days when high school friends—Christians—hugged me saying, "Your guys did great!"

Many Jews during this time expressed their connection with Judaism through philanthropy and community involvement. Religiously, they identified themselves as Jews; politically, they identified themselves as liberals. In the 1960s and 1970s, Jews were profoundly socially active. Images of Abraham Joshua Heschel marching arm-in-arm with Martin Luther King, Jr.; Betty Freidan and Bella Abzug campaigning for women's rights; and the Chicago Seven (including Jerry Rubin and Abbie Hoffman) testified to Jews' commitment to liberal causes. Organizations were launched to save Jews imprisoned and persecuted in the Soviet Union. New forms of *gemilut hasadim*, "good deeds," and acts of *tzedakah*, "charity," became a prominent expression of Reform Judaism, attracting Jews who might not have affiliated with the Jewish community. Performing deeds that improved the world was a way to identify as a Jew.

Concurrent with this was the emergence of *havurot*, small communities for worship, study of Jewish text, and social action. Groups frequently formed as a revolt against synagogues that were perceived to have lackluster services, stilted practices, and arcane beliefs. A section in *The Jewish Catalogue* (1973) describing components of a *havurah* reads,

> You begin with a shared dissent from existing Jewish institutions and their modes of participation, and a group decision to initiate an alternative model .... The *havurah* should experiment with traditional religious observances and rites of passage, as well as create its own new forms of celebration and commemoration.

Jacob Rader Marcus, professor at Hebrew Union College, described the *havurah* as "a commune of intellectuals ... inquiring youth, and adult 'seekers' ... building a faith tailored to their individual needs" (1993). Each *havurah* was like an extended family that was unified by religious expression. Some were attached to a synagogue; others completely independent. All furthered sociability, religion, creativity, and intellectual inquiry; they offered a healthy challenge to the establishment in the world of the spirit. One *havurah*, Havurat Sholom in Boston, established a rabbinical training institute, partially to keep its students out of the Viet Nam draft but also to expand the revitalization of Jewish learning by creating a welcoming, personal, authentic, egalitarian center for Jewish life.

Other Voices

Avram Kraft, convener and leader of Highland Park, Illinois, Torah Study Group

In 1975, during the heyday of the *havurah* movement, a group of congregants, most from North Suburban Synagogue Beth El in Highland Park, Illinois, formed a group to study Jewish texts. It was a way to honor the memory of my father who had recently died. The ten couples all knew each other. We were in business, medicine, and education. Some were in Jewish education. Some were *frum*, "observant," and some were not. Our ages ranged from mid-thirties to mid-forties. For those of us with younger families, the children joined in the experience. Some of those children have now carried the tradition of Shabbat study to the next generation. Of our original number, eight couples continue to learn together; one couple which made *aliyah* joins us whenever they are in town.

Having decided not to engage a formal leader, the expectation was that each member would come to the table to contribute, raise questions, and delve into the conflicts from classical commentaries or from independent thought. Our bi-monthly gathering gave us an opportunity to *schmooze* and "catch up" and discuss current matters of local, *shul*, national, and international interest. We usually spend two hours together, 4:00 to 6:00. When Shabbat ends before our study ends, we make *havdalah*.

We studied agreed-upon selected texts in Hebrew and met consistently on Shabbat afternoons as long as at least three couples were in town. Over the last thirty-five years, we studied three books of Torah; five texts from the *Nevi'im*, "Prophets"; and portions of books of *K'tuvim*, "Writings," associated with specific holidays.

When each text was completed, we held a formal celebration, a *siyyum*, a meal at a local *kosher* restaurant.

Presently, we are embarking on a journey with *Daniel* to visit the lion in his den. We will even try to engage the Aramaic text. Notably, we dwelled on letters, words, and phrases when we started our text explorations (*Bereshit*, "the beginning," was a seven-year excursion). We are more attuned to the ticking clock thirty-five years later and tend to study shorter selections more hurriedly. There are so many questions yet to be answered. So many more texts to learn.

It was a good time to be Jewish in America. While religion was valued, it did not make heavy demands on life. Children's Jewish learning was thriving, the day school movement was growing, and a core of adult Jews was committed to learning. But in the early 1970s, there were growing signs of the challenges that lay ahead. Some of these were highlighted in 1971 by the first National Jewish Population Study. This drew attention to the declining number of Jews in America, to the growing rate of intermarriage, and to other signs of weakening Jewish identity. Jews were enjoying the prosperity of a thriving economy. We were also suffering a spiritual decline.

Lessons for Today

1. Adult education is not just about learning Judaism; it is about survival.

2. Since the 1970s, Jewish population in America has been shrinking. Jewish learning has the potential to stem the flow caused by apathy, not antagonism.

3. Jewish learning in the context of synagogue life remains an expression of Jewish identity.

4. Besides joining a synagogue, Jewish identity has been expressed through social service, philanthropy, Israel-related activities, and participation in self-directed groups for learning, prayer, and socializing.

5. American support of Israel since the founding of the state has been shaped by pride and the desire to connect with Israel's Jews; education must convey the enduring values of the Jewish State while recognizing temporary social, religious, and political tensions.

6. Service learning is an opportunity to integrate Jewish education with the performance of acts that improve the world.

7. Leaderless groups that socialize, celebrate, study, and pray rely on individual commitment and group loyalty. With that in place, they can persist for decades.

Chapter II

Surviving Freedom

What the fathers no longer hand down the sons must get as best they can—they must study it .... The passion to hand down can be replaced only by the passion to study, the passion of the fathers only by that of the sons, who must work unremittingly to regain the approach to the ancestral treasure, and thus re-establish the bond of memory that joins the community together. — Martin Buber, from "A Syllabus for the School for the Jewish Youth of Berlin," 1932

In 1949, historians Oscar and Mary Handlin wrote in the *American Jewish Year Book*:

> The events of the Second World War left the United States the center of world Judaism. The future of the Jews everywhere will be determined by the attitude and the position of the five million Jews who are citizens of the American Republic.

With the end of Eastern Europe as a center of culture and education, there was a vacuum to fill. It created an opportunity to build a new strong American community on the foundation of Jewish adult learning.

American educators in the 1940s and 1950s had already realized their responsibility to build this new center for Jewish life. Imitation of the Judaism of parents and close community could no longer be the factors motivating Jewish identity, practice, and belief. Personal experiences and knowledge would be the basis of how the next generations would lead their lives. Although attention to adult learning had taken a back seat to the rigors of life during the Depression and World War II, commitment to learning never faltered. Innovation continued in synagogues, Zionist organizations, Jewish community centers, and the central agencies of Jewish education. Millions of dollars were spent on anti-defamation work, especially to educate Jews and Christians about Jews' beliefs, ethics, history, and religious practices. Jewish

9

leaders knew it was important to remind Jews frightened by anti-Semitism in America who they were and about the richness of their heritage. This kind of education strengthened self-esteem and helped preserve our Jewish past.

In 1940, Dr. Louis Finklestein, chancellor of the Jewish Theological Seminary, launched the National Academy for Adult Jewish Studies. It was intended to expand adult learning in Conservative synagogues. As Finklestein wrote, the academy was founded

> to perform a double function. A broad knowledge of historical Judaism will bring psychological reassurance to the Jew of today by showing him the present crisis in its proper perspective. A study of the Bible, Talmud, and medieval and modern Hebrew literature will also indicate the manner in which Judaism, and indeed civilization, can be saved in periods of crisis.

Organizations like B'nai B'rith, the National Council of Jewish Women, the American Jewish Committee, and the American Jewish Congress established departments of adult education. Learning was a popular dimension of meetings and a supplement to social activities and community social action projects.

The Nazi's destruction of Jewish libraries in Europe spurred concern about the condition of Judaica collections in American libraries. The New York Public Library, the libraries of Columbia and Yeshiva universities and the Jewish Theological Seminary, and YIVO Institute for Research took the lead in preserving Jewish writing, documents, and books which were the legacy of Eastern Europe. They also expanded their English language literary collections that contained new thinking and writing about Jewish life and culture.

While Jewish education was influenced by American educational practices, teachers and scholars who fled here from Eastern Europe brought their own knowledge, skills, and inspiration with them. Great teachers—such as Rabbi Abraham Joshua Heschel, Emil Fackenheim, Joseph Soloveitchik—helped establish America as a new cultural, intellectual, and educational center for Jews. Of the Jewish Theological Seminary, for instance, Charles Silberman wrote in *A Certain People* (1986),

> Rarely before and never since did one academy serve as the home for just about all the masters of a scholarly discipline within its own walls .... It can take credit, almost single-handedly, for the transmission of the tradition of Jewish scholarship from Europe to America.

While most Eastern European models of adult learning have been adopted by the Orthodox community in America, the European model that has had the most influence on adult Jewish learning in other denominations is Frankfort's *Freies Judisches Lehrhaus*. Franz Rosenzweig saw Jewish learning as a means of self-perpetuation, a weapon for survival at a time when German Jews were finding their spiritual and intellectual homes outside of the Jewish world. The *Lehrhaus* which opened its doors in 1920 was a way to counteract assimilation and spark a renaissance of Jewish life. Rosenzweig's model of a school that welcomes people from across the community became highly relevant once again as we Jews faced the threat of assimilation—the consequences of acceptance and status in a free American society. For many young adults today, Judaism is one thin thread of the tapestry of life they are weaving. It is not sufficient to draw them to institutions, friendships, business relationships, or Jewish peoplehood.

Rosenzweig headed the school in Frankfort until his death in 1929. Although its activities diminished with the rise of Hitler, Martin Buber revitalized it in 1933. The school became an expression of resistance to the Nazis. Its doors were forcibly closed in 1937.

Throughout Europe, myriad other centers for Jewish learning—the *shteibele*, the *kehillot*, *yeshivot* where Jewish men had gathered for centuries to learn and to teach—also closed. The tragedy of the destruction of European Jewry has been captured in countless documents and images. One that touches me deeply is the image of empty, silent halls of study that were once filled with the sounds of Jewish learning.

American Jews faced a tremendous challenge in these years. In *American Judaism* (2004), Jonathan Sarna quotes a phrase from Van Wyck Brooks who spoke of "a postwar Jewish hunger for affirmation, for a world without confusion, waste, or groping, a world that is full of order and purpose."

Among the American-born leaders of the time, Rabbi Mordecai Kaplan was a strong, compelling voice for adult learning as an entry point to a more ordered world. In 1948, he wrote:

> Our main concern in popularizing adult Jewish study should be to make it relevant and vital to present realities. We cannot create a demand for Jewish knowledge unless we are prepared to help the Jew find some meaning in the events in which he plays a part and to cope with the problems that beset him as a Jew .... [I]t must be made relevant to the problem of overcoming the centrifugal tendencies in Jewish life which threaten to disinte-

grate Jewish solidarity, to vitiate the Jewish ethic, and to minimize the worth of the Jewish religion .... Jewish adult study must concern itself with Jewish literacy as a means to Jewish experience.

Starting in the late 1940s, the inspiration of the new State of Israel spurred greater participation in adult education. The founding of Israel also led to what some have called the "Hebraist-Zionist" takeover of Jewish education. Children now attended "Hebrew schools," not "afternoon schools." Interest in improving the teaching of Hebrew led to *Ivrit b'Ivrit*, "Hebrew in Hebrew," in which all instruction was in Hebrew. It also led to new curricula for summer camps that used Hebrew as their spoken language. Reading and speaking Hebrew became a symbol of an educated Jew. It was seen as the shortest road to the Bible and the prayer book. For a while, it enhanced the professionalization of teachers. Its demands, however, on teachers and students were unrealistic: mastering Hebrew required more time than was available. The effort to make Hebrew the top priority of synagogue schools collapsed in the 1970s although celebrating Hebrew language continued through music, dance, and literature. Today, successful Hebrew study continues in day schools, public schools, and *ulpanim* (Hebrew language institutes), where adequate time is devoted to it.

Expanding Adult Jewish Learning in America

Between 1965 and 1970, events on a national level had focused attention on adult Jewish learning. In the Fall of 1965, a study by New York's City College history professor, Oscar I. Janowsky, revealed inadequate standards, planning, and accountability in Jewish adult learning programs. There was a lack of strong educational leadership other than that of rabbis. Janowsky recommended creating effective adult education materials, determining the best ways to teach adults, and developing better-informed leaders. He specifically addressed the need to promote the importance of serious, sustained study for adults—especially among parents who could then enhance the education of their children.

In 1967, building on Janowsky's work, Samuel I. Cohen, the membership director of B'nai B'rith, wrote about adult Jewish education as an emerging and integral part of American Jewish life since the end of World War II. He specifically looked at the impact of national Jewish organizations such as the American Jewish Committee, the

American Jewish Congress, B'nai B'rith, and the National Council of Jewish Women in promoting a deeper understanding of Judaism. To him, this was indispensable for the future of American Jewry. The work of these organizations, he concluded, reflected the realization that adult learning was the new frontier in Jewish education.

In 1969, Judah Pilch, the head of the National Curriculum Research Institute of the American Association of Jewish Education (AAJE), acknowledged growth but noted that statistics on the number of participants were sparse, and there was little data on what adult Jewish educators would like to achieve. He made a strong case that professionalizing Jewish learning would make it more attractive to parents of children in Jewish schools. "A Judaism unworthy of adult study," he said, "is hardly worthwhile preparing children for."

It was just at this time that I began my career in adult Jewish education. The Jewish community was broadening its concern from focus on Israel and Soviet Jewry to surviving in America's free, open society. Synagogues were thriving, women were taking a more active role in Jewish life, and the civil rights movement had established the right of every individual to achieve his or her potential. Economic security coupled with the existing five-day work-week gave adults more discretionary time for relaxation, recreation, and learning.

Growing interest in adult learning put it center stage in the 1970s, when, for the first time in American history, studies showed decreases in its Jewish population. A population survey a decade later confirmed these statistics. The report blamed assimilation and absence of immigration for the shrinking numbers. Sociologists, religious and community leaders, academics and educators all pointed to Jewish learning as the vehicle that could strengthen the community and staunch the flow away from it. Hopefully, this would spur a renaissance in American Judaism—religious, spiritual, and communal.

Awakenings

In 1982, William McLoughlin, history professor at Brown University, described an "awakening" in intellectual life as "a major cultural reorientation—a search for new meaning, order, and direction in a society which finds that rapid change and unexpected intrusions have disrupted the order of life." As Jonathan D. Sarna, history professor at Brandeis University, has shown in "A Great Awakening" (1995), "cycles of crisis in identity in America are invariably followed by efforts at revitalization."

The cycle of crisis followed by revitalization has occurred twice in the North American Jewish community since 1970. The first crisis—the growing awareness of the threat of assimilation—had been developing slowly since the late 1950s. But once identified in the 1970s and 1980s, it triggered strong responses. This included introducing high-quality adult learning in many settings. As Jewish leaders made more funds available, learning became a growing priority and revitalizing the core American Jewish community was the result. As Sarna wrote,

> Now the emphasis was more on ritual and spirituality ... even as the awakening left countless individual Jews unmoved and had no appreciable effect on the size of the American Jewish community, the changes it wrought on the synagogue, on Jewish education, and on Jewish culture affected Jewish religious movements of every kind .... Adult Jewish education flourished. The success of *The Jewish Catalogue* and Barry Holtz's *Back to the Sources* ... demonstrated a hungering for adult Jewish learning, reaffirming the observation that "the most active periods in the history of adult education have always been those in which there has been the greatest rapidity of change." ... Three nationwide programs of adult Jewish education took off in their wake—the Wexner Heritage Program (1985), the Florence Melton Adult Mini-Schools (1986), and the Me'ah Program (1994) each of which attracted thousands of committed Jewish adults.

The second nation-wide crisis yet undocumented was the recession that began in December 2007. Day schools cut staff and services, central agencies that had sponsored adult learning fired staff or merged with other community-funded organizations. Jewish colleges were struggling. Me'ah, the nationally successful adult learning program created at Boston Hebrew College, was acquired by the Jewish Theological Seminary that took over responsibility for its implementation beyond the Boston area. The Florence Melton Adult Mini-School that, at its peak, was located in sixty-three North American communities was in forty-three in 2012.

These consequences can be compared to what occurred during the Great Depression when Jewish learning suffered, teachers lost jobs, and enrollment in Jewish schools fell. What is comforting is that following World War II, learning expanded. An "awakening" also occurred beginning in the 1980s when leaders and professionals recognized growing assimilation in North America. Our own future appears to mirror that past. Now, in 2012, a young generation of Jewish leaders, parents and educators are fundraising and advocating for adult learning, working to maintain and adapt existing learning programs, and initiating new ones. A new "awakening" is being fashioned by a determined young generation.

Early History of Adult Jewish Learning in America

Learning was part of American Judaism from Jews' first arrival on these shores. At first, it took the form of sermons, conversations, and Torah reading. Gradually becoming more formal, it incorporated lectures, study groups, and classes. By the mid-nineteenth century, Jewish learning reflected the growing Jewish community. Records of *hevrot*, societies for the study of Bible, Mishnah, and Talmud, go back to the 1840s when Shearith Israel Congregation in New York started an adult school called the Hebrew Literary and Religious Library Association. While New York was the largest center of Jewish life in the United States, other *hevrot* existed in Philadelphia, Chicago, and Rochester where there was a tailors' *hevrah* for chanting the Psalms.

Isaac Mayer Wise came to America in 1846. From his home in Cincinnati, Ohio, he set in place not only the structures that would build and sustain the Reform movement—the Union of American Hebrew Congregations (1873), the Hebrew Union College (1875), and the Central Conference of American Rabbis (1889)—but also capitalized on the power of the printed word to enable more adults scattered in communities across the United States to learn about Judaism. From 1854, he edited, wrote, and published *The Israelite*. In the first issue of the newspaper, he wrote,

> The Israelite will favor enlightenment, education, a moderate and rational progress and improvement of our institutions, will cherish the spread of knowledge, the progress of learning, and the triumph of truth.

Due to his passion for writing not only articles but essays, novels, and books of history, the work threatened to overwhelm him. He hired Edward Bloch to handle the publishing. Bloch, in turn, hired Louis Behrman as his assistant. Bloch and Behrman both eventually moved to New York where they established independent Jewish bookstores and publishing houses, helping to create a new American Jewish industry.

In the last half of the nineteenth century, young adults, primarily from Philadelphia and New York, who participated regularly in adult education, saw learning as a way to respond to challenges to life in America. Unlike previous adult learning experiences which had been directed by rabbis and scholars, this grassroots effort was driven by young men and women who had been raised in a democratic society and applied democracy to their education settings. Their leadership and creativity strengthened the Jewish community and countered the anti-Semitism that Jews confronted in America. They chose Hanukkah as a holiday which they felt could strengthen their Jewish identity, slowly turning it into a holiday that was almost able to compete with Christmas. Sabbath observance expanded. *The American Hebrew*, a newspaper established in New York in 1879, emerged as a strong voice of Jewish identity and pride. Women were welcomed into the world of Jewish learning. Led by Rebecca Gratz in Philadelphia, women became Sunday school teachers and spurred the growth of children's education and literary discussion groups like the Female Benevolent Society and the National Council of Jewish Women. For men, the Young Men's Hebrew Association provided Jewish classes. Hebrew Union College was founded in 1875 in Cincinnati and the Jewish Theological Seminary followed in 1887 in New York.

The major cultural reorientation that began in the late 1870s was soon augmented by mass immigration from Eastern Europe. As Sarna (2004) wrote:

> The critical developments that we associate with this period—the return to religion, the heightened sense of Jewish peoplehood and particularism, the far-reaching changes that opened up new opportunities and responsibilities for women, the renewed community-wide emphasis on education and culture, the burst of organizational energy, and the growth of Conservative Judaism and Zionism—all reflect different efforts to resolve the crisis of beliefs and values that had developed during these decades.

In the early twentieth century, the massive stream of Eastern European immigrants gave education a new and distinctive nature. Learning was seen as a critical tool of survival in the New World, whether it was learning a language or a trade. Community centers were a unifying factor as divisions became more pronounced between earlier German immigrants and the new arrivals; and among the growing religious denominations. New York's checkerboard of neighborhoods was divided according to when Jews immigrated to America and which communities they came from. Reform Judaism's rejection of most ritual separated it from the more traditional Orthodox and Conservative movements.

The momentum of Jewish education continued with the establishment of the Jewish Publication Society, the American Jewish Historical Society, Gratz College, the Jewish Chatauqua Society, and the writing of a *Jewish Encyclopedia*. Orthodox Jews continued to study in their *b'tai midrash* and *shuls*. Rabbi Isaac Elchanan Theological Seminary (RIETS) and Yeshiva College were established. While institutions like the Jewish Theological Seminary and Hebrew Union College served Conservative and Reform movements, colleges like Gratz College, Dropsie College, Baltimore Hebrew College, and Boston Hebrew Colleges were more inclusive centers of learning. The College of Jewish Studies in Chicago, for instance, was started in 1924 primarily to serve first-generation immigrants. Its leaders soon realized that the Jewish community at large would benefit from its lectures, classes, and social and recreational activities.

To counter Reform rabbis who were suggesting alternatives to studying Torah and Talmud, the Jewish Theological Seminary and leading Eastern European Jews formed the Orthodox Jewish Congregational Union of America. The Union offered immigrants and young Jews in New York English language lectures and classes whose content was based on traditional Jewish texts. In addition, social and recreational activities brought young Jews of Eastern European descent into a welcoming traditional community. This also rebutted the work of Christian missionaries and settlement house workers who were interested in attracting the new immigrants to Christianity.

Adult learning was also strengthened as part of the establishment of a "double schooling" system for children. Fashioned by Samson Benderly—the director of the newly founded New York Bureau of Jewish Education, and his "Benderly boys," young educators he inspired—the school system included programs for parents. Along with establishing bureaus of Jewish education in major American cities, Benderly and his colleagues melded American life with Jewish tradition by creating free-standing afternoon schools that Jewish children could attend after public school. Double schooling allowed families to experience the good that the greater society offered while still encouraging them to learn about their distinctive heritage. Every member of a family was considered to be a patron of the school and participated in educational and social events. These afternoon schools looked at the family as a whole rather than focusing only on the children. They were a center for serving the entire neighborhood. A model for Jewish afternoon schools followed by Benderly is found in a 1911 Wisconsin state law which stated that a public school could establish evening schools, vacation schools, reading rooms, libraries, debating clubs, gyms, public playgrounds, public baths, and similar activities to serve the entire community. Isaac Berkson, one of the disciples of Samson Benderly, wrote about the Central Jewish Institute which he directed (Krasner, 2011):

> It addresses itself not to child alone, nor to any one age of the population, but regards every member of the family as its patron. In fact, it looks upon the family as a whole rather than the individual as its unit of work .... It is a Community House endeavoring to serve the neighborhood in every way it can .... The Jewish center must carry on activities which make for the physical and social well-being of the people who live in the neighborhood.

Jewish Learning Meets American Academia

In America's academic circles at this time, adult learning became a distinct category in education. It gained sufficient importance to justify the establishment of the American Association of Adult Education in 1926. The first graduate program in adult learning was created at Columbia University in 1930 and included courses in sociology, psychology, education, and human development. No longer was the young adult who had completed elementary and high school education considered to be a finished product. Adults continued to grow and change throughout life, and educational experiences had to be created to address the variety of adults who came to learn.

Malcolm Knowles, considered the father of the science of adult learning, attempted to popularize the word "andragogy" which he defined as "the art and science of teaching adults." He contrasted it with "pedagogy," which is concerned with teaching children. Adults had always been learners although their study was not looked at systematically. In the twentieth century, settling immigrants, job training during the Depression, and efforts to combat adult illiteracy post-World War II had drawn attention to the fact that teaching adults was different from teaching children and prevalent enough to merit the attention of scholars. It was Knowles, however, who did the most to define those differences in the 1960s through 1980. His foundational studies and those that followed were described most effectively in a book by Malcolm Knowles, Elwood Holton, and Richard Swanson (2005) in which they summarized assumptions about adult learners. (1) As a person matures, he needs to know why he needs to learn something before undertaking to learn it—the benefits of learning and the negative consequences of not learning. Teachers need to make students aware of "the need to know." (2) Adults see themselves as responsible for their own decisions, their own lives. They need to be seen by others and treated by others as being capable of self-direction. Although learners may begin with an "I am here so teach me" attitude, good teachers will create learning experiences that will help make the transition from dependent to self-directed learners. (3) As adults mature, they accumulate a growing reservoir of experience that is a resource for learning. Although it increases the challenge of teaching because of the great diversity of learners, it also provides the opportunity for peer learning. Adding to the challenge of teaching adults is the increased need for "un-learning," for becoming aware of assumptions, testing them, and reinforcing or changing them. (4) Adults become ready to learn those things they need to know and to do to meet challenges related to their roles in life. Adult learners are rarely attracted to particular subjects for their own sake but are problem-centered or task-centered.

This developing field modernized Jewish adult learning. Earlier in Eastern Europe and America, adult learning had focused solely on content: What subjects/texts are to be learned? Male learners gained knowledge and skills from texts and from interacting with each other. The academic study of adult learning prompted teachers to ask new questions: What is a literate Jew? What are the characteristics of people coming to learn? What will attract them to educational experiences? What will be relevant to their lives? What is the best way to teach adults? Jewish study was no longer an assumed aspect of the life of Jews so potential students had to be convinced of the importance of Jewish learning. They had to be convinced that it was worth their while to participate.

Today, when maintaining and deepening involvement in the Jewish community is a priority, an important quality to be recognized and reckoned with is that individual needs frequently supersede group identity. The "sovereign self" described by Steven Cohen and Arnold Eisen (2001) is the independent, self-directed individual that educators must attract and serve. Knowing the students and responding to what is occurring in their lives is essential. Beginning with identifying the characteristics of students and what would motivate them to learn, teachers select subjects and strategies that encourage lifelong Jewish learning.

In truth, the ancient Jewish sages sometimes did focus on the nature of the learner. *Pirke Avot,* "Sayings of the Fathers," (5:24) discussed subject matter as it corresponds to the age of the student:

> At five years (the age is reached) for the study of Torah; at ten for the study of the Mishnah; at thirteen for the fulfillment of the *mitzvot*; at fifteen for the study of the Talmud; at eighteen for marriage; at twenty for pursuit of a livelihood; at thirty for physical strength; at forty for understanding; at fifty for giving counsel; at sixty he attains old age; at seventy fullness of years; at eighty he attains spiritual strength ....

That statement reflects an understanding that the learner is always changing. The concentration on content, still prevalent in many settings, prevents many teachers from shaping what is learned and how it is taught to fit the qualities of students including what is going on in their lives. At a time when satisfaction with the experience determines whether students continue or drop out of learning, this is even more important.

Franz Rosensweig, the German Jewish educator and philosopher who established the *Freies Judisches Lehrhaus,* "The Free House of Jewish Studies," was ahead of his time. He instinctively knew to teach what the adults who attended his school wanted to learn.

> To begin, offer only an opportunity to begin—"a space to speak and a time to speak"—a discussion room. Then supply what they ask for. Discussion is a Jewish conversation on being a Jewish human being. Not lectures or speechmaking. The old form of maintaining the relationship between life and the Book—has failed. New "learning" is about to be born. It is a learning in reverse order: a learning that no longer starts from the Torah and leads into life, but the other way around: from life, from a world that knows nothing of the Law, or pretends to know nothing, back to the Torah. All of us to whom Judaism, to whom being a Jew, has again become the pivot of our lives—and I know that in saying this here I am not speaking for myself alone—we all know that in being Jews we must not give up anything, not renounce anything, but lead everything back to Judaism. From the periphery back to the center; from the outside in (Glatzer, 1953).

Adjusting content and strategies to match the interests of students makes the work of teachers more complicated. As a result, teaching adults requires more and more specialized knowledge and skills. For example, it is not enough for teachers to know Jewish history. They must also possess the ability to teach history to adults, and knowing how to teach history is different than knowing how to teach Bible or ethics or literature. This more refined approach to adult learning creates a demand for specialized courses devoted to adult education in Jewish colleges and universities.

The stage was set to expand Jewish adult learning. The challenge came directly from Oscar Janowsky's 1965 recommendations to develop effective adult education materials and unique training for teachers of adults. He was also concerned about educating Jewish leaders. This was the opportunity I was presented to use my knowledge and skills during an exciting late twentieth-century revival of American Jewish learning. Bruce Springstein once attributed his success to being able to swim in the currents of history. This was the world that I entered, the world in which I would swim.

The expansion of adult Jewish learning in America is shaped by history, sociology, education, and religion—both in the Jewish community and the wider society. It is driven by the commitment and creativity of individuals and institutions and enriched by intellectual contributions from Israel. The American roots from which it evolved were sparse; the Eastern European roots were no longer available to us. It is a uniquely American experience driven more recently by those who come to learn. In the following pages, I will explore centers for adult learning that have been adapted or created to serve learners the past four decades. In historical perspective, they embody the reinvention of adult Jewish learning in America.

Lessons for Today

1. The Judaism of each generation is constructed on a foundation of positive personal experiences and Jewish knowledge.

2. "A broad knowledge of historical Judaism will bring psychological reassurance to the Jew of today by showing him the present crisis in its proper perspective. A study of Bible, Talmud, and medieval and modern Hebrew literature will also indicate the manner in which Judaism, and indeed civilization, can be saved in periods of crisis" (Louis Finkelstein, 1940).

3. Learning can be made part of all kinds of Jewish gatherings—even if it is only a portion of the environment or the program materials. It complements social activities, meetings, cultural events, and social action projects.

4. "We cannot create a demand for Jewish knowledge unless we are prepared to help the Jew find some meaning in the events in which he plays a part and to cope with the problems that beset him as a Jew .... It must be made relevant to the problem of overcoming the centrifugal tendencies in Jewish life which threaten to disintegrate Jewish solidarity, to vitiate the Jewish ethic, and to minimize the worth of the Jewish religion" (Mordecai Kaplan, 1948).

5. "As Jews, we have to understand and love our ancestral culture and religion. As American Jews, we have to contribute to the moral and spiritual life of our country. As citizens of the world, we have to be in a position to act intelligently on all matters that pertain to the well-being of mankind as a whole" (Mordecai Kaplan, 1956).

6. Adult Jewish learning can provide insight during a crisis—personal or communal.

7. Every member of a family is a customer of the afternoon school. Family and parent education play a vital role in shaping the Jewish future.

8. When engaging adults in Jewish learning, keep in mind that for most adults today individual interests and needs supersede group identity.

9. "New learning is ... a learning in reverse order: a learning that no longer starts from the Torah and leads into life, but the other way around: from life, from a world that knows nothing of the Law, or pretends to know nothing, back to the Torah" (Franz Rosenzweig, 1920).

10. Each consecutive American generation has redesigned and delivered a custom-made version of adult learning that celebrates the new and respects tradition.

Thriving in America

Who Is Coming to Learn?

Moses received the Torah at Sinai and transmitted it to Joshua, and Joshua to the elders, and the elders to the prophets, and the prophets handed it down to the members of the Great Assembly. — Pirke Avot, I:I

Chapter III

Learning throughout Life
Stories and Case Studies

8. Every Israelite is under an obligation to study Torah, whether he is poor or rich, in sound health or ailing, in the vigor of youth or very old and feeble. Even a man so poor that he is maintained by charity or goes begging from door to door, is also a man with a wife and children to support, is under the obligation to set aside a definite period during the day and at night for the study of the Torah as it is said, "But you shall meditate therein day and night" (Joshua 1: 8).

....

10. Until what period in life ought one to study Torah? Until the day of one's death, as it is said, "And lest they (the precepts) depart from your heart all the days of your life" (Deuteronomy 4:9). Whenever one ceases to study, one forgets. — Maimonides, *Laws Concerning the Study of the Torah*, Chapter 1

Entering a Florence Melton Adult Mini-School classroom on a snowy day in Chicago, I hear the hum and chatter of eager students greeting each other and catching up on the week's events. As they brush off the snow, pour themselves a cup of coffee, and take their accustomed seats around the table, they never fail to warm my heart. There are young mothers who ask to keep their cell phones on just in case they are needed back home and recent empty-nesters who call themselves "the post-carpool generation," and senior citizens who forget their infirmities while they study. I never take for granted the wonderful diversity of students before me, all of them sharing a love for Jewish text and a sense of wonder at the way it touches their lives. They represent all ages; they come from all parts of the world; they are at different stages of their Jewish journey. I am in awe of the representation of life before me, and I am challenged to teach in a way that will meet their unique needs. From them, I have learned that there are common experiences

25

and desires on which I can build, and that these are a result of living in North America in the twenty-first century.

The motivations that lead people to make serious commitments to Jewish learning and the results of those commitments are as different as their lives. Here are several stories that further illustrate the variety of those who come to study:

❧ When Ruth Weinberg came to America from Antopole, Poland, in 1920, she was exposed to Jewish learning that was entirely new to her. Describing her ability to attend a Jewish school, she said "It was like a jail was unlocked!" Ruth was the youngest of three siblings. Her sister had learned cooking, sewing, embroidery, and homemaking from her mother. Ruth was not interested. Because her father believed in education for girls, her sister also attended a Jewish school. Ruth, still young, would follow her brother and sister to school and long to go inside. "I would stand outdoors by the school," she said. "I wasn't on the roof like Hillel. I stood on the porch. But like Hillel, I could not get in. I was too young. It was the tragedy of my young life." In America, Ruth became a scholar, a valued student at the College of Jewish Studies in Chicago, a teacher, and a model in her community. At the college in the 1930s, she organized a strike by women who demanded the right to study Talmud like the male students. The strike was so successful that several years later a younger student told her, "Of course, we study Talmud. Don't women here always have the same right to do that as men?"

❧ On an evaluation form for the Union of American Hebrew Congregations' Regional Retreat, "Encountering God in Your Life," one participant commented, "This is the first time I have ever had the chance to learn and talk with others about my relationship with God. It wasn't anything we talked about at home or in school when I was growing up nor do my friends and I speak about it now. It just seemed like this is something Jewish people didn't do. This retreat created a time and space to reflect and share ideas about something that is important in my life. I think I know what it means to have a good relationship with a parent, a child, a husband, and a friend, but I've never taken the time to think about what it means to have a good relationship with God."

❧ Hannah and Craig moved to Denver from the East Coast. At first, they pursued their careers in volunteer management and medicine, along with fishing, hiking, and skiing when time allowed. As they were beginning a family, they decided it was time to connect with a community of Jewish peers with whom they could share the joys and challenges of parenting. Because of their backgrounds—Craig had been raised Orthodox and Hannah had been raised Conservative—they were attracted to a program at their Jewish community center called "Jewish Baby University." This included classes about Jewish parenting as well as the nuts and bolts of having a first baby. There were also social activities and Shabbat dinners. Seven years later, their social group is primarily composed of parents who had been in this group. They share play dates, birthday parties, mothers' nights out, and family holiday dinners.

✻ Jean was a diligent student. She attended the Florence Melton Adult Mini-School every week, read the texts before every class, and between classes e-mailed me questions related to lessons. In a conversation toward the middle of the year, she shared a moment in class that was very meaningful to her. We had read Rabbi Yitzhak Greenberg's essay on Jews' delivery from slavery in Egypt. The fulfillment of God's promise of redemption from Egypt has been a source of Jewish optimism and resilience for millennia. "It was just what I needed," Jean explained. She had been divorced the past summer and was trying to pull her life together. "I either had to go into therapy or sign up for Melton. I made the right decision!"

These "case studies" illustrate the diversity of people whose lives are changed by learning. They attend lectures and classes, learn in *hevrutah,* or study on their own at home through reading, online learning, and video-conferencing. They participate in workshops, book or film clubs, parent and child activities, and peer-led groups. The number of adult Jewish learners in the United States has grown steadily since the 1950s. It is estimated that the number of students enrolled between 1990 and 2012 in national programs like the Florence Melton Adult Mini-School, Me'ah, ConText and the Rohr Jewish Learning Institute exceeds 250,000. More adults than ever are continuing their Jewish learning and an increasing number of organizations are making this possible.

There are many explanations for this growth. Chief among them is that the numbers of potential students have grown. Leisure time has expanded, and learning makes use of that time in a meaningful way. Baby boomers, who manage to change every decade they enter, are reaching retirement age; and the children of baby boomers, many of whom send their children to synagogue schools and day schools, are participating in family education activities and making time to learn so they can share Judaism with their children. Living in the age of Google, they are accustomed to having easy access to information. Learning programs and experiences that appeal to them organize the specific information they are seeking in a convenient and attractive way.

Through the last forty years, like other commodities, adult learning has responded to the growing diversity of life. Adults are accustomed to personalizing smart phones, computers, iPads, automobiles, and entertainment centers. They make choices according to their preferences. By recognizing the broad spectrum of needs that learning can fulfill and designing experiences and programs that reflect them, institutions and organizations are able to attract more potential learners and keep them involved.

The proliferation of organizations that are providing learning experiences and educational activities also increase the number of learners. While creating competition, multiple sponsors—in business language—stimulate the market. Adult learning is more visible and more accessible to potential students. It is part of the mainstream of Jewish life and is perceived as a valid and valuable way to express Jewish identity.

What follows in this chapter and the next is a portrait of Jewish adult learners and the variety of purposes that learning fulfills for them.

Parents: Sharing a Heritage

In the 1980s, growth of family education created a new entryway into Jewish learning. Cherie Koller-Fox in Boston, Harlene Appleman in Detroit, Jo Kay in New York, and Ron Wolfson, Vicky Kelman, and Joel Grishaver in Los Angeles were among the educators across the country who acted on the belief that a combination of efforts in the synagogue and in the home determined the success of children's education. In 1989, the Shirley and Arthur Whizin Institute for Jewish Family Education was created to develop family educators and to study and exchange knowledge about this field. Family education is now so essential a part of Jewish education that it is almost taken for granted. Positive experiences not only reinforce children's education but also motivate many parents to continue their own learning. In 2010, family education received another vote of confidence and opportunity to expand when the Covenant Foundation allocated $100,000 over two years to support Jewish Family Education 3.0: The Next Generation created by Shevet: Jewish Family Education Exchange. It will be used to train a new generation of family educators through conferences, use of social media, digital media, and other technology. All of them believe, as Menachem Mendl of Kotzk did,

> If you truly want your children to study Torah, study it yourself in their presence. They will follow your example. Otherwise, they will not themselves study Torah, but simply instruct their children to do so.

A sign of growing sophistication of parent and family education is adaptation of learning experiences to specific life stages of parenting. A program for new or expecting parents, many of whom may be entering the Jewish community for the first time as adults, differs from programming for Jewish parents who have enrolled their children in a Jewish preschool. Parents of children in congregational elementary synagogue schools and day schools have different concerns than parents of teens. Not only are the content and styles of teaching different, but also the timing and location of learning experiences and the strategies to market these programs.

Couples expecting children and parents with very young children have been one particular focus of programs and research. Young couples are having children later in their lives, many when they are in their thirties. They want to connect with others who face the same rewards and challenges that come with having children. Their involvement with work and the mobility of our society often make it difficult for them to find a community of like-minded friends. Coming together to learn and share activities with their children can be the beginning of life-long connections with the Jewish community.

Working with parents of children from the time of pregnancy to three years old is of great interest to educational and religious institutions. This is clearly a moment when lives are in transition, and, consequently, when individuals are open to community support and opportunities to learn. Going by names such as Baby University, Lamazel Tov, Sholom Baby, and Mom2Mom, programs frequently begin with prenatal programs, personally delivered welcome baskets from Jewish community organizations, and invitations to join other expecting or new parents in specially-designed experiences. In his research at Brandeis and Tufts universities, Dr. Mark Rosen (2006), describes the types of programs these young parents are seeking.

⚜ Parenting and Child Development
Some programs are purely secular, offering practical information to help parents make the transition to parenthood and bond with their children. Others combine parenting information with some Jewish content.

⚜ Developmentally-appropriate children's activities
Sometimes the primary orientation of a program is for children rather than parents, and age-appropriate activities are offered.

⚜ Social time
Almost all programs provide time for parents to socialize.

❧ Jewish learning
Central agencies of Jewish education, rabbis, Jewish educators, Jewish community centers, and synagogues offer programs primarily designed to give parents a stronger background in Jewish tradition and enable them to bring Judaism into their homes.

❧ Clinical/peer support
Some new parents have personal difficulties such as post-partum depression or marital conflict. Others are overwhelmed by the responsibilities of new parenthood. Jewish Family Services sometimes offers support for individuals or groups by trained professionals or peers.

Mothers and fathers of preschool age children are another important group. The Jewish Early Childhood Education Initiative (JECEI) was inspired by the model of Reggio Emilia, a community in Italy that recreated itself around the goal of excellent education for young children. Although JECEI ended its major initiatives in 2011, it provides a model worthy of imitation. It addressed parent and family education based on Jewish principles through which people view and experience their lives and the world. It recognized that teachers and families together create a learning community and nurture the social and emotional growth of everyone involved. Adult Jewish learning offered families the knowledge to design a Jewish home and, in JECEI's words, "to make their life journey a Jewish journey." Between 2004 and 2011, the organization worked directly with Jewish early childhood centers throughout the country to create an educational and social environment welcoming to all Jewish families to advance excellence, and to reach children and their families at a point when they are receptive to Jewish learning and involvement with a Jewish community. At the end of 2011, JECEI's website celebrated its accomplishments. JECEI had:

❧ Created a model for excellent Jewish early childhood education, which has been validated in peer-reviewed academic articles and by independent research

❧ Engaged about 6,000 families, 8,000 children, 1,000 teachers, and thirty-two Jewish early childhood schools

❧ Constructed a data-driven system allowing the impact of the Jewish early childhood program to be measured with tools to be utilized by outside evaluators or through self-assessment.

❧ Created a rigorous accreditation process that resulted in seven accredited Jewish ECE schools that are models of excellence for their geographic areas.

At the same time, the website noted that "although the program will not be maintained with the full model intact, our rigorous research, learning, and ideas are being made available through our website." Whether the discontinued funding was the result of the financial downturn or the dissatisfaction of the funders, it represents the loss of a standard-setting organization at an important entry point into the Jewish community for parents of preschool children.

Other Voices

Diana Ganger, coach and consultant in organizational and educational settings, former program director at JECEI.

One of the important ideas in Judaism is the centrality of the family. As such, excellence in early childhood Jewish education means having the family as an active partner.

Creating a learning community centered in the school is a result of this vision. Families are developing their identities and beginning to explore values that will guide them. This is an opportunity for schools to provide "windows" through which to see possibilities for raising a child with a soul and "mirrors" for families to see themselves by observing and conversing with other families. The school staff plays a central role by modeling learning and open dialogue and by responding to families' questions and needs. Schools partner with parents to decide how and when to build relationships and to learn and grow together.

As an example: In one school parents met in the evening to discuss Jewish Big Ideas and their relevance to parenting. The group met around small round tables covered with tablecloths and spread with flowers, snacks, and coffee. (This is a model for creating sacred space, an intentional way of creating a feeling of welcome, relaxation, and belonging). The conversation, based on texts on Shabbat, was about the meaning of sacred time and space. The couples reflected on their own ability to create sacred times and spaces. They talked about awe and wonder and how it could bring meaning and depth to their lives. These sacred moments add quality to their relationships with each other and with their children. Teachers shared their efforts to bring more wonder into the classrooms. Afterwards, one parent reported that she bought a round table for her family of six as it created a different Shabbat atmosphere, and another parent stated that her continuing discussions with her husband about Judaism added to their relationship.

Baby Boomers: Personalizing a Heritage

In the 1960s, "Hell, no. I won't go" was chanted by young adults at anti-war rallies. Leap ahead fifty years and congregations are coping with the same phrase, "Hell, no. I won't go!" The Jewish baby boomers are the largest generation alive today. They are the ones who powered innovation and created *havurot* in the 1970s, grassroots organizations for social, educational, and religious purposes. They fought for human rights and integration and, except in history books, never knew a world without the State of Israel. Wade Clark Root called this group, born between 1946 and 1964, "a generation of seekers." Arnold Eisen, then a professor at Stamford University and Steven Cohen, a researcher at the Hebrew University of Jerusalem, described them in *The Jew Within: Self, Family, and Community in America* (2000) as independent-thinking individuals seeking a personalized form of Judaism. When offered opportunities to join Jewish congregations or participate in community-run philanthropic efforts, boomers often react with their practiced refrain, "Hell, no. I won't go."

One explanation is that affiliation implies commitment to a consistent activity over an extended period of time. It represents deciding what is right and proper rather than being open to a variety of alternative activities. It assumes that individuals have stable interests that can be met by one institution. It restricts change and limits experimentation.

However, certain forces have balanced these strong individualistic tendencies. Baby boomers have grown up in the Information Age. They have a need to know and cannot tolerate their own ignorance. With the expansion of leisure time and the increase of learning opportunities, baby boomers have found there are advantages in learning in a community—clarifying questions, sharing answers, and being moved forward by others when one's motivation falters. As more baby boomers approach retirement, they are setting aside leisure time for learning to satisfy curiosity and fulfill social needs.

For many, "getting ahead" in the work world has been replaced by "catching-up" in previously neglected areas of their lives. Some attend adult learning programs in congregations; some enroll in classes sponsored by organizations and institutions that do not require commitments like membership dues and building funds. Independent learning programs—for example, the Florence Melton Adult Mini-

School and the Rohr Jewish Learning Institute—have attracted the unaffiliated who insist on remaining that way.

As many of these baby boomers reach their mid-sixties and seventies another very important motivation for Jewish learning emerges. Enjoying good health and more leisure time, grandparents once again become teachers of the youngest generation. The opportunity that presents itself has sent many grandparents back to learn basics of Judaism, to discover the best of Jewish children's literature, and to find Jewish settings to share Judaism with their grandchildren. Recognizing this growing group of adults, synagogues are adding specialized programming like holiday arts and crafts workshops, *tzedakah* projects, and mixed generation choirs. The Jewish Community Centers of Chicago sponsor weekend retreats for grandparents and their grandchildren.

Other Voices

Sharon Morton, Director of Education Emeritus of Congregation Am Shalom, Glencoe, IL, having served as their educator for thirty-two years; founder of Grandparents for Social Action and the Social Action Resource Center and Network.

We become teachers of the younger generation when we think about our legacy. What do we want that legacy to be? I went to the funeral of the mother of a friend. An adult grandchild stood up and with tears said, "I'll always remember my grandmother's chocolate chip cookies." Of course, the moment was poignant. But when I left the chapel, I thought, "What would I want my grandchildren to remember about me?" They will never remember anything I cook.

One week later, I went to a meeting of the American Jewish World service, and met Ruth Messenger. In a short private conversation, she told me about a philanthropy fund she had for her grandchildren. *That was it!* I put $125 a year in the bank for each of my three grandchildren. We went on a family vacation during which I taught them the words, "philanthropy," "philanthropist," "philanthropic," and "*mentsch*." At the end of two days, they each stood up, raised their right hand and said, "I am now a life-long philanthropist and will do philanthropic things because I am a *mentch*." Then each of my grandsons received a certificate with a gold seal saying they were a member of the MIMAST (stands for Michael, Matthew and Steven) philanthropy club. That same week, I took the boys shopping, and they found mittens on sale for fifty cents. "Wow, we are having a mitten drive in school. This is a great project for our philanthropy money!" And those three young boys spent two hours selecting mittens, big and small, girls' and boys'. It was delightful. Since then, each time they choose a project they report to me what they want to do and why. They have learned about matching grants and accompanying service projects. This situation was the beginning of "Grandparents for Social Action," an organization focused on the role grandparents play in teaching grandchildren about Jewish life and values.

When grandparents study Torah with their grandchildren, they can read stories like Rebecca at the well or Abraham welcoming strangers to his tent or the many sayings in *Pirke Avot* about the importance of philanthropy and good deeds. Grandchildren will learn that they have the power to make their lives meaningful, and grandparents can enjoy seeing grandchildren become learners and participants in a beautiful world that they will help to create.

Senior Adults: Savoring a Heritage

A 2008 report on aging from the United States Census Bureau contained a chart projecting the proportion of Americans sixty-five and older in 2008, 2020, and 2040:

	65 & older	75 & older	80 & older
2008	12.8%	6.2%	3.8%
2020	16.5%	6.9%	4.0%
2040	20.8%	11.6%	7.3%

Jewish institutions are preparing for this future. Settings for learning for seniors are expanding in synagogues, extension classes, community centers, and independent and assisted living facilities. They are part of efforts to support "healthy aging." Learning in later years keeps the mind active, creates social connections, and provides the pleasure that comes with exercising critical thinking, reason, imagination, and creativity. It creates strong communities of people who have the ability and interest to continue to learn about life and connect with each other.

Most Americans are familiar with Elderhostel (now Road Scholar) which has provided educational retreats and travel to over 4 million adults fifty-five and older since 1975. A successful series of Jewish programs for seniors based on the Elderhostel model were sponsored by the Midwest Region of the Union of American Hebrew Congregations (now Union for Reform Judaism). Trying to avoid negative connotations of aging, the series was called "The Institute for Mature Adults."

This was one of my most enjoyable teaching experiences, and I found students wise, colorful, and enthusiastic. The four-day, midweek program at Olin Sang Ruby Union Institute in Oconomowoc, Wisconsin, was filled with learning, recreation, prayer, and laughter. Whether talking about God, writing ethical wills, studying Jewish texts, or learning about Jews in the entertainment world—humor, stories, hobbies, and new friendships enriched those days. The relationships created with the wonderful people participating, both professionals and participants, enriched my life.

At the Institute, a woman who was a mother and a grandmother summed up what she wrote in her ethical will by describing "a life of action":

Seek—truth and justice
Explore—your talent and opportunities
Celebrate—life as a Jew and an American
Support—your family, friends, and country with love and understanding
Trust—yourself to do your best
You can **Make Life Happen** by being committed to **Action**.

Besides the more serious messages for the next generation generated in the workshops on writing an ethical will, conversation with various participants during retreats provided me with great advice for coping as a "mature adult."

"As long as you are learning, you are still alive. Keep growing."
"Believe in God. It can't hurt."
"Marriage is for better or worse, but not for lunch."
"Always have room in your life for the unexpected."
"If you think about doing some kind of good deed, just do it—don't waste time wondering about it."
"Don't put anything in writing that you don't want the world to know."
"Don't hold on to anger—it takes too much energy."
"Use every excuse you can to celebrate."

When Malcolm Knowles began writing about adult learning, he contrasted it with children's learning. One of his observations was that children learn information for future application. Knowledge does not have to be put to use immediately. On the other hand, he writes, adult learners are practical learners. They want to learn something that fulfills a particular need and that will benefit their work, their appreciation for leisure activities, their status. He was not aware of the Jewish pursuit of *Torah l'Shemah*, "learning for its own sake," nor was he considering the recreational learning of senior adults. There is little that compares to learning for pleasure whether by studying with an outstanding teacher, by examining a subject in depth, or by suddenly discovering an elusive truth.

As seniors enjoy longer healthy lives, they participate more frequently in adult education activities. Recent research has shown that the brain is similar to a muscle. If you use it, it maintains its elasticity and its strength. Along with Sudoku and crossword puzzles, stimulating lectures and classroom learning exercise the brain in beneficial ways. Scientists are uncovering new secrets about the brain. When an older person participates in new learning, the brain acquires new "plasticity," the ability to reshape itself and improve how it functions. The emphasis is on the word "new." By attending classes, adult learners move out of their comfort zone and participate in a challenging, stimulating, and sustained activity.

Other Voices

Susan Buchbinder, Director of Religious Life for Council for the Jewish Elderly-Senior Life in Chicago, Illinois.

When I began working in the field of aging services thirty years ago, I was a twenty-four year-old who had recently graduated with a Masters in Social Work. My friends were concerned that the work would be depressing. I told them, actually, that the work was quite fulfilling and described how I learned new things every day from these folks who were so much older than me. I learned how I did—or did not—want to age. I got to know Marion, a little lady who, no matter how many curves life threw at her or no matter how many losses she experienced, looked at what was good in her life. She always helped others, no matter how she felt on a particular day. She became a role model for me about how to age with dignity and grace. I also learned how not to age by interacting with elders who were not able to find the positive in life and who fixated on the things dragging them down—even if there was nothing they could do to change them.

In recent years I have discovered joy in learning with the elders in long term care and assisted living residences run by the Chicago Council for the Jewish Elderly-Senior Life. While in college, I taught children in several Hebrew and Sunday schools. Most of time, I felt unsuccessful. I did not have the skills I needed to motivate and engage them. I know that my teaching has come a long way since then, but I find learning together with elders (you notice I did not say, "*teaching* elders") a much more successful rewarding experience. They are motivated, enthusiastic, and able to express themselves beautifully.

I have had the privilege for the past three years of overseeing a Jewish adult learning program for elders. I have marveled at the way the older folks soak up knowledge and are always are reaching out for more. One ninety-one year-old woman—I will call her Dvora—often tells me how important learning is to her. "You have to keep learning until you die," she says. Another student—a gentleman—in reference to the mature approach to text and Bible study in our classes, asks almost every instructor, "How come they never taught us this in *cheder*?" I witness, on a regular basis, how intellectually top-notch, mature Jewish study can rejuvenate the people I work with, people I love and dearly respect.

Reaching the New Emerging Adults

The most recent focus in adult learning is the challenge presented to professionals to attract young adults in their twenties. There are so many of them who would be open to Jewish learning and its rewards were they to make room for it in their busy lives. How do we capture their attention? Many have already demonstrated an interest in participating in Jewish-related learning and activities in their college years —enrolling in Jewish studies classes and, most notably, participating in Birthright Israel—a free, inspiring trip to Israel. Thousands more were active in Hillel. How do we transform learning from a college experience into a lifelong pursuit? How do we transform engagement in a short term experience into a lifelong commitment?

In addition, many twenty-somethings may not have had a Jewish experience since their *bar* or *bat mitzvah*, confirmation, or camp, and there are growing numbers of others who are Jewish by birth but not raised in any way that affirms their identity. For these young adults whose lack of Jewish identity is more apathy than rejection, attending a cultural event, serving as a volunteer in the Jewish community, or participating in Birthright Israel can be the step into Jewish life that could become a journey were there meaningful next steps toward involvement in Jewish pursuits.

"Emerging adults," are a recently identified life-phase. During the past ten years, sociologists have investigated this potential new stage in adult development between adolescence and adulthood. In 2001, in an article, "The Myth of Maturity," Terri Apter wrote about "thresholders," young adults who were not adolescents and had not yet taken on the responsibilities of adulthood. In 2007, *New York Times* columnist David Brooks referred to this time as the "odyssey years." By delaying marriage, having children, and permanent employment, the eighteen to twenty-five year-old takes advantage of an opportunity to explore the world, to investigate life-style possibilities, and to figure out who they are. Most are optimistic and enjoy the great number of choices before them. They continue their education, travel, volunteer, take breaks, fall in and out of love, and pursue a variety of careers. Some researchers extend this stage of life into the thirties. Although many of these sociologists—like Jeffrey Arnett in *Emerging Adulthood: The Winding Road from the Late Teens through the Twenties* (2004)—predict that this is a new stage of human development that will be repeated in future generations, others take a wait-and-see attitude arguing that it is the product of the particular time in which we live.

When it comes to Jewish learning, emerging adults' strong self-focus and their desire for introspection and exploration provide both opportunities and obstacles. Jewish researchers observe in them openness to examining Jewish identity and Jewish perspectives on the meaning of life. These young adults want to create a personalized version of Judaism and experiment with various ways it can be expressed.

Emerging adults are open to spiritual experiences whether through music and the arts, meditation and prayer, studying Jewish text, or nature. In 2003, Bethamie Horowitz studied Jewish adults in the New York Federation area. In the process of investigating how being Jewish fits into people's lives and how a relationship to Judaism evolves over a lifetime, she discovered an important characteristic of today's young Jewish adults. Unlike some in preceding generations who reacted to their grandparent's or great grandparent's immigration to America, the desire to fit in to society, and the Holocaust and its consequences, young adults today do not reject Judaism. That assumes previous involvement or at least an awareness of it. Assimilation into American society and the failure of many Jewish educational institutions—outside of the Orthodox community and day school and camping in the less traditional communities—have left many entering adulthood indifferent to Judaism. Horowitz observes, however, that they are open to influence.

There are critical periods and moments in life that offer opportunities for institutions to play a role if only institutions can be open and available in a way that meets changing needs and concerns.

There are numerous reasons why it is a challenge to attract this group to formal Jewish learning. It may be best understood in their own words. One example comes from a conversation with a college graduate just entering the working world. When asked why he and most of his friends do not attend learning programs offered by the Jewish community, he responded, "I have just finished eighteen-plus years of school. Can't I go out for recess for a while?"

In a phone conversation with a twenty-something, I asked, "Why do you prefer working as a volunteer in the community to attending a class on Jewish ethics?" Without a pause, he responded, "The class benefits me. I want to be able to do something beneficial to the world."

The difficulties in attracting this group also reflect their resistance to affiliation, to paying dues, and to committing to one organization. In their study of young adults, Steven Cohen and Ari Kelman (2007) contrast unmarried Jews, twenty-five to thirty-nine, with parents of school-age children. Of unmarried Jews, 22 percent belong to congregations, 5 percent pay dues to Jewish community centers, 7 percent are members of other Jewish organizations, and 5 percent contributed $100 or more to their local Jewish federation campaign. Of parents of school-age children, 82 percent belong to congregations, 38 percent pay dues to JCCs, 42 percent belong to other Jewish organizations, and 23 percent donate $100 or more to their Jewish federations.

A selection from a blog by David Bryfman that appeared on eJewishplanthropy.com in 2010 elaborates this challenge:

A lot of younger Jews in the United States are even more influenced by American values than by a particularistic Jewish perspective. They view Israel as a foreign country, and their attitudes towards Israel are refracted through the lens of American sensibilities about war, race, and human rights. Their cultural references come from American pop culture. They understand ethical imperatives as obligations to humanity rather than applying first to their own community. And at least half of them have non-Jewish relatives by marriage.

The words and deeds of the organized Jewish community, however, barely register these changes.... [T]he response has often been superficial, temporizing, or panicked rather than substantive. Institutions tout their Facebook pages and Twitter feeds as tokens of how up-to-date they are. They create groups exclusively for young adults, as if this age cohort simply needs special attention and activities .... The problem is that they hold on to two assumptions that are largely no longer true. One is the belief that if individuals try out an organization and like what they see, they'll become involved for the long term .... The other, more serious assumption is an implicit distinction between who's "in" and who's "out," with the object of bringing people "in." That's evident in the language we constantly hear about "welcoming," about creating "points of entry." But American Jews, by and large ... feel, and rightly so, that they have a world of choices available to them and they need only choose the ones best for them.

In spite of Bryfman's critique, many established organizations are offering programs designed especially for younger adults. Federations' Young Leadership Division broadened programming to include more cultural events, health and fitness activities, wine tasting and cooking classes, and social service opportunities. A network of new agencies called Gesher City connects young Jewish adults based on self-determined interests and activities.

National/international programs like Next Dor and Moishe House have shown that it is possible to attract and serve these young adults. Both are nondenominational, peer-directed, community, or home-based efforts that empower twenty-somethings to create their own communities. Next Dor is funded by Synagogue 3000 and local synagogues, foundations, and funders. Moishe House is supported by the Charles Schusterman Foundation and by local resources. Although activities are rarely located in synagogues, community centers, or other traditional settings, these organizations consider themselves to be a conduit between their participants and the established Jewish community. Next Dor has introduced the idea of synagogue satellites, communities of young adults that do not pay synagogue membership dues but share commitments to the same causes.

Moishe House is unique in that the international office responds to local young Jewish leaders who choose to establish a shared residence. In return for rent subsidy and a program budget, residents host between three and seven programs a month in their home. These programs include Jewish learning, social service projects, general culture and social events, and spiritual and Jewish communal activities. They take advantage of local resources and encourage participation in national programs like conferences, service learning, and Birthright Israel. At the end of 2011 there were forty-four Moishe Houses in fourteen countries with 51,387 participants in their activities.

There are local efforts, many like Next Dor that are loosely affiliated with congregations. The Riverway Project based out of Temple Israel in Boston sponsors programs that combine social activities with Shabbat services, pop music, and dinner—soul food. A weekly Torah study class, Torah and Tonic, provides a setting for socializing and learning. These are activities designed to complement and not substitute for other ways to participate in the synagogue community.

Operating since 2003, Brooklyn Jews has attracted young people who want "a meaningful connection to Jewish life, culture, and practice." Congregation Beth Elohim offers young adults ways to learn, to pray together in small neighborhood groups, to connect with Israel, and to recapture "the kind of Jewish community they once may have felt in summer camp, a youth group, or semesters abroad when Judaism and Jewish identity were real, relevant, and alive." They have recently offered a special form of membership for the member of Brooklyn Jews that includes free use of a gym and swimming pool, discounted activities and classes, and priority admission (after full members) of children to nursery school.

In regard to the many young adults who do not participate in these experiences, some claim that if the Jewish community is patient, the majority will become part of the community when they become parents. As young Jewish Americans accept more adult responsibilities, they will discover that they can enhance their lives without having to choose between the values of the American mainstream and Jewish values and Jewish ways of living. Pursuing meaning, spirituality, and community is compatible with being an American—and with being a Jew. This message, however, must reach them through planned systematic efforts on the part of the organized Jewish community and the young members of that community who want it to change and grow.

Lessons for Today

1. Adult learners prefer classes that organize information they are seeking in a convenient attractive way.

2. Many young adults affiliate with the Jewish community when they marry and have children. Effective parent education is tailored to serve specific interests and needs that reflect stages of parenting.

3. Reflecting a concern for the future of the American Jewish community, many funders and adult learning professionals are directing their attention to working with emerging adults.

4. Identifying and acting as a Jew used to be accompanied by membership or affiliation. Today this is only one way to express Jewish identity. Young Jewish adults are attracted to nondenominational, peer-directed, neighborhood-based activities that do not require them to join an institution or attend activities on a regular basis.

5. Jews do not have to choose between the values of the American mainstream and Jewish values and ways of living. Pursuing meaning, spirituality, and community is compatible with being an American—and with being a Jew.

6. As baby boomers retire over the next decades and join the present group of senior adults, a third of the Jewish population will be retirees. Many of them are—or will become—lifelong Jewish learners.

7. The numbers of individuals participating in adult Jewish education have increased, but less than 50 percent of the core Jewish community is enrolled in learning activities. The percentage drops as connections to the community decrease.

Chapter IV

Seekers of Equality, Belonging, and Meaning

We must create a climate of elucidation ... of pronouncing our people's waiting for meaning ... by discovering and teaching the intellectual relevance of Judaism, by fostering reverence for learning and the learning of reverence .... — Abraham Joshua Heschel

Responding to the historic and sociological events of each decade and the desires growing out of individual lives, Jewish adult learning in America is unique in every generation. Children react to the world created by their parents. They have their own dreams and visions to fulfill. The last four decades of adult learning have been shaped both by the changing journey of adulthood and by unique groups of learners who demand and deserve attention.

Women: Claiming a Heritage

This all began for me when my neighbor, Dee Berg, invited my family to help decorate her Christmas tree. When I declined and asked why she celebrated Christmas, not Hanukkah, she explained that she always likes to do something this time of the year. "It's easier and more fun," she said, "for the kids to pick out and decorate a tree than to buy candles for a candle holder. Besides, I don't know how to light the candles and say the prayers, and there is no place to find out."

That was the beginning of what was eventually known in Chicago's northern suburbs as JET, or Jewish Effectiveness Training. My two children were in school all day, leaving me with time on my hands, women's liberation on my mind, and the question, "What am I going to be when I grow up?" ringing in my ears. A friend, Fran Alpert, was in the same position. Fran possessed a dedication and love for Judaism, a teacher's certificate, and a flair for public relations. We had lunch together in front of her fireplace in January 1973 to plan our future. By March, we were ready to teach young mothers how to create a Jewish home. Classes included learning about Shabbat and religious holidays by exploring rituals, history, and literature; Jewish cooking; and activities parents could enjoy with their children. Our flyer for the course also advertised "Consciousness-raising sessions—what does being Jewish mean?" The first class consisted of eighteen women; it was held at a local Jewish Community Center.

From the outset, we wanted to connect students to past family experiences so we asked each student to write down her earliest memory of a Jewish experience. There were memories of a *Zaide*'s long silky-fringed *tallis,* of homemade noodles, of newspapers spread on a freshly washed floor on a Friday afternoon to protect it from the drips and spills of pre-Shabbat cooking, of a white-haired grandmother with black lace on her head lighting candles. One woman recalled bouncing on her father's shoulders in a noisy parade around the synagogue sanctuary. These memories had colored the women's feelings toward Judaism, and now they wanted to create memories for their own children. Sharing these stories called attention to the fact that they were continuing something that had been a part of their parents' and grandparents' lives. They were also continuing certain traditions that were thousands of years old.

In another class, we discussed the meaning of the blessings over the Shabbat candles. We gave them two candles to be lit at home on the next Shabbat, one candle for each version in the Torah of the commandment to observe Shabbat. Students were offered the option of taking extra candles to light representing each of their children, a practice in some homes. We demonstrated how to light candles and explained why you cover your eyes before reciting the blessings. As we were to discover on a number of occasions, many students knew what to do, but not why. Frequently, we were asked, "Why?" and sometimes could only toss the question back to our students. There were always a healthy combination of poets, pragmatists, and cynics in our classes to provide an exciting range of answers.

As expected, the students who had never lit candles felt awkward doing it. One woman had lit candles alone in her bedroom because she was so self-conscious in front of her family. We spoke about the woman's responsibility to welcome Shabbat for the entire household and the value of their children witnessing it. It was also important, we agreed, that the children see us attempt to learn something new. One student talked about practicing the blessing and the ritual motions before the dinner hour. Another spoke of her husband's pleasure that she was doing this. Another mentioned that she had silenced her giggling children by saying, "I don't care if you think it's funny, but don't interrupt me!"

We had theoretical questions like "What is the source of the prayer?" and practical ones like "If we go out after dinner, can I blow the candles out?" We told the two women who had not lit candles that they should do it the coming Shabbat, and that they were behind one week's assignment and were expected to keep up with the class. We noted with amusement the encouragement from their classmates: "Try it! You'll like it!"

What we were experiencing in these young mothers was a hunger for knowledge of Judaism they had not had access to as adults. They were learning about Judaism on a sophisticated level in a way that was relevant to their present lives. They were motivated by a desire to create Jewish homes and to talk about Judaism with their children, most of whom were attending congregational schools or day schools. Many of our students had grown up in Jewish communities where education for girls was considered less important than for boys. Many had not celebrated a *bat mitzvah*; all of them wanted their daughters to be as well educated as their sons.

One of our students' favorite classes was led by my grandmother, Dinah Pershin, who was then in her seventies. In a student's kitchen, she demonstrated how she baked challah. One student transferred my grandmother's handful of flour into a measuring cup before adding it to the mixture in the bowl. That way, she could record the recipe more precisely. And I can still hear Grandma's voice that accompanied the handfuls of flour going into the bowl: "*Vun, tu, drei, fir.*"

My grandmother's presence reminded us that a world was slipping from our grasp. These young mothers wanted to carry on traditions that were part of their family memories. They wanted to make them part of their children's memories, but first they had to learn them.

OTHER VOICES

Fran Alpert, master Israel tour educator and teacher in Jerusalem.

As a young mother, my growing sense of Jewish commitment was fulfilled through JET. Torah study became peer-oriented as we created a lesson plan of basic Jewish life and observance. Our enthusiasm for all things related to Jewish life—hands-on challah baking, Bible study, and life-cycle education—provided young mothers with a supportive first step in building a Jewish home. Not only did many of those first JETers continue their exploration, but several became deeply involved in many areas of Jewish life in Chicago and elsewhere.

Leading the JET classes propelled me toward a more focused path to deeper learning. My sense of worth as an educator was more firmly grounded, administrative skills in planning and execution of programs became more defined, and the "art" of working with a colleague took on new dimensions. Forty years after the JET class, I am still deeply satisfied when a former student stops me in Highland Park, Chicago, or Jerusalem and says, "I still remember your JET class. It made a difference in my life."

Nachas? For sure, but also the highest compliment a teacher can receive.

The women I have met in JET classes and elsewhere over the years are committed to living a full Jewish life. They are claiming their heritage through study and by bringing Jewish rituals and prayers into their homes. They are ensuring that their daughters—and their sons—receive the spiritual inheritance to which they are entitled. In spite of all the changes in society and the Jewish community, it is primarily women who remain responsible for the education of children. They want to be good mothers, good Jewish wives, and be better informed, contributing members of their community.

In the early 1970s, the women's movement affected all of us. Many women held part- or full-time jobs and also had major responsibility for maintaining their home. Feminism made us conscious of the multiple challenges women faced. It inspired us to join in study and prayer and to advocate for women's equal participation in Judaism. One group—the Jewish Feminist Organization—was founded in 1974 as an intellectual, philosophical, and political movement to achieve equality for women. Women's *Rosh Hodesh* groups and women's retreats thrived. Congregation-based adult *bat mitzvah* classes allowed women who had not celebrated a *bat mitzvah* as adolescents to do so now. At model *seders*, women read from a feminist *haggadah*. We welcomed biblical women, as well as the men, into the *sukkah*. We subscribed to *Lilith Magazine*, studied prayers from women's *siddurim*, wrote midrash, and read books and articles about women and Judaism. There were women's study groups like Jewish Effectiveness Training that offered instruction and discussion on how to create a Jewish home. *Sisterhood is Powerful*, published in 1970, was not about synagogue sisterhoods but was the focus of many conversations among Jewish women. Dramatic changes in Judaism occurred when the Hebrew Union College ordained the first woman rabbi in 1972. The Reconstructionist Rabbinical College followed by ordaining its first woman rabbi in 1974; and the first female rabbi in the Conservative movement was ordained in 1985.

As the Jewish Feminist Organization declared in the preamble to their 1974 constitution, we were committed

> to the development of our full human potential and to the survival and enhancement of Jewish life. We seek nothing less than the full, direct, and equal participation of women at all levels of Jewish life—communal, religious, educational, and political. We shall be a force for such creative change in the Jewish community.

Now, at the beginning of the second decade of the twenty-first century, efforts to establish the equality of Jewish women are moving in new directions. Today, most young women affiliated with liberal denominations are hardly aware of what previous generations experienced. Women serve as Reform, Conservative, Reconstructionist, and Renewal rabbis across the country. As heads of congregations, day schools, and camps, they are reshaping the institutions in which they work. Others are creating new institutions. They are presidents of congregations and chairpeople of committees that shape Jewish life. Research on who attends the Florence Melton Adult Mini-School reports that that 79 percent of those enrolled are women. Growth in trends as diverse as spirituality, Jewish cooking, modern Midrash, healing services, and congregation support groups is frequently attributed to women.

The status of women has been raised in congregations to the extent that some are now concerned that it is resulting in the feminization of Judaism where men cede too much responsibility for leadership and participation in learning and worship to women. Books are being written that address the need to increase the involvement of men in synagogue life. They include recommendations for more gender-defined activities, separate classes, and varied approaches to marketing.

The most dramatic changes are in the Orthodox community. Women's prayer groups, partnership *minyanim*, and women's *yeshivot* testify to the access women now have to Jewish resources and experiences. They are accepted by some in the Orthodox community as spiritual and intellectual leaders. The first egalitarian Orthodox *yeshivah*, Yeshivat Hadar, opened in New York in 2009. That same year Yeshivat Maharat was founded to educate women to become rabbinic authorities. Founded by a woman ordained by Rabbi Avi Weiss, head of Yeshivat Chovevei Torah, it is the first Orthodox institution in Jewish history whose goal is to ordain Orthodox female religious leaders. Subsequently, the Rabbinic Council of America passed a resolution against women's ordination—its opposition based on tradition, proper gender roles, and perception that it is against the value system of the Torah. However, a more recent debate in the national spotlight reflecting the sensitivity of the issue was centered not on the ordination of a woman but rather on the title reflecting her new status.

Efforts continue to enhance the role of women in all sectors of Jewish life. Adding to the recognition of Jewish women in North America today is the Jewish Women's Archives in Boston. The Archives uncovers, chronicles, and transmits the history of Jewish women in North America. Its staff creates learning materials for all ages that commemorate and celebrate Jewish women and their efforts to achieve equality. Online, the Archives offers an encyclopedia, exhibits, book and film guides, and a blog, all of which are dedicated to the role of women in America. The knowledge, pride, and self-respect generated are a form of advocacy that speaks to women—and men—of all ages.

Challenges still exist. A study of 2,500 Jewish professionals in 2010 revealed serious inequality in salaries between men and women. Two-thirds of Jewish community professionals are women. Their median age is forty-eight. Sociologist Steven M. Cohen's research showed that these women are paid on average $20,000 less per year than men in comparable positions. On this front, the Jewish community, both men and women, have work to do.

Intermarried Adults: Adopting a Heritage

While leading a workshop for parents of high school students, I used a metaphor I had relied on in several other settings. Jews today, I said, perform a sacred task. Each person provides a link between the past and the future in our chain of tradition which extends back to Sinai. Then one young woman said, "I am the first person in my family in this chain. I converted to Judaism. I am just a charm on the bracelet." This triggered an intense discussion about all of us standing at Sinai, about the privileges and pleasures of Jewish life, and our responsibility for the next generation regardless of when we became part of the chain.

In reality, we are living in a time when most non-Orthodox Jews are "Jews by choice." We decide for ourselves what kind of Jews we want to be and whether we want to remain part of the Jewish community. Once making that choice, we link ourselves with all that happened to the Jews who lived before us, all that is happening to Jews today, and all that will happen in the future. Each one of us inherits the richness of experience and learning; each of us passes it on to others.

On another occasion, a man who chose Judaism told me that he had gone through a conversion ceremony and a Jewish wedding, but not until spending more than two years learning in the Florence Melton Adult Mini-School did he feel that he was truly becoming a Jew.

Another time, a woman married to a Jew and just beginning the conversion process shared her distress over the decision of her congregation that as a non-Jewish member of the family, she could not open the ark at her son's *bar mitzvah*. "That is why Jewish study is so wonderful," she said, "no one argues or objects to my learning Torah."

Often adults who are new to Judaism bring their born-Jewish partners with them, Jews who would not otherwise have chosen to attend classes. Many people who had been in conversion classes discovered that these whetted their appetites for more knowledge. They are among the most highly motivated Jewish learners.

Frequently, non-Jews attend classes and participate in Jewish experiences. Moishe House (described in the previous chapter) recognizes that non-Jews are part of many Jewish social circles and welcomes them to participate in activities. In the Mini-School, there was a couple who wanted to teach about the Jewish roots of Christianity in their church, a brother and sister who knew that their ancestors had lived as Jews in Spain, and the grandparents of children being raised Jewish by their daughter who had converted to Judaism. These grandparents wanted to learn how to share Shabbat, holidays, and rituals, as well as Jewish stories with their children and grandchildren.

The social networks that develop in classes especially influence intermarried couples. For those couples who deliberated about whether to raise their children as Jews, having Jewish friends tipped the scales toward Judaism. Classmates also affected whether parents enrolled their child in a Jewish preschool. While peer relationships may help establish connections with the Jewish community, something more is needed to sustain and deepen these connections. Meaningful encounters with program leaders and teachers who take a personal interest in parents are important. These encourage and guide parents to continue their Jewish explorations.

The number of people who enter the Jewish community as adults has grown significantly over the past four decades. Some enter the community through conversion, others out of curiosity or at the urging of a close friend. Some may be non-Jews who live in Jewish homes or who work in Jewish organizations. All this is at the core of the question of "Who is a Jew?" and has consequences for ritual within our various denominations, as well as for citizenship in Israel. Jewish practice and language is changing, not only to include respect for non-Jews living among us but also those men, women, and children who are on the way to becoming Jews. In some Reform congregations on Yom Kippur, a prayer of gratitude is recited for the non-Jews in the congregation who support the Jewish life of their family members. Perhaps *havair toshav*, "friend living among us," is a better term than what is sometimes used today—*gair toshav*, "resident stranger."

Spiritual Seekers: Deepening a Heritage

I attended the first meeting of a Florence Melton Adult Mini-School class in October 2001 at the Fourteenth Street Y in New York. To get there, I walked by a fire station next door to the Y where bouquets of flowers, notes, and pictures memorialized firemen who had sacrificed their lives on 9/11, just several weeks before the class. As the class began, the teacher asked students why they were there. A daughter and mother were studying Judaism together. A young man serving on a synagogue board wanted to know more about his Jewish community. A Russian immigrant wanted to learn what it meant to be Jewish. I was moved most by one student who began by describing the view from her apartment window:

> I look outside and see space where the Twin Towers once stood. I need to be in this class to allow myself time to think about what happened and to look for answers to the questions I am now asking. Something was taken from me that day. I want to try to find it again.

The answers to the young woman's questions are elusive. Not knowing them challenges our life as spiritual and religious human beings. Seeking for answers—looking for something healing in a fractured world—provides a path when we feel helpless. We cannot explain why tragedy occurs. Similarly, we cannot prove that God exists. By searching, however, we open ourselves to the possibility of rediscovering meaning in life and evidence of God.

I learned the most about spiritual seeking within the context of Judaism from a series of retreats I led with Rabbi Alan Bregman, Director of the Midwest Regional office of the Union of American Hebrew Congregations (UAHC, now the Union for Reform Judaism). We called the experience "Encountering God in Your Life." Introducing the program at a UAHC Kallah at Brandeis University, we told the twenty participants that we were setting aside time and space to think about our personal relationship with God and about finding meaning in the world. We would be looking at the profound and painful aspects of life and God's role in them. We would not discuss theology or try to convince anyone to believe in God. We were inviting them to explore the possibility of God acting in their lives. The next three days included journal writing, art, music, meditation, storytelling, study, and discussions.

Using five Biblical texts as starting points, we traveled on a metaphorical journey from darkness to light. The first stage of the journey, based on God telling Abraham to travel to an unknown land (Genesis 12:1), led to a discussion about taking risks—its dangers and rewards and what provides security and comfort when we explore what is unknown. That led to the story of creation in the first chapter of Genesis: the world emerged out of chaos and confusion. Each person drew and shared with the rest of us a timeline of their lives illustrating periods when they were unsure, insecure, or troubled—when they felt alone. The third text—Jacob wrestling with an angel (Genesis 32:25-33)— laid the groundwork for a discussion of victories and defeats participants had experienced. Elijah hearing a "still small voice" (I Kings

19:11-13) provided an opportunity to recall when participants had personally heard such a voice. The final exercise started with a discussion of the priestly blessing and, specifically, the word *ya'er*, "shine," as in "May God cause His countenance to shine upon you"(Numbers 6:25). We talked about moments of clarity, insight, and understanding.

We found over the ten years we led these retreats that there is a yearning to connect with something beyond an intellectual understanding of the world—a longing for something sacred permeates everyday existence. It connects us to a wholeness that is greater than us. As a result of encountering parts of life which are rarely considered, participants in the retreat gained insights into the meaning and purpose of their lives. They also discovered new sources of strength.

There are differences among "theology," "religion," and "spirituality." They are, however, interrelated. From a teacher's perspective, the theological question, "Do you believe in God?" is the most difficult to answer. If it is not clearly "yes" or "no," there is resistance to the question and commonly a retreat to the answer "I'm not sure." The religion-related question, "Where in Judaism do you find a connection to God?" is easier to answer and results in a discussion of meaningful rituals, prayer, life cycle events, and holiday celebrations. The spirituality question, the one most easily answered by the majority of Jewish learners, is "When in your life have you felt close to God?" It meets with the least resistance and allows for a variety of answers, some tied to Jewish life and some to nature, humanity, and the broader, created world. All three categories are elements in a relationship with God.

I have seen that the cerebral can be a starting point for the spiritual. In the Florence Melton Adult Mini-School which is strongly committed to conveying Jewish literacy, studying text leads to discussions about our relationship to God and about experiencing the spiritual through prayer, Israel, nature, and ethical behavior. Classical and modern texts contain responses to questions about revelation, providence, what happens after we die, and why there is suffering in the world. God, who no longer appears in a burning bush or a pillar of smoke, still can speak to us through Jewish texts.

Over the years I have taught adults, I have seen growth in students' comfort as they address questions of spirituality. For some, even saying the word "God" can be awkward. As "God language" is used more frequently in our culture, it creates an openness, perhaps even a need, for these kinds of discussions. I have also learned that experiencing God can be contagious. By hearing others speak about their searching and about their spiritual discoveries, students open up to the possibility of this happening to them, too. Many of us are, in fact, looking for ways to overcome the tensions, confusion, and anonymity of modern life.

Students have spoken of not finding a Jewish place where they can talk about their souls and their seeking. Because other cultures have been more responsive to this need, Jews have looked beyond the Jewish community for guidance in spiritual learning, meditation, and contemplation. Few Jewish professionals have had formal preparation enabling them to discuss matters of a theological or spiritual nature. Until recently, it was rarely included in the education of rabbis, cantors, and educators. Fortunately, this is changing.

No description fits all spiritual seekers. They cannot be categorized by age, gender, or religious background. Men and women are equally capable of discovering their soul—and that of the Jewish people. Spirituality can be achieved by looking inward or outward, in formal prayer or creative expression, through the intellect or through emotion. That so many people I have met throughout my career have found evidence of God, wholeness and meaning in life, is for me one of the strongest proofs of God's existence.

Leadership: Assuring a Heritage

When a rabbi suggested that the president of her congregation sign up for an adult learning program that might interest him, the lay leader joked, "Rabbi, I thought we had an agreement. You don't have to participate in my board meetings, and I don't have to participate in your classes and worship services."

Underlying this story is a question that must constantly be addressed: Why should leaders who are already giving considerable service to Jewish life also devote time to Jewish learning? The question goes back to Talmud *Kiddushin* 40b:

> Rabbi Tarfon and the Elders had been dining ... in Lod when this question was presented to them: Is study greater or is practice greater? Rabbi Tarfon's opinion was sought and he said, "Practice is greater." Rabbi Akiba's opinion was sought and he said, "Study is greater." The opinion of the whole group was sought and they said, "Study is greater, for study leads to practice."

Individuals who lead congregations, organizations, and institutions need to be encouraged to study Jewish text to enhance their experience as leaders and to link what they do to ethics and values of Jewish life. Some of the most respected Jewish leaders of the past decades have been inspired by programs like CLAL (Center for Leadership and Learning) and the Wexner Heritage Program, programs that united Jewish learning and leadership.

Throughout our history, each generation of Jewish leaders has approached Torah in light of its own experiences and integrated it into the Jewish world. By studying, leaders learn from those who came before us: they question, they reflect, they wrestle with ideas. New students receive the tradition, and then pass it on to the next generation. They do all this within a community of leaders, all talking, arguing, agreeing, and disagreeing. They listen and affirm; negotiate and compromise with one another. The multiplicity of ideas encourages mutual understanding. It opens up conversations and sharing insights into problems of the time. Learning texts teaches us how to be part of a community that debates important issues about life and that supports, challenges, and works toward answers together. In the process, groups develop a shared language that comes out of Jewish tradition. Texts also provide models of leadership and tales of how others learned from one another and from their mistakes. They have the potential to raise the level of discussion from management of the community's resources to the level of inspired leadership that incorporates eternal ideas and vision for the future.

Jewish leaders integrate learning into their lives. At a time when Jewish education is perceived as one way to halt assimilation and strengthen the Jewish community, such leaders set an example, modeling good judgment, generosity, intellectual growth, and respect for the Jewish past. They frequently become advocates for Jewish education and for Jewish teachers. They influence policy and funding of Jewish education.

In an ideal world, learning would be a natural component of Jewish leadership. It would be seen as a reward rather than another onerous commitment to fulfill. The reality, however, is that those who work with leaders must find effective ways to motivate them to participate in Jewish learning. Torah study at the beginning of meetings sets a tone for the work ahead; when done effectively, it can lead to continuing participation in learning. Another setting is the leadership retreat. I attended a mid-career Leadership Retreat sponsored by the Center for Leadership and Learning (CLAL). During a concentrated period of time—only five days—I studied Jewish sources with eminent teachers, interacted with other Jewish education leaders, and was pushed to my creative limits by assignments that linked learning to work. To this day, the high level of learning that focused on models of leadership and contemporary responsibilities influences my professional life.

A community leader recently confided that he could not imagine his professional life without ongoing learning. For him, as for Jews through the ages, study is a blessing. A specific prayer articulates that for us: "Blessed are You, God of the Universe, who has made us a holy people by commanding us to occupy ourselves with words of Torah." Study has made us holy. It has made us unique. The joy of discovery and the exhilaration of meeting an intellectual challenge are fulfilling rewards. In addition, pursuit of Torah enables us to discover what it means to be a Jewish leader created in the image of God.

Who Is Not Participating: Ignoring a Heritage

A challenge to contemporary teachers and leaders is how to shape institutions and organizations so they attract and serve the rainbow of Jewish life beyond the present core Jewish community. The 2001 Jewish population study paints a disappointing picture. While 47 percent of the highly-affiliated Jewish population participates in learning, only 29 percent of moderately-affiliated Jews and 6 percent of unaffiliated attend. Only the active core of the Jewish community is taking advantage of the proliferation of opportunities to learn and the improved quality of the experience.

Attracting the marginally-affiliated and the unaffiliated is made even more difficult because of the growing distance between the centers of Jewish life and the periphery. There are debates between those supporting "inreach" and those who advocate for "outreach." Do we dedicate our time, money, and energy to enriching those who are identifying themselves as committed Jews—however that is defined—or to attempting to bring those outside of our existing institutional world into the community? There are more of these marginal Jews today than ever and they are socially and psychologically more removed from the center. In addition, they drift easily in and out of organizations and Jewish experiences.

Diversity and Response

The two chapters just completed only begin to explore the great diversity of expression of Jewish identity. Jews of all ages—including those who choose to affiliate with a particular denomination—are defining their own ways of being Jewish. Within any synagogue, there are many pathways to a Jewish life. In the broader Jewish community, a Jew can choose to be part of a group that focuses on philanthropy, community service, culture, meditation, yoga, or the environment. Each offers opportunities to act out Jewish identity in ways meaningful to the individual. The important consideration in the present context is that learning can be part of them all.

The following chapters illustrate how key institutions in American Jewish life attempt to respond to these challenges—some of them succeeding and some not. The efforts continue as the concern for the American Jewish future grows.

Lessons for Today

1. In spite of all the changes in the Jewish community and Jewish life in America, it is primarily women who remain responsible for the Jewish education of children.

2. Jewish women have not yet achieved equality with men. While women make up two-thirds of all Jewish community professionals, they are paid on average $20,000 less per year than men in comparable positions.

3. There is a yearning among many Jews to connect with something beyond an intellectual understanding of the world.

4. There are multiple Jewish pathways for Jews on a spiritual journey. We can become aware of forces beyond what is human through Jewish rituals, Jewish theology and philosophy, Jewish text, community activities, and prayer and meditation.

5. God can speak to us through Jewish texts.

6. Being part of a group who study text and wrestle with ideas teaches leaders how to debate important issues and to support or challenge one another as they work towards answers together.

7. The debate over how to use diminishing community resources—for inreach or outreach—continues and is taking on new urgency as the

distance between the center and the margin increases and the numbers of Jews outside conventional boundaries increase.

Chapter V

The Synagogue
Adapting to New Realities or Not

So picture the synagogue not as corporation or marketplace for programs, but as Pisgah, the summit of human life, whence from every side we see promise, hope, and meaning. — Lawrence A. Hoffman

*T*he vitality of Judaism in America will be determined by the way synagogues adapt to the changing Jewish community. In the 1960s, suburban synagogues were serving the needs of Jews who had left the ghetto-like life of urban settings and had followed other prosperous Americans to the suburbs. Reform and Conservative Congregations offered what members needed to sustain their Jewish identity without impinging too much on their American way of life.

In 1972 Marshall Sklare addressed the form Jewish education took in a suburban Conservative congregation.

> The flexible structure of the Conservative education has proven to be highly popular. It has provided a Sunday school curriculum for the children of minimalist parents, as well as a reduced Talmud Torah program for those interested in more intensive training. Thus, whatever the desires of parents—except if they belong to that small minority which insists on a very thorough Hebrew education—their needs can be met. If the boy attends Hebrew school, he can be taught enough so that he will be competent to perform at the *bar mitzvah* rite …. The educational program for the young serves to compensate for the declining interest in worship among the adults. In addition, the parents of the children who are registered in the school represent a group which can be enrolled in the congregation.

North Suburban Synagogue Beth El in the 1960s housed a school in which over 1000 students—preschool, kindergarten through high school—were learning. Beth El was a growing, thriving Conservative congregation that was the subject of some of Marshall Sklare's research. My responsibilities as its Assistant to the Director of Education included teaching parents as well as other adults enrolled in continuing education classes. The Jewish Theological Seminary had recently produced a Parent Education Program that paralleled what children were learning in Conservative synagogue schools, day schools, and special education programs. The formal curriculum covered holidays, prayer, and Jewish history and equipped parents with the vocabulary and basic knowledge they needed to participate in Jewish conversations with their children—reinforcing what they learned in school.

A series of workshops and activities for parents of preschool children prepared them to share Jewish moments with their children at home. Activities on Shabbat and holidays brought the family into the synagogue to learn and to celebrate. There were a *sukkah* party, a Passover model *seder*, a Shabbat *seudah shlishit*, and an *erev Shabbat* dinner preceded by a Jewish cooking class and making centerpieces. There was also an opportunity for mothers of preschoolers to come into the congregation after morning carpool for a cup of coffee and discussions on creating a Jewish home. Since these groups met while children were in nearby classrooms, from time to time there were mother-child activities like baking challah and *hamantashin*, decorating the *sukkah* and playing *dreidel*.

Further along the spectrum of parent learning, there was a B'nai Mitzvah Parent Institute. During the year prior to a child's *bar* or *bat mitzvah*, parents learned about Shabbat, the Shabbat prayer service, *mitzvot*, and Jewish beliefs about God, Torah, and the Jewish people. There were discussions on their child's education and the upcoming *bar/bat mitzvah* ceremony and celebration. During joint parent-child activities, families studied the *parshiot* ("portions" of the Torah read at the *bar/bat mitzvah* service) and rehearsed *brachot* ("blessings") and rituals surrounding the Torah reading.

Another early venture into ambitious family and adult learning was a 1982 family *kallah*, a Thursday through Sunday retreat held at the congregation. Joining with Rabbi Neil Gillman, Rabbi Mayer Rabinowitz, and Amy Eilberg, then a rabbinic student and later to be the first woman ordained at the Jewish Theological Seminary, the Beth El staff and lay leadership, established goals and activities for the *kallah* scheduled to take place just prior to Passover. The records list the goals as:

🌿 Making families aware of their homes as a setting for Jewish education.

❧ Motivating families to use the Sabbath and festivals as opportunities for education within the home and the synagogue.

❧ Transmitting skills and knowledge related specifically to observing Passover in the home.

❧ Creating a model of an intensive family education weekend which could be used by others.

The event was held in the synagogue, not a retreat center, in spite of misgivings about losing the audience. Thinking was that this model could be duplicated more easily by other congregations which might not have access to a retreat center. It allowed leaders to focus on education rather than logistics, plus it was considerably less expensive, and freed funds for the educational program.

The *Haggadah* served as the "textbook" and the *seder* table as the "classroom." Using lecture, text study, small group discussions, games, socio-dramas, music, and art, sessions included the Exodus as the founding myth for the Jewish people, the *Haggadah* as *midrash*, the *seder* as a family "happening" and Passover in music, literature, and art. Some sessions were for parents and children together, others divided them into separate groups that also reflected different ages of the children. In some sessions, parents taught their children what they had learned. Seventeen families participated.

The experience was intended to be a beginning of a process. At a discussion held after Passover, families reported how this Passover was different in light of what they learned at the conference. They spoke of their home being transformed and asked for workshops and materials on *Shavuot*, the High Holidays, *Sukkot* and Hanukkah. The *kallah* began a year-long family education experience that was repeated for other families in the years that followed.

Family education has remained central in congregations. Over a decade later, a task force on continuing education met to examine existing adult programs at Beth El, to study successful activities elsewhere, and to make recommendations on how to increase numbers of synagogue members participating in Jewish learning. It recommended a more inclusive definition of "continuing education," a broader perspective on how and where adults can learn, and a cataloging of distinct learning groups within the community. Educating parents of children in the synagogue school and nearby Solomon Schechter Day School were high on the list of priorities. Besides workshops, classes that parallel children's learning, and Jewish parenting classes, the task force recommended the creation of a "family school." This would provide families with the option of attending Sunday school together. It was instituted for the pre-*b'nai mitzvah* family group. The model continues to be popular today.

Educating Adults in Synagogues of the Twenty-First Century

The Jewish adult education world has changed dramatically over the past four decades. As indicated in Chapters III and IV, the diversity of people who participate has expanded, and their search for answers to practical and existential questions has intensified. Keeping in mind adults' unlimited freedom to design their lives, the Judaism lived by the majority of affiliated Jews is one that they have created for themselves. Denominational movements tolerate the variety of expressions of Jewish life among members. Many who choose to join congregations do not expect to comply in their personal lives with the boundaries of a movement. Indicative of weakening adherence to movement standards, many join because of what Marshall Sklare was already calling "congregationalism." Their allegiance is not to an ideology or a complex of organizations but to their rabbi, their friends, and the educational, social, cultural, and religious activities centered in a convenient synagogue—the congregation's ability to meet their personal needs.

Demographic changes in America add to the variety of people who affiliate with synagogues. Increased longevity of seniors and the generation of baby boomers, the bulging "pig in the python" demographic, have raised the average age in many congregations. Young adults, who are commonly delaying marriage and children until their late twenties or early thirties require different programs and different means of affiliation. Many resist affiliation all together. Historically-strong congregations are graying and experiencing shrinking membership. Affiliation with synagogues averages around 45 or 46 percent around the country, with New York coming in at 43 percent and, according to a 2010 study, Chicago at 37 percent.

The question is whether synagogues can adapt to these new groups and individuals and still assume the role of guiding religious growth. Can a synagogue expand to accommodate both seniors and emerging adults? Are there ways to affiliate other than by paying membership dues? Can those living out their "sovereign self" feel welcomed in a "commanding community?" Synagogue professional and lay leadership are struggling with the tension between attracting new members and fulfilling the expectations of a movement dedicated to what is best for the Jewish community. The paradox exists that in order to meet institutional needs—maintaining or growing membership—congregations have compromised what is known to be necessary for strengthening Jewish life. Of late, even required time devoted to children's education that prepares them for *b'nai mitzvah* has been cut back in order to compete in the membership marketplace.

Many believe that parent, family, and adult learning is the best pathway by which a synagogue can expand membership. A non-judgmental setting that encourages exploration, questioning, and social exchange for learners, be they the oldest or youngest members of a congregation, may be the best option for supporting growth. Varieties of learning opportunities extending to the arts, social service, and travel to Israel can supplement what seems like meager expectations for the formal Jewish education of members. Efforts to create positive identification, understanding of traditions, and continued involvement in the Jewish community must extend beyond now limited classroom time.

In the spring of 2009, the United Synagogue Regional Office in Chicago convened a think tank to examine Jewish education in congregations and to recommend changes that echo these sentiments. One recommendation echoing the observation above was to broaden the field being examined to include not only "formal education" in the classroom but also "informal education." Expanding how learning is defined encourages professionals to think more systematically about the educational potential of multi-faceted experiences. It increases opportunities to learn and adds new, accessible entry points. The strict boundaries between what is thought of as "education" and the rest of synagogue life are being leveled. Two specific examples that were discussed at the United Synagogue think tank were (1) using all aspects of Shabbat observance—cooking, *oneg Shabbat*, three Shabbat meals, prayer, formal study, *havdalah*—as opportunities for congregation learning; and (2) setting aside one month during the year when classes would ordinarily be meeting for educational art and cultural activities inside and outside of the congregation.

A second priority of the think tank reinforced decades of commitment to parent education. The recommendation given highest priority by multiple breakout groups recognized that synagogues have the responsibility to educate parents—and parents and children together—so that the home supplements and reinforces what is taught in congregations. It was seen as a way to motivate commitment to Jewish education and the synagogue and to strengthen the Jewish identity of the individual and the family.

When comparing the 2009 Think Tank with the 1972 Passover Retreat and the recommendations of the 1995 Adult Education Task Force, consistent principles of excellence emerge. All three settings model or advocate for parent education and the blending of formal and informal education. The primary focus is children's education and the enhancement of it through parent education.

These unchanging priorities indicate, on one hand, their essential role in synagogue life. On the other hand, this raises some important questions. Is this enough? Are we merely reinventing a wheel that may not even be taking us where we want to go? If efforts since 1972 have not stemmed the flow of individuals from the committed core of the Jewish community, are we overlooking opportunities to increase the reach and effectiveness of parent, family, and adult learning? In addition, there is the question of whether the increasing numbers of congregants who no longer have children in school are being adequately served. These adults, who will continue to make up a growing proportion of synagogue membership, are part of the lifeblood of a congregation and are an important part of the model of a Jewish community.

In 1996, Rabbi Lawrence Hoffman, a professor at Hebrew Union College and one of the founders of Synagogue 2000 (now Synagogue 3000) that seeks to strengthn Jewish life in synagogues, wrote:

> We have planned for children only. In our understandable anxiety to pass on Judaism as their heritage, we neglected its spiritual resources for adults, leaving ourselves with no adequate notion of how we, too, might draw sustenance from our faith as we grow up and grow older. Worse: we were often the very children for whom our parents over-planned, so that we should have known better from our own experience. We are living proof that their pediatric approach failed: seeing no models of religious Jewish adulthood, we learned that Judaism is for children, so that many of our friends do not even have the basic commitment to a Jewish future and Jewish learning and life that we possess. And worse yet: we are commit-

ting the same error with our children, devoting all our institutional efforts on their childhood education, while ignoring our own adult needs.

The consequence, said Hoffman, was

little understanding of Judaism as an adult faith, with adult consciousness, adult intellect, and answers to the challenges of adult life. Our synagogue is largely if not wholly driven by children.

Beyond Parent Education

There are unintended outcomes of the prevalent synagogue practice of relegating continuing education to a category separate from parent education. It limits the opportunity for integration of the two settings for learning and limits possibilities of a natural transition between family education and adult education when children leave the synagogue school. In addition, adult learning frequently assumes a lower priority reflected in less funding and the lack of systematic planning, evaluation, and professionalism. A majority of congregations do not have a staff person, other than the rabbi, overseeing continuing education. This separation of responsibilities and lower attention to adult learning reinforces the perception of synagogue life being focused on the religious school and a family's education and association with the institution culminating with a child's *bar/bat mitzvah.* Unless a conscious effort is made to create a transition from adult learning tied to children's learning to "independent" adult learning, synagogues have a greater chance of losing the parents as learners—and a greater chance of losing the family as members of the congregation. In addition, the decisions of professionals and leadership send the message that this religious community plays to the young at the expense of other members—a model that was antithetical to Jewish tradition. The institution whose purpose is to perpetuate sacred Jewish values is surrendering—perhaps unintentionally—to the modern world.

In remedying this, synagogues need to become more aware of what differentiates them from other Jewish institutions. The synagogue is the only institution that has the potential to serve a sustained community throughout the life cycle—birth, marriage, death; the years, the weeks, the days, the moments. It has the potential to be a central, stable presence when almost everything else in life is changing at a more and more accelerated rate. It can support adults at all stages of life through worship, ritual, social, and learning experiences that encourage and guide Jewish growth over five, ten, twenty, fifty years—

over a lifetime. In addition to celebrating joyous occasions and providing support in difficult times, what would it be like if congregants could take advantage of this sustained relationship to construct a deepening relationship with Torah, a continuous path of learning?

Successful Congregational Models

There are notable positive changes in many congregations. What follows are examples of synagogues that embrace both parents and children and the post-carpool generations. Characterized by systematic planning, adult learning as a funding priority, excellent teaching, and growing professionalism, these synagogues are adapting to changing membership and the demands of contemporary Jewish life.

Reform congregations are constructed around the character of their constituency as well as the dreams of leadership. Consequently, pursuit of the American way of life while maintaining Jewish identity shapes their approach to learning. Social and intellectual freedom is embodied in a culture of choice, ideally informed choice based on knowledge of Jewish options. As a professional on the Committee of Lifelong Learning of the Midwest Region Union of American Hebrew Congregations (UAHC, now the Union of Reform Judaism or URJ), I was part of the mobilization of the talents and resources of Chicago area congregations to create effective programs for adult learners. An operating principle of the committee was collaboration—sharing ideas and human resources and encouraging congregants to attend programs in neighboring temples and community settings.

One product of the deliberations of the committee was a community-wide publication of adult learning opportunities which appeared in the local Jewish newspaper two times a year. It also resulted in the publication of a booklet of best practices in adult learning, a compilation of ideas that had been tried and proven successful. Two of the entries highlighted the celebration of learning in contrasting settings. The first is an informal, leaderless discussion group based on curriculum guidelines created by a rabbi. The gatherings emphasize personal seeking and social interaction. The second is a formal, goal-oriented classroom setting leading to a certificate recognizing the learner's achievement.

> **Searchers Groups.** A growing interest in searching for Jewish identity and the inspiration of a UAHC Biennial theme of spirituality led to the formation of Searchers Groups .... As [leadership] hoped, Searchers provided a

meaningful education experience and developed, as well, a sense of community and belonging.

Each Searchers group has about a dozen participants ... composed of a cross-section of congregants—young, older, long-time members, new members, those who are active, and those who attend only High Holiday services. The groups are led by lay facilitators chosen on the basis of their warmth and ability to lead groups democratically and who were ready to explore Judaism along with the group. These leaders attended two training sessions on group facilitation and solving problems that may arise ....

The format of each Searchers session includes: (1) Prayer: Each session begins with sharing experiences brought to mind by a selected prayer: *Shema* created an opportunity to talk about Jewish belief and strength in a time of need. The reading of the *Shehehiyanu* prayer stimulated discussion of having learned or done something new. These discussions create closeness among members of the group, and the prayers bring a religious awareness to sessions, raising them above the level of a support group. (2) Text: the rabbi has chosen Jewish texts and articles of Jewish interest to be read and discussed following guide questions that are provided focusing on the meaning of the texts and their application to life. (3) Refreshments and socializing complete the evening.

The program was introduced during the rabbi's High Holiday sermon. One hundred seventy-five members submitted registration cards agreeing to participate in six sessions over three months. Meetings were extended by twelve more sessions in the initial year and by Shabbat and holiday meals. Groups continue to meet many years later.

Jewish Educational Development (JED) is a certification program for adult Jewish learners. The course of study requires learners to design a personalized series of learning experiences that add up to 135 hours in two major subject areas to be chosen by each participant. The curriculum guidelines determined by a committee of rabbis and adult educators encompass three major questions: What do we do as Jews? What do Jews believe? How do we make Jewish decisions? After the initial pilot year, Hebrew language was added as an additional area of study.

Each learner participating in JED is assigned an advisor to review the learning contract and monitor progress on a yearly basis. Learning is not limited to what is taught at the congregation. It can be independent study—including on-line learning, classes at other institutions, or educational travel. On completion of the 135 hours of study, a participant is honored by their congregation.

Another model synagogue education experience grew out of participation in a 2009 think tank to plan a Center for Spiritual Growth in a local synagogue. Bnai Jehoshua Beth Elohim (BJBE) was moving to a new location. Rabbi Karyn Kedar seized this as an opportunity to re-fashion a synagogue for the twenty-first century. The congregation's programs would provide multiple paths for the search for meaning and purpose. Rabbi Kedar's goal was for the synagogue to become, "a third place—beyond home and work—that connects people to one another, God, and their essential self." Think-tanks were convened to plan centers for adult learning, Israel studies and the Hebrew language, social justice, and centers specifically for men, women, and children. This think-tank was to initiate learning and programming to meet the needs of spiritual seekers.

A group met to brainstorm ideas and programs. During the introductions, Rabbi Kedar asked participants to describe what influenced their spiritual seeking. Think-tank members came from very different beginnings: an Orthodox Jew, a Christian, a non-observant Jew, a small-town Jew, a lifetime member of BJBE, a Conservative Jew. A shared desire for spiritual wholeness led them along many different paths: social service, therapy, Buddhism, Orthodox study, academia, teaching, meditation, yoga. All had come together motivated to design a center for spiritual journeys. The questions needing answers were challenging: What do the diverse stories have in common? Is "spirituality" the best word for what was described? Is *kedushah*, "holiness," a better word? Is gender still an issue? Should sessions be offered that would introduce four different pathways to spiritual growth so those interested could pursue one path in depth? How is participation to be encouraged?

Although finding God and experiencing a spiritual moment is for some a spontaneous surprise, the Center for Spiritual Growth that was created as a result of the committee's work provides alternative, structured ways to discover meaning and God in our lives. The members of the task forces embody some of those alternatives. One person had found God and meaning in the action, symbols, prayers, and music that comprise rituals; another found them by studying Jewish theology and great thinkers; another by listening for God's voice in Jewish text. A fourth person found spirituality in community activities and by doing *mitzvot*—both of these starting with relationships among human beings. Others found spirituality by looking inward through meditation, yoga, and care of the human body. The members of the congregations are on parallel journeys within one home.

Other Voices

Alan J. Levin is an Education Specialist; and Joan Glazer Farber, an Adult Learning Specialist for the Union for Reform Judaism.

We are two people engaged in adult Jewish growth who often feel the frustration of evaluating our success by the number of participants attending sessions. We look at the demographics of the participants. Are they all older adults? We question what program would change that profile. We recognize the need for adult study and personal reflection, and we are refreshed when we step back to judge our successes one adult at a time and look at ways we impacted on lives in our community. As we reflected together the following examples struck us and gave us motivation to keep moving.

A secretary at a Jewish organization who after trying a six-hour speed course on reading Hebrew found the motivation to join a *bat mitzvah* track in her congregations and to continue her study at a deeper level.

A gentile man was so moved at a community *kallah* experience that he continued to attend this winter study retreat for six years and convinced his church to follow the *kallah* structure.

An elderly woman who used a walker drove out in a blizzard so that she would not miss one of her adult classes.

A participant in the URJ Summer Kallah learned how to lead a *shiva minyan*, a service for mourners, using the weekday *nusach*, liturgical melody. Her rabbi had been asking her to join the *minyan* team for years.

A learner who studied *Pirke Avot* in classes and on his own designed a six-week course on the texts he loves and discovered he enjoys teaching as much as learning.

The success of adult learning opportunities should not be based on the number of learners in the room, but in the impact the experience had on each of the learners in attendance.

In 2009, North Suburban Synagogue Beth El organized a Lifelong Learning Task Force. Driven by a new source of funds and the work of an Educational Vision Task Force, the group met to determine how to best serve the congregation's adult learners. Their work included research to define cutting edge adult learning including the growing role of technology, focus on evaluation, and changing demographics. In relation to the latter, it was concluded that there was a growing population within the congregation that had the potential to begin or to enhance their Jewish learning.

Among the recommendations of the Task Force were many that recognized the need for the synagogue to adapt the adult learning to an evolving Jewish environment.

֍ Identify multiple effective entry points or "doors" for all current and potential adult learners and "keep them in."

1. Website to portray the outstanding quality of our adult Jewish education program ....

2. The use of the concierge (a person to help individuals determine a path of learning)

3. Varying the content, type of class, and time offered.

Include programs that satisfy the expressed needs of our congregant students; seek input from potential learners as to desired programs, classes, and learning options including but not limited to

   a. Hebrew, texts, tefillah/prayer, film book clubs, Israel, art, cooking

   b. More informal study, perhaps sometimes in private homes

   c. Classes with fewer sessions

֍ Offer programs with broad appeal

1. More congregation-wide and multi-generation programming

2. Use of the idea of "immediate application of knowledge"

3. Social action, hands-on learning, and interactive program options

֍ Use of technology—website

1. To portray the quality of adult Jewish education and enable easier use of the website

2. To reach out to potential members: college students, emerging adults, home-bound adults, snowbirds, and other groups to be identified

3. To make available class and programs via audio, video, podcasts, etc.

4. To allow congregants access to Jewish learning content from our rabbis, from the Conservative movement, and from other distance learning centers ....

֍ Take advantage of "outside" partnership opportunities by maintaining current and creating new programs which partner with other organizations to provide what we cannot do alone ....

֍ Institute a recognition program to celebrate the ongoing individual studies of our adult learners

֍ Create a method to evaluate each year's programming and set a goal of finding the next fifty, one hundred, one hundred and fifty adult learners

Other Voices

Sandy Starkman is a member of North Suburban Synagogue Beth El since 1982. She is chair of the Continuing Education Committee.

I am Hebrew school educated and I enrolled in a few Jewish studies and Hebrew language classes in college. After graduate school, my husband and I joined a synagogue where I attended a weekly Hebrew language class for seven years, scholars' lectures, and an adult education class when my schedule allowed—although few in attendance were close to the age of my husband and me. A few years later, I enrolled in the two-year Florence Melton Adult Mini-School and continued in graduate classes for another seven years! I have been a student in our rabbi's Talmud class for more than seventeen years and engage in many learning opportunities both at our synagogue and in the community.

I realized early in my life that continual study of Jewish texts and Hebrew language was very important. We enrolled our children in Jewish day school. I wanted them to have the skills and knowledge I didn't possess—and not having to go to afternoon Hebrew school was a bonus! For some reason, I wasn't intimidated by my lack of knowledge. I now know this is one of the significant barriers to adult Jewish education—the feeling that it is not something attainable or even approachable if one has little Jewish background.

My volunteer work in adult education in our congregation began when I served on an adult education task force in 1995 and then became a member, co-chair, and finally the chair of the continuing education committee. We are responsible for implementing all the present task force's recommendations possible within constraints of the budget and staff. We also have the responsibility to see that what we were implementing followed "best practices" in adult education. My most recent volunteer position commenced in 2009, when I chaired the Lifelong Learning Task Force set up to determine the use of the funds from a major financial gift to the synagogue. Adult education at North Suburban Synagogue Beth El has been recognized for excellence in adult Jewish education the last eight years by the United Synagogue of Conservative Judaism.

There has been a shift in thinking about adult Jewish education from simply trying to provide a variety of classes and scholars' lectures to responding to what our congregants want and how best to provide it for them. This involves a variety of settings and different types of learning modalities. We are sensitive to barriers to entry and know there is much competition. Our goal is to elevate the status of adult Jewish learning and to communicate its importance in order to create a larger, wider, and more diverse cohort of congregants who will study, observe more *mitzvot*, and continue on their Jewish journey. The task force came up with some basic strategies to help us "get the next fifty, one hundred, one hundred and fifty learners."

We are no longer the youngest students in our congregation classes, but over one third of our members are under the age of fifty. We would like to engage them in adult Jewish learning over the next few years.

We are inspired by the quotation: "The Teaching isn't beyond reach ... not in the heavens ... but very close to you ..." (Deuteronomy, 30:11-14). This means that Torah and Jewish learning isn't just for God, priests, or our clergy. It is for everyone, and we are obligated to learn and to study.

The Jewish world is changing but so is congregational adult learning. In response to new population groups, new priorities and interests, new translations of texts and technology, there is a new understanding of what comprises good teaching and learning in synagogues. As a result of the fading of the Jewish neighborhood and weakening observance in the Jewish home, the twentieth century belief that the future of Judaism lies exclusively in the congregational school no longer dominates our thinking. The education of parents, grandparents, neighbors, and leaders creates new models and teachers for children that will help create that future. Offering well-planned, high-quality learning experiences for all adults will strengthen synagogue life. The image of the lifelong learner has sustained Judaism in the past and will continue to do so. The discussion on this vital aspect of adult learning is continued in the final chapter about the future.

Lessons for Today

1. The synagogue is the only institution serving Jews throughout their life—birth, marriage, death; the years, the weeks, the days, the moments. The synagogue has the potential for being a central, stable presence when almost everything else in life changes at a more and more accelerated pace.

2. To remain relevant, Jewish institutions must evolve as the Jewish community changes. In the process, however, tension arises between maintaining existing boundaries and adapting to new realities. How does an institution balance the competing demands of the individual member, the individual institution, and the movement?

3. Children's Jewish education encourages parents to participate in Jewish learning and experiences. Without the reinforcement of a Jewish home and community, the impact of children's education will be small.

4. In the synagogue, learning is the most effective way to achieve balance between the individual and the community, between personal desires and the demand of tradition.

5. Synagogues adapt to changing membership and the demands of contemporary American life through systematic planning of education, adjustment of funding priorities, excellent teaching and growing professionalism.

6. By directing resources only to family and parent education and making it a higher priority than post-carpool adult education, congregations are reinforcing the perception that adult synagogue life is tied to children's learning. Consequently, membership may end when children leave the school.

7. That same tendency presents a model of a Jewish community that preferences the young over the old, the married over the single, parents over childless couples.

Expanding National Adult Learning Initiatives

Case Study of the Florence Melton Adult Mini-School

It is clear that we must address ourselves to a massive effort to match the special needs of Jewish adults in bold and creative ways never attempted before! Toward a goal for a more enlightened Jewry, it is proposed that the commission, as its prime responsibility, undertake the task of designing a special kind of adult school. — Florence Zacks Melton

Chapter VI

Meeting the Challenge of Educating Jewish Adults

Ben Bag Bag said: Turn it over and over for everything is contained within it. Delve into it. Grow old and frail in it. Do not depart from it for there is no pursuit better for you than it. - Pirke Avot 5:26

*F*lorence Zacks Melton knew in 1980 that she was creating an educational institution for which the American Jewish community was waiting. After Jewish identity had been totally altered by the Holocaust, a homeland had been established in the Middle East, Israel had achieved an astounding military victory in 1967, and the Jewish community in the Soviet Union had been rescued, new answers were needed for old questions: What does it mean to be a Jew? What purpose do Jews serve in the world? How do we live as Jews when boundaries that had limited us disappear? With persecution, anti-Semitism, and homelessness no longer defining us, with new options rising out of freedom and democracy in America, we needed to know what it meant to be a good Jew.

At the same time, rabbis, lay leaders, and educators were putting a tremendous amount of energy into making Jewish education attractive to a community that was becoming apathetic not only to Jewish education, but to Judaism itself. More Jews—because of intermarriage, distractions, or negativity—had little or no connection to a Jewish community. It was becoming evident that much of the Jewish education that had replaced the home and the community was not succeeding. Institutions as they had existed for decades were no longer meeting the needs of new generations of Jews.

Florence Melton's determination to change the situation was fueled by her concern for the vitality of Judaism and, in addition, the shrinking number of Jewish adults who would enter the world of learning through existing institutions to savor the richness of Jewish life. How could Judaism be introduced to those who have wandered away? Could we encourage adults to give Judaism a chance, to open their minds, hearts, and souls to its riches? Could adult learning become an entry—or re-entry—point into Jewish life?

Be Open to Inspiration

Florence Melton dropped out of high school in Philadelphia in the late 1920s to help support her family. Her parents had come to America to escape pogroms in Russia. As a child, she learned about Judaism and generosity from her grandmother who spoke to her in Yiddish. As Florence Melton recalled:

> My grandmother was the guiding light in my life. Although she was practically blind, my grandmother could see joy in everything. She found joy in just being alive: joy in her family, joy in her work. Her joy was in every small incident .... It is no small coincidence that her name was Freyda, the Yiddish word for "joy." From my beloved grandmother, I also learned the greatest lesson in my life. She always used to say, "Giving is part of living."
>
> Her kitchen had a huge, black leather couch in it. Everyone in Camden, New Jersey, knew to send a weary wayfarer to her home. There would always be a warm meal and a night's rest on that black, leather couch.
>
> Under the worn patch of linoleum in her bedroom—where there was a little hole in the floor—my grandmother had a *knippel*, a secret cache of painstakingly saved coins she kept bound in an old handkerchief. This *knipple* was there to help a child, grandchild, or a needy stranger.
>
> When people ask me what is my philosophy, I tell them it goes something like this. I have been to the blessing bank many times over a long period of time and I have learned that, when you accumulate a large inventory of blessings, the inventory must be turned. The inventory means nothing unless you turn it, and the more you turn it, the more people benefit from it.

Florence raised two sons and helped her first husband establish a family business. She was active in her Conservative congregation in Columbus, Ohio, and became a leader in the Columbus Federation. Through all this, she had an innate hunger for learning, especially for Jewish learning. When she was seventy, she decided to set aside time to learn more about Judaism. She discovered that there was no place where she could study in a systematic way that would allow her to wrestle with such questions as "What does it mean to live a good Jewish life?" "What does a Jew believe?" "How did we get to this point in history?" With these questions guiding her, she created what she felt was missing from the lives of other Jewish adults.

Discover a Dream and Make It a Reality

In 1980, Florence Melton wrote a proposal to take to institutions that could create her Jewish school for adults. Her proposal for the Mini-School—that's what she called her project—was based on her concern that many Jewish adults

> are either alienated from the mainstream of traditional Jewish life or are marginal Jews. If we are to reverse this trend, it is clear that we must address ourselves to a massive effort to match the special needs of Jewish adults in bold and creative ways never attempted before.

Her premise was

> that if a Jew knows Hebrew, enough to read the prayers, if this Jew understands the prayers, knows the holidays, learns concepts of the Bible and Jewish history (preferably contemporary history which has relevance), that Jew can be said to have achieved a basic or beginning Jewish education with which he/she can function as a participating member of the Jewish life in the community.

The proposal also stated that there is a direct relationship between Jewish life and the degree of Jewish experience and knowledge of its adults.

As envisioned, Melton's Mini-School would take adult education to another level; the schools would treat education as a serious business—not a recreational activity. Florence, a successful entrepreneur, was applying her business knowledge to adult learning. A lifetime spent in the marketplace gave her the experience and confidence to design and promote a new kind of adult Jewish learning. It would introduce the idea of a school for adults and be built upon a sequential curriculum that contained the components of basic Jewish literacy. It would also provide social benefits and attend to individual interests. The idea of a "school"—not "classes" or "programs"—embodied the principle that this was a long-term investment for the community and the individual, not a flash in the pan that would survive for a few years, then disappear. She wanted to create a new institution which would be available when adults were ready to learn.

Melton's school would be operated by local organizations serving the entire Jewish community—a federation, a bureau of Jewish education, a Jewish community center. Later, other community-based organizations like day schools and Jewish colleges and universities joined the sponsoring group as did consortia of synagogues. In one case, an individual synagogue that opened enrollment in the Mini-School to non-members was permitted to sponsor a school. Much later—too much later, the implementation of that model expanded to include numerous individual congregations.

Each school would have a director accountable for running the school according to standards in a manual that guided the director's work. Director responsibility would include conducting training sessions for teachers about the philosophy of the school and how to implement the curriculum. The Mini-School, its staff, faculty, and curriculum would be multi-denominational so Jews could learn together and understand how we differ as well as what unites us. Students' tuition and teachers' salaries would be determined by each community with the cost of classes depending on other funding that subsidized the school.

People have questioned the wisdom of Florence Melton insisting on calling her creation the Mini-School. That word had disparaging associations with mini-skirts, mini-cookies, and mini-meals. And yet, Florence Melton would respond firmly, "This is what it should be called. Participation in a serious two- year program could be very intimidating. By calling it a 'mini-school,' it's less frightening." Years later, confronted again by students and teachers insisting that this "maxi-" experience should not be diminished by the "mini-" prefix, Florence finally agreed that it may not been the best choice but it was too late to make any changes. As the businesswoman observed, "It is now our trademark!"

Between 1980 and 1984, Florence traveled across America and eventually to Israel to find the right institution to produce the Mini-School's curriculum and to serve as the base for implementing the school. She was ready to fund research and the creation of the curriculum, but the idea was not easy to sell. Her first choice was the Jewish Theological Seminary (JTS) in New York or the University of Judaism in Los Angeles. Florence's husband, Sam Mendel Melton, had endowed the Melton Center at JTS, and she admired its work. JTS, the University of Judaism, and eventually Hebrew Union College were skeptical about the idea. Her money, they insisted, could be better used elsewhere.

Eventually, Melton turned to the Samuel Mendel Melton Centre of Jewish Education in the Diaspora. This was located at the Hebrew University in Jerusalem. There, Dr. Seymour Fox seriously considered her proposal. Sharing the doubts of the American leaders, he nonetheless sent a scout to North America to survey the interests of potential students, adult education teachers, and local sponsoring institutions. His report was negative. American Jewish adults, he said, particularly the unaffiliated Jews Melton would like to reach, would not make this kind of commitment to Jewish learning. In spite of his report, Seymour Fox agreed to write a curriculum and guide several pilot schools refusing to accept Melton's money unless the Mini-School proved successful.

In fall 1986, three pilot Mini-Schools opened in the United States. One was affiliated with the Educational Alliance in New York; one, on Long Island, was located at the Jewish Community Center in Commack, New York; and the third was affiliated with the Board of Jewish Education and the Jewish Community Centers of Chicago. As the Chicago BJE Highlights reported:

> For one evening each week, our class joins in search for our Jewish legacy: the history and culture of the Jewish people, Jewish language, ideas, values, and practices. We explore Jewish classical texts including the Bible, Talmud, and the *Siddur* and debate age-old and contemporary Jewish issues. A goal of the program is to integrate learning into family life and to help adults grow as effective Jewish parents. Parents and children attend special seminars and join in family retreats at a camp setting.

I directed the 1986-1988 Florence Melton Adult Mini-School pilot project in Buffalo Grove, Illinois. The program was an immediate success in terms of enrollment. We had hoped for fifteen students. Fifty registered! Florence was right. American Jews were ready for the Mini-School.

Four years later, over 1,000 students were enrolled in classes in twenty Melton Mini-Schools from San Francisco, California, to Washington, D.C. In 1989, I became the North American Director of a rapidly growing network of Mini-Schools. At the time, the usual practice was to assign implementation of Israeli-created programs to *shlihim*, staff members of the Jewish Agency who traveled to America from Israel to run programs here. Alan Hoffmann, the new director of the Jerusalem Melton Centre for Jewish Education in the Diaspora, saw the need for an American to help local communities establish schools, train directors and teachers, and oversee the operation of the various schools. This created a new style of partnership between Israel and North American Jews: a three-way partnership—Hebrew University, the North American Melton Mini-School office, and local institutions that sponsored Mini-Schools. The schools were built on the best that each party has to offer: The Florence Melton Institute at the Hebrew University provided the research, curriculum development, and management of the international project. The expansion of the organization, professional education, and oversight of schools was the responsibility of the North American office. And each local sponsoring agency or institution provided administrative, financial, and educational resources. All of these came together to create a phenomenon now respected around the world.

There were challenges to overcome. Local sponsors had to be convinced to hire a school coordinator. Later, as a reflection of increased importance, responsibility for the quality of the school and its position in the community, the title was changed from "coordinator" to "director." Turning the Israeli and American staff into a unified team was not easy. The Israeli university scholars and leaders who were primarily observant men were working with American female educators affiliated with non-Othodox movements. Leadership styles varied. We only half-jokingly referred to the Israelis' style as "recruit and shoot" while we practiced "befriend and tend." A significant change in operations, reflecting more financial needs than available expertise, resulted in the shifting of responsibility for professional development from North America to Israel in 2009. It negated Alan Hoffmann's initial efforts to place the responsibility for American site expansion and professional development in the hands of Americans.

Learning from Success

In January 1990, Jewish Educational Services of North America (JESNA) devoted an entire issue of the *Pedagogic Reporter* to adult learning. Recognizing that "adult education is emerging as a vital aspect of the American Jewish experience," JESNA challenged communities around the country to invest in adult learning. It recommended that Jewish academic institutions include study of adulthood and the training of adult educators so rabbis and communal professionals could better serve the growing number of people who wanted to learn.

Later that year, Dr. Gaby Horenczyk, a professor at Hebrew University, published the first research conducted on the Florence Melton Adult Mini-School. It reinforced the importance of adult learning. As Horencyk wrote,

We may be dealing with a highly important educational, cultural, and social Jewish phenomenon. The rapid growth of this school and the vast interest it has created suggest that adult Jewish education programs in general—and the Mini-School in particular—seem to respond to a vital and widespread emerging need among American Jewish adults.

Horenczyk found that the majority of the students in the Mini-School were between thirty and fifty-five. Compared to the average American Jews, Mini-School students were more involved with Jewish friends (70 percent compared to 50 percent) and participated more in Jewish religious observances like attending *seders*, fasting on Yom Kippur, lighting Hanukkah candles, observing laws of *kashruth*, and belonging to a synagogue. Responding to questions on why they had enrolled in the course, 90 percent said they came to "broaden their Jewish knowledge." This was more important than "exploring identity," "spiritual searching," or "meeting Jews." "Being a more knowledgeable Jewish parent"—being role models who can transmit Judaism to their children—also ranked high.

Horenczyk's research confirmed that we were attracting people already involved in the Jewish community—not the unaffiliated or those who did not identify as Jews, Florence Melton's original target group. This remains a growing challenge. After the first few years, we had stopped offering a course called "Vocabulary of Jewish Living." It had proven too elementary for most students although, at the present time, this course or a similar one has been re-introduced in several schools as a "pre-Melton" program in an effort to attract people with weaker background in Jewish learning.

Many Mini-Schools communities achieved Florence Melton's goal: creating a long-lasting institution conveying Jewish literacy. New schools joined the network each year increasing not only the numbers of students but also the number of purveyors of adult Jewish learning. The initiative coincided with efforts made possible by the sponsorship of Morton Mandel in the 1980s and 1990s to "maximize" adult Jewish learning in Jewish community centers. Although prior to this, JCCs had minimal formal adult education opportunities for staff or members, the synchronicity of the JCCs and the Mini-School benefitted them both. By 1993, there were twenty-two schools. Within three years, five more joined. By 2001, there were sixty-three.

The Mini-School entered a new stage when Dr. Yonatan Mirvis was appointed head of the Florence Melton Adult Mini-School Institute at Hebrew University in 1991. Besides overseeing curriculum development and graduate seminars—educational travel in Europe and Israel—which began in 1992, Mirvis opened schools in Australia, England, South Africa, and Hong Kong. He created the Gandal Institute for Adult Jewish Learning in Israel for non-Orthodox Israelis who want to remedy their lack of knowledge of Judaism but feel uncomfortable in synagogues and more traditional *yeshivot*.

With his background in adult education and business, Dr. Mirvis transformed the Mini-School into a not-for-profit franchise that introduced new language, new standards, and a new way of doing business.

Other Voices

Dr. Yonatan Mirvis, International Director, Florence Melton Adult Mini-School Institute, Hebrew University of Jerusalem.

The definition of "social entrepreneurship" ... is the successful development of an innovative product or process for the enhancement of social value. What social value does the Mini-School aspire to achieve? In defining desired social value in the educational realm, we grapple with dual issues: social value defined as meeting needs determined by customers and social vision as determined by the providers—educators who have an ideological position.

Our students perceive that Jewish cultural literacy is a prerequisite to "fully functioning" in the Jewish realm. For many students, the Mini-School is the only way they can achieve Jewish cultural literacy. While many synagogues and cultural organizations offer adult education, these are usually short courses that fail to provide the much-needed comprehensive context and background knowledge. The Mini-School, through its comprehensive sequential courses, provides context for the students that allows them to differentiate between major and minor issues, an understanding of the key overarching issues. All this helps students feel that they have a broad sense of the big picture.

For educators, meeting the students' quest for cultural literacy is extremely important. However, they have a social vision that they bring to the educational encounter. This vision is based on an ideological stance regarding Jewish learning as central to the Jewish ethos. Teachers also subscribe to the importance of imparting this ethos to students. This ethos is rooted in the traditional importance attached to the study of *Torah liShmah*, "study for its own sake." In non-Orthodox circles until the end of the twentieth century, synagogue attendance, social action, and support for Israel were championed as the main focus of Jewish commitment. Serious Torah study was relegated to the domain of the religious "clergy." The Mini-School's vision makes Jewish learning central to Jewish commitment. A successful Mini-School should encourage students to be passionate about their Jewish learning, to embark on a path of learning outside of the Mini-School classroom, and to continue on this path far beyond graduation. This path of learning should become a focus of their Jewish commitment and inform their other realms of Jewish commitment.

The desire of the educators to enhance an appreciation for Jewish learning will be reflected in students

- Participating in learning in addition to their Mini-School courses. These may range from a weekly *parashah* class to courses on contemporary topics.
- Continuing their studies after graduating from the Mini-School either in the form of the Mini-School graduate classes or other educational frameworks.
- Becoming champions for Jewish education. Appreciating the ethos of learning makes them natural supporters for growth of Jewish learning in their communities.
- Recruiting their friends for serious learning encounters.
- Initiating learning opportunities for others or becoming Jewish educators themselves.

The franchise system has been successfully used in the Mini-School taking into consideration the demands of its very sophisticated implementation and its impact on the school culture. The franchise fee paid by local communities has increased over the years and after the financial crisis of 2008 became an obstacle to recruitment of new communities and the continuation of others. At the same time, however, the programs available to franchisees increased—growing numbers of graduate curriculum and the Foundations classes for parents became available as part of the fee. There is also a lower fee for smaller communities.

Over the years, new schools have been created while others have closed. Financial considerations, particularly since 2008, have been the most common cause for closing schools. Tight budgets require reassessment of priorities as growing numbers of unemployed Jews seek help from communal organizations. Another issue is the change of leadership in small communities where the success of the school often hinges on the commitment of two or three people.

As of 2010, close to one hundred-thirty communities have at some time sponsored the Mini-School, some of them closing and then reopening after a hiatus. It is likely that the Florence Melton Adult Mini-School will continue as a resource for lifelong learning for many decades to come.

Other Voices

Susan Dickman, Director of Operations of the North American office of the Florence Melton Adult Mini-School from 1992-2002.

Sometimes in life, if you're lucky, opportunity knocks. You just have to hear the knock and answer it. In 1990, a meeting at our home included Dr. Betsy Dolgin Katz from the Board of Jewish Education (BJE) of Metropolitan Chicago; my husband, Marvin, who was then president of the BJE; and Dr. Alan Hoffmann from the Samuel Mendel Melton Center at The Hebrew University. The purpose was to discuss expanding the Florence Melton Adult Mini-School (FMAMS). The school was under the auspices of the BJE. Three test sites had proven the school could succeed. An agreement was reached that the BJE would manage the expansion of FMAMS in North America. I served the coffee.

A couple of years later, I met my friend, Betsy Katz for breakfast. She had carried notebooks to our meeting explaining Melton, the methodology, curriculum, values. She said that Melton had grown so much since that 1990 meeting at our home that she needed someone to help her in an administrative capacity. Would I be interested? It was only a two-and-a-half day a week position with no summer work. I said, "No!" That night I told my husband about the offer. He (kindly) asked, "Well, are you ever planning to go back to work?" True, I had taught high school English but what did I know about adult Jewish education? I was about to learn.

From January 1992 until March 2002, I worked at the North American FMAMS office. Looking back, I see that I was part of a corporate build-up. When I arrived, we were already running twenty-two schools. When I left, we had sixty-three! Along the way, we acquired a Board of Directors, a formal budget, a system of expansion, improved curriculum, and quality people with whom to work both in the national office and at The Hebrew University of Jerusalem.

The office was so elementary when I began that, looking back, I just shake my head in wonderment. I was hesitant to give up my electric typewriter, but little by little, I was pushed into the computer age especially when a grandson of a BJE staff member came into the office. On the way to his grandfather's office, spotting my (still trusty) typewriter, he exclaimed, "Where's the screen?"

My first assignment was to research the feasibility of an idea Florence Melton suggested: taking a cruise with the coordinators of the sites (they are now called "directors") that would allow time for them to enjoy the travel, but also to study, to devise new policies for the schools, and to get to know each other. This never occurred. The costs were too high. But as we discussed this, I thought, "What have I gotten myself into?"

I had gotten myself into one of the richest experiences of my life. We worked hard. We met people who enriched our lives, challenged us, taught us, and became friends. Many I would not have met if not for the Mini-School. The staff meetings were exciting, full of repartee among Betsy, Jane Shapiro, Judy Kupchan, Rabbi Michael Balinsky— people whose brains are never in neutral. Along with Susan Gottlieb, I instituted the initiatives that sprung from those meetings. The flow of ideas never stopped. Along the way, we laughed a lot, cried some, respected each other, and developed a camaraderie that was easy and comfortable. We loved coming to work! At one of the national meetings, someone asked if the staff really liked each other as much as it seemed or was this just a façade? It was never a façade. None of us would have known how to do that.

And then there was Florence, our founder, a woman ahead of her time. She kept in touch with all of us at the office, came to visit, and was a perpetually upbeat, inspiring influence. As I was retiring from my position, Florence wrote me a poem (one of her other many talents). I framed it and hung it at home next to my certificate from the Hebrew University that I earned as a student in the Mini-School.

A prayer in the Reform liturgy says, "Help me to walk with good companions." I have done that, and I am so much the better for it.

Creating Unity in Diversity:
A Shared Vision and Mission

At the International Florence Melton Adult Mini-School Directors Conference in Israel in 2007, a session described the vision that unified all staff in the Mini-Schools, no matter the community or country in which they lived. The vision helped us evaluate our work, guided problem solving, and was a driving force moving the school into the future. Directors, faculty, and students debated who we were, what we were becoming, and what an adult Jew should learn in the Mini-School. They shared stories of the school's strong impact. The discussions illustrated how our vision of Judaism, of a Jew, of our curriculum, and of our teachers shaped a dynamic, successful institution.

In Melton, Judaism is taught as a response to humanity's quest for meaning and value in life, a combination of ideas and ways of living that developed out of our biblical and historical experiences. Judaism is a result of what we have learned—collectively—as we have searched for goodness and purpose.

The FMAMS envisions a Jew created in the image of a transcendent power. This individual is a learning Jew who studies Jewish texts as part of a search for meaning. Such study includes the freedom and ability to question, explore, and draw conclusions about life and Jewish identity. A Jew may not find the answers to every question but will come closer to finding meaning through a life that includes learning. This would describe what would be the ideal graduate of the Mini-School.

Jews are different from others with whom they share universal truths because of the rituals they observe and the curriculum they study. Our studies include Torah, Mishnah, Talmud, the great Jewish books, creative inspiring works that enrich our lives. They contain a variety of approaches to the essential questions of life and can be studied again and again, each time touching us in new ways. This search for meaning involves a variety of masterworks—narrative, poetry, law, parable, history. The primary purpose of each is to instruct in the way of goodness. They allow us to infuse our frequently chaotic lives with order and meaning.

A most moving example of this came right after the tragedy of hurricane Katrina that destroyed much of New Orleans in 2007. The FMAMS listserv carried a letter written by the father of one of our Mini-School teachers. He was a knowledgeable Jew who had somehow found order in a very chaotic life. He wrote about how he had fled three times to save his life, first from the Nazis, then from the Communists, and now from Katrina. Each time he not only survived but built a better life for himself. "Providence," he said, "had made this possible." Here was a Jew searching for life's goodness and meaning, a man whose potentially chaotic life was transformed into a sacred narrative based on his character, his attitudes, and his knowledge of Judaism.

Being an educational institution, the Mini-School also has a vision of a Jewish teacher. A good teacher models what a learning Jew can be. A teacher is someone who embodies a love of learning and learners and the ability to create an environment for questioning and experimenting with ideas. The Melton teachers' goal is to share knowledge and create understanding, not necessarily to engender faith and motivate observance. He guides the students in their questioning, searching, and defining their Jewish lives. The students take their knowledge and understanding and translate it into their reality.

Norman Lamm, a modern Orthodox rabbi and scholar, tells about attending the class of the late Rabbi Soloveitchik, a great scholar and head of the Isaac Elchanan Theological Seminary at Yeshiva University:

> He was extremely demanding. We would come into his class ready for intellectual battle—and we shriveled up. We would put our *Gemarot* (Talmud texts) in front of our faces and peek over them, so he would not recognize us and call on us. Unfortunately, he very often caught me. I remember on one occasion when he had been developing a thesis for some time, he asked me "Lamm, what did *tosofos* (medieval commentators) say?" I was intimidated, so I repeated what he had said the previous day. I thought, "He is going to be pleasantly surprised." But he erupted like a volcano, and said to me, "I know what I am saying. I do not need you to tell me! What do *you* think?" His greatness as a teacher was that he wanted a student to learn to think along the lines of his method, but not simply repeat his conclusions parrot-like.

Rabbi Soloveitchik could teach in the Mini-School.

The Directors Manual presents a more detailed statement of the Mini-School's mission. It reads:

> The Florence Melton Adult Mini-School is a world-wide network of schools promoting adult Jewish literacy that is a partnership between the Hebrew University, its North American office, and Jewish communities. The study of Jewish texts provides ways to understanding key ideas and to acquire the tools and confidence to enter into the Jewish conversation. Through study and participation in this conversation, learners examine diverse expressions of what they can be as a Jew, develop a love of learning, become part of a community of learners, and develop a relationship with Jews across time and geography. Our network is committed to pluralism, community-building, professionalization of adult Jewish learning, evaluation, research, innovation, and Israel-Diaspora partnership.

Innovation and Adaptation: A Pathway to Jewish Literacy

The idea of a sequential, systematic curriculum for teaching adults was rare in the 1980s. Then, as in many settings today, rabbis and scholars were teaching subjects based on their interests and skills.

Florence Melton recommended a curriculum that depended less on the decisions, skills, and charisma of individuals and more on carefully determined educational goals. Lessons were designed and sequenced to build on the inherent logic of subjects that were being taught and the qualities and needs of students.

To determine the curriculum, a team of professors at Hebrew University debated what an educated adult Jew should know. In the Mini-School, the answer to that question has multiple dimensions.

1. At the most basic level, educated Jews should know Jewish language and how to use it properly. This language expresses Jewish ideas, beliefs, and ethics. It describes the Jewish calendar and life cycle. It outlines Jewish history and describes institutions.

2. Literacy is also knowing how and where to find answers to Jewish questions and how to study texts that have informed and shaped Jewish life.

3. Literacy equips Jews to assume the responsibilities and privileges of Jewish life. They can lead a *seder*; help educate their children; navigate family events like *bar mitzvah*s, weddings, or funerals; argue over a Jewish text.

Paulo Freire, a pioneer in adult learning, describes the illiterate as living in silence, as marginal human beings. Jewish population studies identify large numbers of people who identify as Jews but who stand outside the doors of institutions and lack the knowledge and confidence to speak and live as participating Jews. As the case was with Freire's population, attaining literacy can be liberating. It can give individuals the choice to live Jewish lives. Jewish literacy rescues them from silence.

Diane Schuster, describes ways in which all Jewish learners go from being "silent knowers" to "constructed knowers." "Silent knowers" are aware

> that their experience as Jews has left them Jewishly illiterate and thus has made them feel uncomfortable, if not unwelcome, in Jewish learning settings. Because they have never seen themselves as part of the "Jewish conversation," these adults cannot fathom that they can actually study Jewish texts or participate in meaningful discussion of Jewish ideas.

At the other end of the spectrum are "constructed knowers" who

> have developed their critical thinking, analytic stills, and meaning-making abilities to the point that they are able to construct new meanings and as-

sert their independent ideas with a sense of personal authority. These learners take intellectual risks and bring their insight and experiences to the creation of new knowledge; at the same time, they are able to integrate Jewish ideas into their own lives and way of thinking.

This is what Rabbi Soloveitchik wanted Rabbi Lamm to become. In between, and relevant to the curriculum and the learning that occurs in the Mini-School, adults are exposed to Jewish texts, learn methods of textual analysis, and become part of a group of Jewish learners. The focus on Jewish knowledge—on attaining literacy—was the natural choice of the Hebrew University. As an academic institution, its mission was not encouraging increased observance. Its mission was to communicate knowledge and the means to acquire it.

Yonatan Mirvis wrote about the educational goals of the Mini-School. He describes three potential approaches to adult education and the Mini-School's choice of teaching Jewish literacy. "The Competency Approach" provides lessons on practicing *mitzvot* and Jewish customs. Its goal is to help students become more comfortably integrated into the Jewish community through their observance of rituals. Much of this approach involves learning through experience—demonstrations, role modeling, spiritual practice—about the "practical" areas of Jewish life. "The Relevancy-Meaning Approach" is designed to create personal connections between students and Judaism. It is based on studying texts that become meaningful as participants discover the texts' relationship to their lives. The students' world provides the framework for the subject matter. The teacher presents the tradition, selecting texts and ideas that engage students, and encourage them to connect the ideas and practice to their lives.

The third option is "The Literacy Approach." According to Mirvis, deepening Florence Melton's thinking, Jewish literacy is needed since

> Adults, who are often experts in secular areas of knowledge, feel embarrassed by their lack of Jewish knowledge. They do not understand the logic of the tradition, they cannot distinguish between the major and the minor, and they feel that they are outside of the Jewish conversation. The way to alleviate this problem is to organize the subject matter in a coherent, logical manner and introduce the adult to the world of Jewish learning so that s/he will be able to understand the issues from within.

While the Mini-School emphasizes the literacy approach to learning, the other two approaches described by Mirvis are part of the Melton experience. The names of the Melton courses reflect attention to what is relevant and what is competence in living a Jewish life—"The Purposes of Jewish Living," "The Rhythms of Jewish Living," "The Ethics of Jewish Living," and "The Dramas of Jewish Living through the Ages." In class, students frequently discuss how a topic connects to their lives or the reasons behind Jewish practices. Communities periodically offer workshops on the how-to's of holiday and life cycle observance. In truth, the definition of Jewish literacy for American adults has changed. The inclusion of texts of prayers, arranging lessons to follow the Jewish calendar, and discussions of God and spirituality have found their way into the curriculum in response to the interests and needs of students and teachers.

The Mini-School experience also embodies additional approaches to learning discussed by Daniel Pratt in *Five Perspectives on Teaching in Adult and Higher Education* (1998). He describes the Apprenticeship Perspective on learning that addresses the role of the teacher and learners in modeling alternative ways of being Jewish as well as ways to study texts and to disagree and debate respectfully. The Developmental Perspective cultivates students' ways of thinking. Very often in Melton classes, information will be introduced that encourages a student to examine their assumptions about Judaism, consider alternative ways of thinking, and change (or decide not to change) a belief or behavior. Melton classes include "unlearning" as well as learning. The Nurturing Perspective is expressed in and out of the classroom in a teacher's efforts to increase the comfort, confidence, and self-direction of learners.

Of the five original Mini-School courses, four courses are still used today. The first-year classes provide a foundation for those studied the second year. Ideas are introduced that are developed more fully and in greater depth as the two years proceed.

Year One

❧ "The Rhythms of Jewish Living" introduces beliefs and practices of Jewish life based on the observances of the year, the month, the week, and the life cycle. An underlying value is *kedushah*—the "holiness" or special quality of Jewish living that makes us unique. The emphasis is on the underlying ideas rather than on the particulars of religious observance.

❧ "The Purposes of Jewish Living" provides an overview of the theological foundations of Jewish life. The course is devoted to the purpose of creation, of life, of particular Jewish beliefs and observances. It is the course that addresses why we are here on earth and why we do what we do. Because this frequently involves conversations about God, which may be a problem for many, students are asked to suspend their disbelief and not let it prevent them from discovering messages that may be relevant and meaningful and will at least help them understand the perspective of others.

Year Two

✿ "The Ethics of Jewish Living" examines how to take the beliefs studied in "The Purposes of Jewish Living" and apply them to our lives. Based on texts from Torah, rabbinic literature, commentaries through the Middle Ages until today, the course emphasizes God and the commandments as the foundation of core principles of human behavior. The principles are applied to specific, practical areas of human conduct and the challenges of moral issues that confront modern society such as abortion, euthanasia, sexuality, and suicide.

✿ "The Dramas of Jewish Living through the Ages" examines events, experiences, and issues throughout Jewish history. Its goals are to strengthen students' Jewish historical national memory and to use knowledge of the past to shed light on life today. It utilizes texts, maps, timelines, and summaries of historical contexts in which the events examined occurred.

Mini-School graduates beginning in 1992 were invited to participate in a two-week Israel Graduate Seminar. This is sometimes referred to as the Fifth Course. Participants enter a new expansive "classroom," the State of Israel. The Biblical land; the modern state; the nation that is both religious and secular; and, always, it seems, a land in an existential crisis is seen in its complexity and depth. Students bring along their newly-acquired learning, sense of adventure, curiosity, and desire to make Israel a part of their lives. They study classical texts, history, and contemporary literature with one eye on the text and the other on the land, the walls, the physical traces of history, the institutions, and the artistic representations of the culture. Many see it as the culmination of their two years in the Mini-School and their passport to more learning. The original Israel experience for Melton students has expanded to include educational tours on various themes for "returnees."

Building on Successes: Continued Learning in Graduate Courses

Initially, Florence Melton envisioned a two-year introduction to lifelong learning with the understanding that local communities would create challenging follow-up education opportunities for Mini-School graduates. Her ideal was that after two years in the Mini-School, students would have learned that Jewish texts, history, and ideas are so rich and rewarding they merit a lifetime of commitment to learning. Florence Melton did not want the schools she founded to compete with congregations or community centers and the Mini-School staff at the Hebrew University agreed. They already had their hands full creating, revising, and maintaining the four Mini-School courses.

In fact, many communities did initiate courses appropriate for Melton graduates. Most common was studying classical texts; studying Jewish history was a close second. Students' motivation to continue was not only related to their love of learning. They had developed a habit of weekly study that they did not want to abandon, and they had made friends whom they wanted to see. As a poster in a school on Long Island cautioned: "Warning: Jewish study can be addictive. Habit-forming. Results can last a lifetime."

But not every community was offering graduates challenging, high-quality classes. So the Mini-School launched the Rachel Wasserman Scholars Curriculum in 2004 specifically for Melton graduates. One series of courses, for example, consists of ten-week units devoted to the in-depth study of Torah text; another explores Jewish civilization. The numbers of graduate students continue to grow. Although writing and implementing of these graduate classes has become a core activity of the Mini-School, there is no long-range plan for graduate curriculum development. Until classes are tested in the field it is difficult to know if they actually build upon the higher level of knowledge and the interests of the learners. An opportunity is lost when the most highly-motivated learners who now anticipate only high-quality adult learning sponsored by the Melton school are disappointed by their graduate experience.

Other Voices

Morey Schwartz, Director of Curriculum Development for the Florence Melton Adult Mini-School, Jerusalem.

By 2004, it was evident that in eighteen years the Mini-School had created a new need. We had created Jewish adult learners with strong appetites for learning who wanted us to feed their newly-discovered spiritual and intellectual hunger. In January 2005, we brought together experienced adult educators, Mini-School directors, and education experts to recommend what that next level of education should look like. Those deliberations led to the first Rachel Wasserman Scholars Curriculum courses.

At the beginning of 2009, I received an email from one of our teachers.

> I am writing to let you know that whereas I was *impressed* with *Shivim Panim* [a reference to a statement describing "seventy faces" of Torah] prior to class last night, I ... and the *Shivim Panim* students ... now am *in love* with it! The change occurred as we studied "the Expulsion of Ishmael" ... through the lens of the four works of art you provided, as well as other artworks (including several by Chagall) that I brought along to class ... the artworks helped students build closer emotional ties to the text and also provided them with greater insights into how and why midrash—whether textual or "visual"—fills in the gaps in the Torah. When we spring-boarded off the artworks back to some of the written commentaries, the students' text study skills seemed sharper and their recall of things they have learned in Melton over the past four years (the length of time this class has been at it!) simply began to pour out like water released from a dike. Morey, we were intellectually and spiritually on fire!

In the spring of 2010 I had the privilege of sitting in on a Scholars Curriculum lesson in Houston, Texas. Listening to the caliber of the questions, the thoughtful answers, and the heated discussions, I was truly in awe! Our graduates are most certainly climbing the ladder of literacy. Where do we go from here?

Adjust to New Trends: A Changing America=A Changing Curriculum

Each Melton course has been revised at least four times, reflecting the changes in society and the needs and interests of students as defined by an effective, although unsystematic, evaluation process. One should not take for granted the time, energy, and financial resources devoted to evaluation and revision of curriculum. A guiding principle of Melton since its inception has been maintaining the alignment between students and society and the curriculum. The expression of the goal of each course will never be finalized. An analysis of the evaluations and consequent changes in the curriculum reveal a changing portrait of the Jews in America—particularly the core of that community.

Turning to Text

When the curriculum was first written, there were two text-based courses, "The Purposes of Jewish Living" and "The Ethics of Jewish Living." In other courses, students studied "about" Judaism. Holidays, Shabbat, and life cycle events could be learned from selections from *The Jewish Catalogue*. *The Jewish Catalogue*, first published in 1973, was a popular introduction to the practice of Judaism that included laws of observance, cartoons, photos, and descriptions of Jewish life.

But students, enjoying the richness and authenticity of studying primary texts, asked for them in all four courses. Many teachers introduced these into their classes on their own. After meetings between the national staff and local teachers, these texts and others formed the basis of revised curriculum. The multitudes of translations of classical texts that exist today have not only made texts more accessible to learners but have undeniably attracted more learners and deepened their knowledge and connections to Judaism.

Text study is considered "authentic" learning. Primary texts have status in the minds of students whether they are written by contemporary scholars or have been passed down through history. Students are aware that the biblical texts and others that followed them have been studied since Ezra gathered men, women, and children together to hear the reading and interpretation of Torah. They have defined Judaism for millennia. The knowledge and skills students acquire allow them to enter into discussions knowing that this can potentially shape their Jewish lives. For students and their classmates, texts create a shared language and starting point for defining their beliefs, their behaviors, and their associations with the Jewish community.

Melton curriculum writers had to grapple with serious questions as they were selecting texts for the curriculum. They defined "text" in its broadest sense—a primary source written by, about, and for Jews. Texts from the *Tanach* (the complete Bible—Torah, Prophets and Writings) are used extensively. The Talmud, Midrash, and rabbinic writings from the Middles Age until today are included. Great commentators on Torah and Talmud like Rashi (Rabbi Shlomo ben Isaac); Maimonides (Rabbi Moshe ben Maimon); Nachmanides (Rabbi Moshe ben Nachman); and the mystic and codifier of Jewish law, Joseph Karo, all contribute insights to the topics being discussed. The curriculum also includes contemporary commentaries and essays from leaders of the various denominational movements as well as prayers; poetry; selections from short stories; and, more recently in the graduate curriculum, works of art.

Since many different texts can be used to accomplish a particular goal, the question often arises about which text and what type of text should be used—a narrative, a legal text, a commentary, a poem? Over the years, criteria for choosing texts have emerged.

❊ The text must speak directly to the goal (or goals) of the lesson.

❊ It should be accessible given the background of the learners.

❊ It should arouse curiosity by asking a compelling question or presenting a problem to be solved.

❊ It should stimulate discussion and debate possibly by introducing an idea contrary to one already presented in a lesson.

❊ Because of the pluralistic nature of the Mini-School, the texts should represent a variety of positions within Judaism.

On one hand, students are entering into a process that has gone on for generations. But because they are studying texts in English, they are once removed from what could be considered genuine Jewish learning. Hayyim Nahman Bialik, the Eastern European Hebrew poet laureate, wrote at the beginning of the twentieth century, "Reading a text in translation is like kissing a bride through her veil." The Mini-School Student Readers that contain the texts students study include both the English and the Hebrew version of documents. The presence of Hebrew is a statement of the ideal and is intended to motivate students to learn Hebrew in the future. In the 1990s Florence Melton created "Hebrew for Chocolate" an innovative approach to adult Hebrew education based on a system used to teach languages to Americans in government service. It had its advocates and experts in the Mini-School but did not persist. Since then, the teaching of Hebrew has not been a priority. It leaves the question unanswered as to whether knowledge of the Hebrew language should be an element in Jewish literacy—specifically in graduate classes of the Florence Melton Adult Mini-School.

Exploring Spirituality

As Gaby Horenczyk's research testified, students in 1989 were not motivated to study because they were searching for God and spirituality. In some settings, teachers avoid theology and discussing relationships with God, insisting that "spirituality" is not even a Jewish word. It is now, however, part of the vocabulary of the majority of our students, though its definition remains ambiguous. Students in their evaluations of the Mini-School now say they are looking for a dimension of life that goes beyond our everyday existence. They are seeking meaning and purpose in their daily activities, social relationships and community.

Texts serve multiple spiritual purposes in Melton classes. Some stimulate discussion on Jewish behavior, on our outer life. In examining the purposes of ritual and the sources of ethical behavior, students understand why we do what we do. On the other hand, texts also turn thoughts inward to the value of being Jewish, of being a good human being, and connecting to community and to God. Thus, texts can be sources for contemplation of our inner life.

The revisions of Melton curriculum have added lessons that focus on the nature of God and on our relationship with God. Texts have been incorporated that encourage thinking and discussion about holiness and connections between the material and spiritual world. An entire lesson in the beginning of "The Purposes of Jewish Living" uses the texts describing creation as the beginning of a discussion about God's relation to humanity in the Torah. A text from the Babylonian Talmud introduces the discussion of human beings imitating the qualities of God:

> What does the written verse mean, "You shall follow after the Lord your God" (Deuteronomy 13:5)? Can a person follow after the Divine Presence? Has it not already been stated, "For the Lord your God is a consuming fire" (Deuteronomy 4:24)! Rather, [the verse means] to follow after the attributes of the Holy One, blessed be He ....

Texts of prayers are now part of the curriculum, although this had originally been avoided. Initially, there was a concern that including prayers would imply that we were trying to make students more "religious." For the same reason, early versions of "The Rhythms of Jewish Living" did not follow the Jewish calendar. Holidays were organized according to themes. Many teachers independently rearranged the curriculum because they could not conceive of teaching

Pesach in the fall and Rosh HaShannah in the spring. In light of the fact that most students observed the major Jewish holidays, coordinating lesson content with the calendar was an opportunity to explore spiritual life. Although discussions of personal beliefs are integrated into all four courses, expanding "The Purposes of Jewish Living" from a fifteen-week course to a full year after eliminating "Vocabulary of Jewish Living," is partly a response to the growing interest in what Jews believe and in spirituality.

Recognizing Women's Contributions

Several interests that were priorities of American Jews 1980s were not included in the original Melton courses—such as the role of women in Judaism. Noticeably absent from the original calendar and the life cycle units of "The Rhythms of Jewish Living" were the observance of *bat mitzvah* and *Rosh Hodesh*. Sometimes referred to as the women's observance, *Rosh Hodesh* commemorates the beginning of each Hebrew month. The celebration of *bat mitzvah* and growing equality between genders has made it an important moment on the monthly calendar for women to meet and study.

The history course did not include women in Jewish history and such modern developments as ordaining women as rabbis. This was remedied in the revised "Dramas of Jewish Living through the Ages" curriculum, And when contemporary texts were originally added to courses, none were written by women. In this case too, curriculum writers responsive to teachers' and students' recommendations incorporated women's contributions.

Changing the Approach to Pluralism

Rabbi Yechiel Michel Epstein, known as the "Aruch haShulchan," wrote at the beginning of the twentieth century,

> The debates of the *Tannaim, Amoraim, Geonim* and *Poskim* in fact represent the word of the living God. All of their views have merit from a *halachic* [legal] perspective. In fact, this diversity and range constitute the beauty and splendor of our holy Torah. The entire Torah is called a *shira* [song] whose beauty derives from the interactive diversity of its voices and instruments. One who immerses himself in the sea of Talmud will experience the joy that results from such rich variety.

All this relates to pluralism. The promotional material of the Mini-School initially referred to courses that taught "classical, nondenominational Judaism." Course content was based on the Judaism which existed before the Enlightenment when denominations, as we know them today, did not exist. That pre-Enlightenment Judaism became the basis of modern expressions of Jewish life. This perspective created a problem. It did not take long before students and teachers made it clear that in North America today, studying only texts from pre-Enlightenment Judaism does not represent the shared heritage that led to the establishment of Orthodox, Reform, Conservative, Reconstructionist and other expressions of modern Jewish life. Since Mini-School students perceive pre-modern Judaism as Orthodoxy, the label they attached to those Jewish classical texts was "Orthodox."

Although teaching about common Jewish roots remains part of Melton's curriculum, changes were made in what was offered. In exploring traditional texts, the curriculum offers multiple Jewish perspectives from the Talmud, Midrash, and later commentaries. In addition, by adding contemporary texts written in the last one hundred and fifty years, the courses affirm the wisdom of various movements. The curriculum also was expanded to include other denominationally-related practices and beliefs: confirmation, celebrating certain holidays for one or two days, various approaches to revelation, different versions of the prayer book, and forms of Shabbat observance. The present approach to pluralism enables students to understand one another and become aware of the diversity of Jewish life. It provides knowledge of the variety of Jewish expression and encourages tolerance of the variety of perspectives that exist in modern American Jewish life. Pluralism is reinforced by the Mini-School's insistence on exposing students to faculty who come from a variety of backgrounds. Directors hire individuals to teach who model one of many ways to be a good Jew and who respect other Jews regardless of their denomination and beliefs.

A striking example of this kind of faculty member was an Orthodox rabbi who taught "The Ethics of Jewish Living." One lesson of this course is devoted to traditional and modern Jewish teachings on homosexuality. Well aware of how difficult it would be to teach this lesson, the rabbi explained his problem to his students and why he had invited another rabbi to teach the lesson for him. The next week, students discovered that the Orthodox rabbi was joining them as a student so he could better understand the more liberal perspectives being discussed.

When the pluralistic curriculum was introduced in 1986, divisions in the Jewish community were not as detrimental as they are today. Since then, our community has changed. The walls dividing political and religious groups have thickened. Intolerance is now a serious problem that can perhaps be eased through greater understanding of one another. There is much we share in the form of the texts we read and the questions we ask. Texts are a common ground on which interaction and understanding are built. A respectful classroom discussion directed toward understanding alternative perspectives can be a model for what is possible in the community.

As the Mini-School approaches its twenty-seventh year, it continues to meet the challenge of rapid change in the North American Jewish community. At the same time, it remains rooted in the texts and beliefs that have ever been the foundation of our identity.

Matching Curriculum Style to Those Who Teach

The Mini-School's curriculum writers realized that the traditional model of writing curriculum for teachers of children would not work for the Mini-School. The original "teacher-proof" curriculum provided Melton faculty with content plus instructions on how to teach: what to write on the board, what questions to ask, and what strategies to use. The highly-qualified teachers attracted to the Mini-School found this to be condescending and patronizing.

The curriculum writers revised the curriculum so it not only matched the abilities of the teachers but it made teaching in the Mini-School a stimulating learning experience for them. The curriculum became a *hevrutah*, a learning partner, for the teacher. Always intending to provide teachers with resources on particular subjects—saving them the time and effort needed to locate materials—the altered curriculum provided the scope of what was to be taught, some suggestions for teaching, and usually more resources than could be used in one hour. It was the teacher's responsibility to prepare by studying the materials and deciding on the specific texts to use and the strategies for teaching. If a teacher sometimes did not have adequate time to prepare or if a new teacher needed the support, more assistance was available in the form of an optional model lesson in the curriculum guide. More recently, additional model lesson and texts that teachers have used can be found on the Mini-School's faculty website along with lesson guides called "Roadmaps" prepared by faculty members.

Expanding Participation: Melton Learning for New Audiences

"If you offer a class on Genesis for everyone, very few people attend. However, if you offer a class on Genesis for left-handed tennis players, almost every left-handed tennis player will show up." Rabbi Alan Bregman, former Director of the Midwest Region of Union of American Hebrew Congregations, was wise in the ways of successful marketing.

That was one of the motivating factors that led the Melton staff to develop commentaries on the curriculum and supplemental materials for unique groups of learners. Over the years, there were adaptations of the Mini-School for community leaders, for Jewish professionals, for teachers, and for parents of young children. Most frequently, these were developed in response to requests from communities which had already identified these potential learners.

A Mini-School program for leaders, developed by Jane Shapiro, Melton's Director of Community Development and a Melton teacher, came from a request of the Jewish Federation of Metropolitan Chicago. As reported in the JUF News, the goal was to "give something back to community leaders who had volunteered many hours of time and effort to support the Federation and other agencies." The Melton curriculum was chosen because it presents a comprehensive, integrated picture of Jewish living and it is committed to pluralism—especially welcome in the Federation world where diverse members of the community meet. Texts about leadership were added to the standard Melton lessons. Special lessons were constructed around words like *hesed* ("compassion"), and *tzedakah* ("righteousness"/"charity"). On trips to Federation facilities, students learned about the agency's services and studied texts that highlight the Jewish dimensions of the agency's work. At the Council for the Jewish Elderly in Chicago, for example, students learned about the Jewish attitude toward the aged and how, traditionally, they are to be treated. At a food pantry, students studied how Jews have confronted poverty and assisted the poor.

A widely-used adaptation of the Florence Melton Adult Mini-School was the Florence Melton Parent Education Program (PEP). This evolved in a unique way. In 2000, the Avi Chai Foundation, a foundation devoted to perpetuation of the Jewish people, Judaism, and the centrality of Israel, asked FMAMS to develop a curriculum for the parents of young children. Avi Chai believed that intensive adult education would influence parents to enroll their children in day schools—which is one of Avi Chai's goals. In 2002, PEP debuted in three communities. By 2006, four hundred and fifty students were attending PEP classes in eighteen schools around the country.

PEP was adapted from the Mini-School's two-year core curriculum. Because PEP classes are made up of parents with common concerns, discussions of parenting and schooling arise naturally and frequently. In fact, PEP students have always been eager to learn how to translate what they learn in class to their homes. We called this "taking the conversation home." The initial flyer sent to potential participants read, "When your children ask the four questions, do you have the answers?" Parents become particularly aware of their Jewish identity when they have children and when children begin their Jewish education. Their experiences in PEP frequently led to more adult Jewish learning as they became aware that Jewish sources have important information to offer about parenting, enhancing family life, and enriching life in general.

While most of the PEP and the core curricula of the Mini-School are identical, classic and contemporary texts were added to PEP to illustrate how the material taught in class is relevant to students' lives as Jewish parents. The texts describing why God chose Abraham include one about his teaching his children. "For I have singled him out, that he may instruct his children and his posterity to keep the way of the Lord by doing what is just and right" (Genesis 18:19). A text included in the lesson on Passover describes the four children who ask questions at the *seder* (the wise child, the wicked child, the simple child, and the child who did not know how to ask) and the responses to their questions. The class discussion was about the importance of listening carefully to each child's questions and presenting Judaism to them in ways that are understandable and meaningful.

Although classes continued to grow, PEP's sponsors and potential participants felt they could attract more parents, who already had exceptionally busy schedules, with a less demanding program. In 2009, a twenty-week course, "Foundations," was taught for the first time in eight communities. The following year, fourteen classes were organized in two ten-week segments—one dealt with themes derived from Jewish holidays, the other with Jewish ethics. Although aware of the difficulties in attracting young parents, communities continue to line up to offer the program. It is hoped that participants in these classes will continue to study by enrolling in the core Melton classes.

It may be time, after twenty-five years, to examine closely the nature of Melton's potential learners. Although there is no research to verify the observations of educators and community leaders, even those who are already involved in Jewish life today may not have as high a level of Jewish ritual observance or knowledge as students in earlier decades. There are more day schools from which younger adults have graduated, but the over 70 percent of children who have had a Jewish education in synagogue schools have a less rigorous experience than their predecessors. In addition, fewer young adults (thirty to forty-five) are joining Jewish organizations. There is a smaller affiliated audience from which to draw. It may be time to create a pre-Melton program that would be a less-demanding entry point for those who identify as Jews but who are not engaged in any Jewish activities.

In 1990, Horenczyk suggested that there were two types of Jewish commitment. "Commitment to continuity" which is concerned with Jewish survival and preserving Jewish identity places little emphasis on specific Judaic content. "Commitment to content" is concerned with specific Jewish ideas and traditions. Horenczyk proposed that Mini-School students were moving from one type of commitment to the other; they realized that continuity could not be achieved without content. They may already have a strong Jewish identity and a commitment to the future vitality of Judaism, but now they were studying Jewish content to understand Jewish traditions and ideas. Fewer of Melton's potential audience in the second decade of the twenty-first century are moving from continuity to content.

The Mini-School has been true to the ideals of Florence Zacks Melton who knew the world was ready for her innovation. Florence died in 2008 at the age of ninety-five. The day before she died she was on the phone working on another one of her dreams: a model for a new type of Jewish high school. Thousands of people have been touched by her accomplishments and her inspiration. Many more will benefit from those thousands of people who now know—and experience—Judaism in a new way.

Lessons for Today

1. Seek out a need in Jewish education and collaborate with others to fulfill it. Keep it simple.

2. If you believe in it, be persistent!

3. Adult Jewish education is a serious business not a recreational activity.

4. Collaborative efforts utilize the strengths of every partner.

5. "Jewish study can be addictive. Habit forming. Results can last a lifetime."

6. An organization's shared vision determines its goals, directs problem solving, and provides a standard for evaluating its accomplishments.

7. Strengthen and sustain an organization through constant Jewish learning, professional education, and research.

8. Although some see learning as a social or recreational activity, most come to long-term education seeking meaning and value in Jewish life as it has developed out of tradition and historical experiences. As they gain knowledge, they acquire the ability and confidence to speak and live as participating Jews.

9. A good teacher of adults models what a learning Jew can be. He/she is someone who embodies a love of learning, learners, and Jewish texts and the ability to create an environment for questioning and experimenting with ideas.

10. Review and renew. The ability to adjust an organization to new trends and to adapt it to changing audiences determines its continued viability.

Chapter VII

Building a Network of
Learning Communities

The person who participates with the community, his outlay is small and his security is constant. For whatever one person does not manage to do, another comes and completes it. — Yehudah HaLevi, *The Kuzari*

The more freely information flows, the stronger the society. — President Barack Obama, China, November 16, 2009

*T*he refinement of technology contributed immensely to the initial success of the Florence Melton Adult Mini-School. It is not certain if the school could have been created, then expanded, without the computers, faxes, and e-mail that were just beginning to make their way into the Jewish education world. Superior communication—and the relationships it makes possible—were indispensible to the Mini-School's emphasis on building relationships—honest, transparent, dependable relationships. These are the basis of a strong, committed learning community—and a successful business.

In spite of the distances that separate Israel from North America and the Mini-School's North American office in Illinois from over one hundred FMAMS schools during its twenty-five years of existence, there is a remarkable similarity among the schools. Although relationships between the Mini-School office and communities that host the schools are formalized in contracts, it is the very human, person-to-person contacts that gave the organization momentum and allowed it to function consistently throughout North America.

As the Mini-School evolved, these relationships served multiple purposes. First of all, people do business with others whom they trust, from whom they can benefit, and whose company they enjoy. The North American staff depended on local professional and lay leaders to adapt the school to specific locations and to establish and maintain the high quality of each school. Creativity within the boundaries set by the school's agreements with FMAMS was welcome; in several instances, what was learned from directors changed those boundaries. One director led the reorganization of the Jewish holiday and life cycle curriculum so it would present holidays according to the calendar rather than being organized according to themes. Another director initiated sharing recordings of classes on the internet. A third started the practice of adding small numbers of first year students to an ongoing second year class—a better alternative than turning potential students away until there were enough students to fill a first year class. A team of British teachers generated ideas that shaped the most recent revision of the "Ethics of Jewish Living" curriculum.

The staff also learned about adult Jewish education from the directors' and the faculties' experiences. Local school directors were encouraged to critique curriculum and recommended practice, as well as to help solve problems. Frequent communication between the national staff and the directors assured that they understood the ideas on which the school was based and helped them communicate these guidelines to the faculty.

Other qualities of the Mini-School culture emerged, such as the transparency that allowed sites to see into the national operation, to be aware of the problems being confronted and what goals were achieved. It created more vulnerability but also more trust. Valuable information was exchanged constantly.

Other Voices

Judy Mars Kupchan, Director of the North American Project of the Florence Melton Adult Mini-School, Melton teacher for the Board of Jewish Education of Metropolitan Chicago.

My work requires me to travel extensively. The reward is visiting many Jewish communities around the United States and Canada. Some communities are suffering in the present dismal economy, some from a dearth of leadership, some from turf wars. But in many Jewish communities, it's a privilege to witness how collaboration leads to the flourishing of ideas and to creatively implementing them.

What I witness is leaders setting the tone that animates the entire Jewish community to behave as a unified whole. Often, a few inspiring leaders shape the character of the community—large or small. I've seen results from the consortium of congregations and day schools in Conejo/West Valley of Los Angeles and the renewal of the Jewish community in New Orleans, in the pride of being a true community that is shared in Melton classes in Raleigh, and in the vibrant JCC in suburban Detroit.

One of the powerful consequences is the learning that emerges from classical sources and from the interaction among the learners. When I observe adults from Reform, Conservative, Humanistic, Reconstructionist congregations—and, often, from "no congregation"—learn and join in "the great Jewish conversation" of the past four millennia, led by an Orthodox teacher who is using a curriculum from the Hebrew University, I am moved by the vision of real community in action. Rabbi Jonathan Sacks has noted in the *Koren Siddur* that a community is a reflection of the entire Jewish people. Our future as a people lies in strengthening one community at a time. Learning together is a means to that hopeful end.

Pirke Avot, "Sayings of the Fathers," instructs us *K'nai l'cha haver,* "Find yourself a companion." The North American staff discovered the deep wisdom of that statement. An exceptional team came together to make Florence Melton's idea a reality. We learned constantly. This was helped by each member of the education staff in North America teaching at least one local Mini-School class each week. We frequently analyzed teaching experiences together and referred to each other as "critical colleagues"—in the sense of questioning each others' ideas and realizing true collaboration was essential to the quality of our work. We wanted to improve teaching for the benefit of our students, but also so we could relate to other Mini-School teachers effectively. This was a unique opportunity to generate knowledge and sharpen skills that would contribute to the improvement of our schools. Through the knowledge we shared at staff development activities in each community, we earned the confidence and respect of our colleagues.

An unforgettable example of this type of collegiality occurred while preparing a lesson on the experience of the Jews receiving the Ten Commandments at Mt. Sinai. I was struggling with strange descriptions of sounds and sights, the ambiguity, and the contradictions within this pivotal moment described in the Book of Exodus. The Israelites moved toward the mountain, then away from it, then toward it again. They "heard" lightning. They were full of awe and fear and love. I wanted to guide students to discover what occurred at this amazing place. Frustrated and confused, I paced around the office, muttering. Jane Shapiro, my colleague, noticed my rambling. When I told her about my problem, she smiled and simply said, "Perhaps, Sinai was just that—strange, ambiguous, overwhelming, incomprehensible. That is the lesson that the text is teaching."

In looking back on those staff discussions, I realize that chance brought together a dream team—a teacher-educator, an adult educator, a rabbi, a scholar and a teacher with fine communication and marketing skills, an educator with a background in psychology, a financial expert, and a business administrator. Our mutual support and respectful critique of each other created a durable product and an exhilarating process.

Other Voices

Jane Sherwin Shapiro, Director of Community Development at the Florence Melton Adult Mini-School, 1992-2003.

Until he died in 1991, my father had a successful real estate business that covered the north side of Chicago and surrounding suburbs. His business was an extension of his family. He cared deeply for his employees and taught them how to sell real estate. He told his staff—and his daughters—that the real estate business was about more than selling something: it was about meeting a basic human need for a home. When he was showing a house, he never failed to pat the dog, to get to know the children, and to make customers feel that they mattered. Each sale represented someone taking on the uncertainty and the possibility of change.

I loved working in my father's office. Sundays would find me filing new listings or marking those with "contracts pending," changing prices, and removing listings which had been sold. I learned abbreviations for school districts I never knew existed: OLPH translated to "Our Lady of Perpetual Help." Snazzy homes, modest homes, condominiums were a portrait of the growing community.

Of course, if a Jewish family was looking for a home, my father put on the full press. As the president of his synagogue, he was on the hunt for new members. One Sunday, he came into the house, handed me a baby and said, "Jane, take care of this baby. His name is Joey. I'm going to show his parents a house around the corner so you and your sisters will have new friends at the synagogue." I was six years old and happily took the baby as Joey's older sister, Nina, went into the next room to play with my younger sister. My father made two sales that day: a house and a synagogue membership. Nina's daughter is now married to my son. My father was not wrong about the pull of home and the deep satisfaction that comes from setting down roots.

So I was amused when I became the director of a new department at the Florence Melton Adult Mini-School. The department was called "Community Development." What a euphemism! It was a sales position—pure and simple. Everything, I figured, I had ever learned about developing centers of Jewish education I had learned from watching my father sell real estate. For several years at Melton, we rode the wave known as "Renaissance and Renewal." Renaissance was born from a concern for Jewish continuity, but also from a wonderful sense of optimism. Now that Yassir Arafat and Yitzhak Rabin had come to an agreement about Israel and Palestine, there would be peace throughout the Middle East. Jewish community money—formerly sent to Israel—could be spent locally for culture and education. Day schools, Jewish arts, philanthropy, Shabbat extravaganzas—all would flourish. It was an exciting climate in which to talk to communities about raising their capacity to offer adult learning.

Community development at Melton picked up steam. In one year, we started fourteen new schools and the numbers and the size of the Melton community grew exponentially. A few techniques contributed to that success. First, was a deeply held and passionate belief in the power of good Jewish education to bring meaning and depth to Jewish lives. Education could transform an individual, a family, a community, the global Jewish world. For me, a Melton class was just like home: it was a basic human need. This sentiment was contagious. Second was a disciplined and systematic approach to building relationships with each community. This made a huge difference. I made it my job to know about each community: the names of its leaders, federation directors, bureau of Jewish education directors, rabbis, how many day schools existed, the names of the people who answered the phones at each agency. I stayed in touch with them, week by week, calling to say hello and ask what concerns they might have, what communal discussions were taking place to advance adult Jewish learning. I helped communities find faculty, recruit students, articulate the right buzz words to make the school a success. Each community mattered to me personally. Acting like a Jewish teacher, my contacts became my students—learning what was at stake if we educated the community well.

While my father always joked that I should be selling real estate, he never failed to be proud of the sales I was making because he knew they made a difference in the Jewish world.

Organizing an Education Community
Makes the Difference

A challenge faced by any project that is national in scope—from Starbucks to Ben and Jerry's—is how to maintain a high quality of service and standards when not physically on the scene. The same applies to the Florence Melton Adult Mini-School. What assures that the reputation and integrity of FMAMS will be preserved? One of Florence's best recommendations was that communities hire a director who would act like a principal of the school. The director's job description is spelled out in the franchise agreement and detailed directors' manual. Directors, with their advisory boards and sponsoring institutions, ensure adequate financial resources to meet all the school's commitments. They also find the right location for the school, schedule classes, recruit students, and supervise everything necessary for running a quality school. The director was our contact person.

Directors hire, evaluate, and supervise the faculty, which must, according to the franchise agreement, be comprised of "committed Jews; knowledgeable and able to teach in a pluralistic setting; and who are qualified to teach the course to which they are assigned." No specific teaching credentials are required. It is sufficient that teachers be the best teachers of adults in their community. This is a change from the more common practice in North America where synagogue professionals or academics are the prime candidates for teaching. The Melton model of introducing students to a broad spectrum of teachers was inspired by the *Lehrhaus Judaica* in Frankfort at the beginning of the twentieth century whose teachers came from diverse backgrounds and had various strengths and various approaches to Jewish text. As Franz Rosensweig describes the *Lehrhaus,*

> It is really enough to gather together people of all sorts as teachers and students. Just glance at our prospectus. You will find an artist, a politician. Two-thirds of the teachers are persons who, twenty or thirty years ago, in the only century when Jewish learning had become the monopoly of specialists, would have been denied the right of teaching in a Jewish House of Study. They have come together here as Jews. They have come together in order to "learn"—for Jewish "learning" includes Jewish "teaching."

Directors supervise FMAMS faculty by observing classes and assuring that all requirements are being met. This can be a challenging task when the faculty often consists of rabbis, academics, and other highly qualified educators—none of whom are accustomed to being supervised. We encourage the directors to build relationships with teachers based on the fact that they know more about FMAMS, its culture, and its curriculum than anyone who is just beginning to teach in the school. The North American staff guide directors on how to observe classes: what to look for, what questions to ask teachers, how to discuss their teaching with them. Directors also bring the faculty together for discussions and seminars about adult Jewish education.

For much of their work, directors are supported by an advisory board composed of rabbis, lay leaders, faculty, students, and FMAMS alumni. Some boards assist with marketing the school or recruiting students; some help with planning extra-curricular activities, such as additional study sessions, fundraising programs, or a seminar in Israel. In some communities, the advisory board hires the school director.

The annual International Directors Conference is held every year alternating between and North America and Israel. It is an opportunity for intensive learning, creative problem solving, and exchange of ideas. The theme of the conference relates to a current issue in directors' lives. In 2006, for example, the conference examined "The Challenges of Collaboration." Every morning, the day began with *limud*, "learning" focused on studying texts. These usually introduced a new curriculum or a new version of the standard curriculum. Sessions the rest of the day spotlighted successful models of collaboration in communities, problem-solving, working with faculty members, and strategic planning. Each conference also is an opportunity to discuss research that enriches understanding of our students and the American Jewish community, Jewish education, and management of the Mini-School.

The 2008 conference was devoted to sustaining FMAMS and recruiting students. This occurred as community finances were especially tight. "Melton: Built to Last," the theme of the conference, examined the strategies of successful Mini-Schools. Many directors shared how they attracted young adults, built large schools in comparatively small communities, and recruited for the Israel Seminar, alumni associations, and special events. A Brandeis professor spoke about leadership and the chair of the International FMAMS Board of Directors spoke about strategies in challenging economic times.

Treating the Faculty as Professionals

Professional learning is an integral part of the culture of the Mini-School not only for directors but also for faculty. Whenever I visited the Philadelphia Melton School, for example, I met with the faculty in a room near the main entrance to Gratz College where classes were held. As one meeting began, students were filing out of the building talking animatedly about what they had learned. Through windows overlooking the parking lot, we overheard clusters of students continuing their class discussions.

The faculty session began by citing research showing that two-thirds of the Mini-School students say their lives were transformed by the two years of learning in Melton schools. One student interviewed said,

> Everything seems much more meaningful. It helped me get over that feeling of "inferiority" I had years ago. I am now involved in many Jewish organizations. As a family, we go to a synagogue much more often now .... It used to be meaningless for me to listen to a *d'var Torah*. It was meaningless because I didn't make a connection. Why were we doing this? Why did we start every meeting with fifteen minutes of this? I was always thinking, "Come on, hurry up, we have things to do." Melton really pulls so much of it together. There is so much more to learn, but now I have pieces of understanding. I can participate in many more conversations. I can celebrate with my family. I really feel a connection.

The session that followed was devoted to how these changes occur. What do teachers do to make this happen? In a typical meeting, faculty members analyze their teaching and relate it to research on transformational education, specifically studies describing how thinking and, consequently, attitudes or behavior of students can change. They provide examples from teaching of how they create opportunities for students to examine their Jewish beliefs and their Jewish life that they may have always taken for granted.

On this occasion in Philadelphia, the discussion expanded when the faculty read a selection from the *Book of Ari*, "The Tree of Life." In part, this reads:

> Behold, that before the emanations were emanated and the creatures were created. The upper simple light had filled the whole existence.
> And there was no vacancy, such as an empty atmosphere, a hollow, or a pit ....
> And it was called Endless Light.

And when upon His simple will, came the desire to create the world ....
He then restricted Himself, in the middle ....
And the light drew far off the sides around that middle point.
And there remained an empty space, a vacuum circling the middle
point ....
There, after the restriction, a place was formed where ... the created
might reside.
Then from the Endless Light a single line hung down
Lowered down into that space, and through that line, He emanated,
formed,
Created all the worlds.

The text became a prism for examining teaching. In the discussion that followed, teachers described how they often had to resist the desire to fill the room with their own knowledge and words. Instead, they withdrew, creating space for the students to question, to argue, to grow, and perhaps to be transformed. The image of the "single line" became the image of a teacher's presence in the classroom encouraging student exploration.

An important message integral to FMAMS is that every good teacher is a learner. No one teaches FMAMS curriculum without participating in an orientation that introduces the Mini-School's goals, what has been learned about students, and how to implement the curriculum and use it as the basis of teaching. Orientation sessions are followed by future meetings in which teachers explore Jewish content, the context of their teaching, the teaching process, and the nature of their students. These sessions are designed to encourage ongoing discussions among faculty when the national staff is no longer present. As Rabbi Michael Balinsky, who headed the design of the faculty's education curriculum, wrote in the introduction to the professional development handbook, "Influencing how faculty learns and encouraging their continuous growth is the key to success." The process he describes involves learning from Jewish texts, from literature on education and adult learning theory, from educational practice, from classroom experiences, and from each other. As faculty encounter all of these, they grow professionally. "What is key to all sessions," Rabbi Balinsky wrote, "is a faculty talking together and, in the process, building a community of reflective teachers."

OTHER VOICES

Rabbi Michael Balinsky, Executive Director of the Chicago Board of Rabbis, Formerly, North American Director of Faculty Development for the Florence Melton Adult Mini-School.

"So Rabbi, which position do you believe?" This question, asked towards the end of a class, gave me pause. The topic of why do people suffer is powerful, important, and relevant to adult student's lives since all of us suffer at one point or another. How do we reconcile our experiences of pain, loss, and tragedy with a God to Whom we speak in prayer and pray to for compassion? We had already studied texts suggesting that suffering is a result of sin; that reward and punishment come in the next world, not this one; that suffering is a divine secret whose purpose is not known to us; or that suffering may serve an educational purpose. Already, initial reactions to some of the texts were "this is ridiculous." The challenging class had forced students to confront difficult texts. And evoked deeply felt responses. After all this came, "So Rabbi, what do you believe?" My response was to pause quietly for a minute. Why did I pause? Why did I hesitate to answer?

While I paused, a student suggested that since all the views presented on suffering were from the tradition, my message was they could pick a view that worked for them. I said this was a possibility, but what I hoped for was something different. I encouraged them to allow the different voices to speak to them. If, as we had suggested in previous classes, ideas of miracles and messiah argue for betterment, growth, and the importance of deed, then the position of Deuteronomy and the Mishnah that suffering is a consequence of sinful deeds contains an important truth. We must consider the nature of action and deed—even if one rejects the theology that suffering is a form of punishment for sin. Suffering can be a moment for education and growth and transformation that God imposes on us to enable us to grow. I wanted them to engage in conversation with the wisdom and texts of our tradition—not to agree or disagree, but to see truth in these texts and their authors. "Rabbi, what do you believe?" I never really answered that for the goal was not to define or convince them of one belief or another, but to create a space to engage in that conversation. This, I humbly suggest, is one worthy goal for adult Jewish education.

Teaching adults is always complex. Teaching Jewish adults is especially complex. Although some people consider teaching to be more of an art than a craft, there are ways to analyze and systematize knowledge that allows it to be shared. You can learn from other teachers' successes and failures. It is important to know why a learning experience succeeds so it can be replicated. Developing a transmittable body of knowledge also provides the resources that enable rabbinical schools and schools of education to offer courses on "working with adults."

A most gratifying aspect of faculty learning was exchanging knowledge among young and old teachers; Orthodox, Reform, Conservative, Reconstructionist, and Renewal-affiliated teachers; experienced faculty and novices. Faculty not only learned about each other but grew in ability to understand different perspectives on Judaism. Knowledge of teaching the Melton curriculum, of Jewish adult learning and Jews, expanded with every conversation. This has been one of Melton's great strengths.

Creating a Learning Community

Six years after opening the first Mini-Schools, an article in the *Chicago Pioneer Press* reported that

> Four years ago, Caryl and Carl Derenfeld enrolled in an innovative course for Jewish adults that promised to give them an understanding of basic Jewish concepts and ethics. Long past the original curriculum, the Buffalo Grove, Illinois, residents are still studying with about twenty other graduates of the two-year program, all of whom received a Certificate of Jewish Studies from the Hebrew University in Jerusalem. What's more, Caryl Derenfeld says her life has been transformed.
>
> "I was on a personal quest to redefine my identity and what being Jewish meant to me," Carol Darenfeld said. "The Mini-School was a catalyst, a spark that began my thinking processes. It was the philosophy course I loved in college that came back in the form of spirituality."

Derenfeld and her fellow students had "become 'family,' creating a community that had a tremendous impact on how I am living my life" and boosting her involvement in synagogue life, the Jewish federation, and the Jewish community center.

Every Mini-School seeks to create a classroom community. Within weeks after individuals come together to study Jewish texts, they begin forging deep relationships that, over time, become the glue that encourages regular attendance in class and are essential to the rewards of the learning experience.

Essential to any successful long-term learning experience are text, people, and consistent attendance. The situation does not always have to include a professional teacher. This has been proven by many successful *havurot* or self-directed groups. Mini-School students, however, meet weekly over two years, thirty weeks a year, usually with different teachers for each of their four courses. There are not many things in life in which we participate over such an extended a period of time with the same group of people. It takes this kind of time, this extensive "quality time," for learning to have an impact and for the creation of a community.

From the first moment a prospective learner hears about the Mini-School, the school's director makes an effort for this to be a personal, positive experience. The goals of the school are made clear through its publicity and, sometimes, through one-on-one interviews conducted by directors with potential students. "Taste of Melton" classes, orientation sessions open to the public, assure that potential students know exactly what they will be doing in class and who their teachers will be. In addition, current students are encouraged to bring potential students to visit classes so they can experience learning Melton-style.

One of the most common reasons students cite for enrolling in a Melton School is to meet others like themselves. Newcomers to a community meet others who are also interested in serious adult learning. Seniors find companionship and a stimulating environment. Husbands and wives or groups of friends want to share their Jewish growth.

The seeds of a learning community are planted early in the students' experience. They are enrolling in a "school"—not in an isolated class or in a short-term experience. On the first day of class, students receive the *Florence Melton Adult Mini-School Readers*, and a class list is distributed so students can contact each other between classes. Sometimes a listserv or Facebook group is organized. Students are encouraged to have a "study partner," someone they can contact if they miss a class and who will collect handouts for them when they are absent.

The fifteen-minute break between the two classes held each evening was intended for students to socialize as well as discuss the class that just concluded with their teacher and other students. It is also a time for holiday celebrations: snacks in the *sukkah*, lighting Hanukkah candles, eating *hamantashin*—or to celebrate a birth, a birthday, an anniversary. On occasion, some schools have mourned the death of a student.

Students often raise questions that can be addressed outside of class time. For that, school directors may plan field trips to a *mikveh*, or a local synagogue, or a museum, or schedule guest speakers who discuss timely issues, or lead workshops on such topics as how to conduct a *seder* or build a *sukkah*. Many schools offer a *Shabbaton*, a weekend of study in a congregation, a community center, or a retreat center. These include the observance of Shabbat and greatly enhance shaping a learning community.

At the end of a student's first year in the school, there frequently is a *siyyum*—a festive ceremony celebrating the achievements of the past year. This gives students an opportunity to discuss their reactions to the course work. Marking their accomplishments and looking forward to their next year in the school can be very satisfying. This is even more pronounced at graduation at the end of the second year when guests frequently include family and friends, all of whom who add to the joy of the occasion.

Creating community may begin with something as basic as the arrangement of seating in a classroom. Conference-table style seating is preferred, with the teacher either being part of the circle of learners or taking a more authoritative position in front of the class. Seating the students in rows with their backs to each other would tell them that it is not important for them to speak to each other.

The most successful teachers create a warm, supportive, non-judgmental environment in which people can question and debate each other. The teacher models listening and dialogue and encourages participation rather than squelching debate. Only in a safe environment can students experiment with ideas and safely make mistakes or change their minds. The best Mini-School classrooms encourage students to enter into each other's perspectives and accept various perspectives as valid. Diversity becomes enriching, not threatening.

Another strategy used by Melton teachers to form a community involves studying texts in *hevrutah*—with one partner or in small groups. This encourages quiet students to express their opinions and spurs discussions that challenge positions, raise questions, and demand explanations. *Pirke Avot*, "Saying of the Fathers," describes this type of learning as two stones sharpening each other.

Observing the results of all these efforts have led to these conclusions on what produces a community of learners:

Stability

Partners or groups meet over an extended period of time. Continuity and consistency are essential. If students attend class sporadically, community may never form. Commitment significantly determines how people feel toward each other and their study. Regular attendance represents shared purpose and shared expectations of progress.

Artifacts

Many schools build class identity by creating "artifacts" such as yearbook-like publications that are distributed at graduation. Others have class t-shirts, song sheets, and holiday guides. Another kind of artifact is oral history—stories of individual students or the school itself that are retold year after year, such as telling of couples who were married after meeting in a Melton class or describing the exciting adventures from Israel Seminars that could fill a book. Stories are part of a common school history that maintains and strengthens a sense of community. In Raleigh, photographs of each graduating class line a corridor in the Jewish community center.

Other by-products include the weekly "roadmap" each teacher creates to serve as a lesson guide. A roadmap can contain vocabulary lists, important names and dates to be discussed, and the questions that will be addressed. Sometimes they include additional references and texts for continued learning.

Ritual

The stability of a community of learners is reflected in how it develops rituals. Learning habits create a sense of order and unity. The act of Jewish learning itself is a ritual, the fulfillment of a *mitzvah*. A Melton student in New York said, "I feel that I am a better Jew because of this program. I am doing something that, as a Jew, I should be doing: fulfilling an obligation to learn. You don't come to a certain point in life and close your mind."

Rituals also unite students. Many observances come up during the Jewish calendar year: studying in the *sukkah*, lighting Hanukkah candles, or eating Israeli foods at a *Tu BiShevat seder*. Sometimes, students begin each class with a blessing that ends with the words, *La-*

asok b'divrei Torah, thanking God for commanding us to study Torah. Or the process of learning itself may become ritualized, the reviewing of the prior class, distribution of roadmaps for the lesson, and the summary period at the conclusion of the hour when the content of the lesson is reviewed. Students might take on roles as leaders, followers, doubters, devil's advocates, compromisers that become part of the routine.

Skills

A community of learners develops a repertoire of common study skills. First are the basic skills required to learn: how to open and hold a holy book, how to locate "book, chapter, and verse" in the Bible; how to make your way through the landscape of a particular Jewish text—reading a page of Talmud, for example. The lesson on the nature of *mitzvot,* "commandments," introduces vocabulary that enables students to talk about them as well as understand their meaning: *mitzvot aseh,* "positive commandments"; *mitzvot lo ta'aseh,* "negative commandments"; *mitzvot bein adam la-Makom,* "commandments relating to human beings and God"; *mitzvot bein adam la-havero,* "commandments between human beings." Students become familiar with texts, commentaries, and scholars who appear repeatedly in the curriculum.

Joy of Learning

A community of learners is also defined by their enjoyment of learning: the pleasure of discovering knowledge previously inaccessible; the "Aha!" moment when the beauty and profundity of a Jewish text is revealed; the excitement of uncovering the treasures cherished by previous generations. Experiencing this in community increases learning and intensifies the experience. With no grades or degrees, this kind of Jewish study is experienced as a reward in itself and provides motivation for continuing learning.

Connecting to a Broader Professional Community

Although aspects of the Florence Melton Adult Mini-School developed slowly as a result of collaboration and cooperation, communication is even easier twenty-five years later. Innovation takes place in networks in which people inspire and motivate each other. They stimulate creative thinking and make constructive demands on each other.

While Melton has its own professional community, for ten years, the Alliance for Adult Jewish Learning provided further opportunity for communication among professionals and lay leaders. The Alliance's national conferences were opportunities to learn, share insights, and be inspired. They brought together people from across North America. Especially for adult educators in smaller communities without much local support, they were important places to exchange ideas and gather education resources. While the ideas and practices shared in lectures and workshops enriched the field and energized practitioners, the Alliance did not continue due to a lack of leadership willing to make the necessary commitment and give the time needed to the demands of programming. It would have been a forum in which expertise of one generation could have been passed on to another, a meeting that encouraged high professional standards, and a center that advocated for the vital importance of adult learning. All this must now be maintained by individual institutions and organizations.

Still, the Alliance conferences while they lasted were an indication of the importance people placed on adult learning and efforts to turn an avocation into a profession. One of the questions often discussed was the definition of "profession." As exemplified by FMAMS, "professionalism" means high-quality work and, consequently, the self-respect and dignity for those who are part of it. The components of a profession that evolved from the discussions are:

❧ Commitment to a shared mission and vision with recognition that there can be a diversity of approaches to achieving these goals.

❧ Knowledge of a shared history reflecting the traditional pursuit of Jewish learning.

❧ Expanding knowledge of the field: personnel, products, ideas about good teaching.

❧ Specialized language with which to communicate the concepts related to adult learning.

❧ Standards: What does "excellence" look like?

❧ Work ethics and values.

❧ Methods of evaluating teachers, students, and programs.

❧ Professional training experiences based on a shared body of knowledge.

❧ Funding for adult learning.

❧ Quantitative and qualitative research.

☆ Publication of articles in a professional journal and on a website.

☆ Extended professional growth—conferences, web learning, mentoring, travel.

☆ Teaching standards for practitioners with certification and other forms of recognition and incentives.

☆ Visibility as a profession at national and community events.

Choosing a Business Model that Ensures Excellence

I entered Jewish education because I was committed to studying Judaism and Jewish texts and wanted to make them accessible and comprehensible to others. Little did I know that, as my career progressed, I would become involved in text-based literacy education, refining it, adapting it to various settings and expanding it in North America. This was not a challenge that Jewish educators in Eastern Europe had faced. It was, however, indigenous to the development of adult Jewish learning in America.

Somehow, I found myself immersed in the business section of the library or a book store and was surprised when I discovered the relevancy to Jewish education of books about Starbucks, Ben and Jerry's, and Southwest Airlines. I found inspiration and optimism in these corporations, in people who take a unique idea and expand it throughout the world. Growth and change—as opposed to stability and conservation—rule. There were countless lessons to learn.

When the first Mini-Schools opened, they signed two-page letters of agreement that defined their relationship with the national office. These documents addressed the yearly cost of participating in the Melton network, the responsibilities of each school, and the responsibilities of the North American office. In exchange for the curriculum and consultation services, each school committed to teaching the Melton curriculum and limiting its use to the FMAMS setting. Directors and faculty had to participate in regular professional education experiences. This partnership allowed each party to do what it did best. It was based on respect for each other's work and on an open exchange of information.

When Yonatan Mirvis became director of the Florence Melton Institute in 1991, Melton adopted the not-for-profit franchise model that exists today. A franchise, unlike a simple contractual relationship or licensing agreement, involves not only rights to a trademarked product but also guidelines for successfully conducting a business. These include how to open and maintain a school and train directors and teachers and benchmarks for accomplishing goals that maximize success. The benefits to Melton franchisees, besides the constant infusion of new and improved curriculum, include an annual site visit from national office staff, marketing materials and strategies, yearly conferences for faculty and directors, an interactive website with resources from the central office and from other communities in the Mini-School network, and toll-free numbers for calling the North American office or the Melton office in Israel. Above all, members of the network benefit from twenty-five years of experience and expertise that almost guarantee the success of the school.

I remember the disbelief from Esther Zimand, the director of the Melton school in St. Louis, when she learned that the Mini-School would become a not-for-profit franchise. "A franchise?" she exclaimed. "This is education! Are we going to turn into McDonalds!?" Her comment reflects a cultural disconnect between the franchise system and the existing implementation practices in Jewish institutions. Melton succeeded as a non-for-profit franchise because of the strong persistence of its Board and Israel and North American staff and because of the ability of the staff to master the administrative and legal intricacies of a franchise. It has never been replicated by another Jewish education business or organization. The preferred model has most frequently been memberships, affiliation, or licensing. That fact alone points to the difficulty of changing an existing business culture.

Dr. Mirvis's decision to franchise the Mini-School was based partly on economic necessity. Florence Melton had always spoken of investing in the initial stages of the Mini-School, then setting up a system that would make communities financially responsible for their own adult education program. The funding from the Melton family could not support running a growing number of schools, a North American office, curriculum writing, educational seminars in Israel, and supervising the international network. Partners were needed to run the program in each community. These sponsoring institutions could seek local funding from federations and philanthropists and would know potential directors, faculty, and students.

In 2004, Martin Mendelsohn, a member of Melton's Board of Directors, warned about some drawbacks of the franchise arrangement. Recognizing "the organizational instability of the franchisees, their changing leadership and set of priorities," Mendelsohn advised that, "when a franchisee's organizational director leaves the position, there is no guarantee that his or her successor will have the same level of affinity and commitment to the franchise as the predecessor." At times, in fact, communities have used a vacancy as an excuse not to hire another director for the Mini-School but rather to operate the Mini-School in a manner similar to their other adult programs. In such situations, we say they must hire a director or close their school. Over the years, only three schools have closed after these ultimatums.

This suggests a second disadvantage of the franchise system. As Martin Mendelsohn wrote, "The franchise has a unique culture which must blend in with the local organizational culture. When there is no blend, this can lead to a number of tensions. This problem proved to be potentially acute when the franchisee offered other adult education courses. In two situations, the Mini-School was perceived to be a counterculture within the organization. Rather than allowing Melton to be changed to be more like other programs, the franchise relationships were ended with both organizations." The major question, then, and one that must be addressed constantly, is, What are the standards of the Mini-School? What cannot be changed? When will flexibility be permitted? What compromises quality? What alters the organization and the learning to the point that it no longer corresponds to the goals of the Melton system?

Despite these challenges and despite the rising costs of operating a school whose funding competes with other priorities in a community, the Mini-School continues to operate successfully. The franchise system has built-in flexibility. As financial pressures have increased Melton has increased its franchisees' benefits by including the graduate classes and the new parent program. In addition, while maintaining the insistence on pluralism, it has broadened its list of potential franchise holders to include more synagogues and synagogue consortia. In this way too, Melton would have access to more already-affiliated adult learners who are the most likely group to enroll in classes.

The Florence Melton Adult Mini-School is unique in the Jewish world. For twenty- five years, it has also been known for the quality of the learning it offers Jewish adults. At the beginning of 2012, it is educating adults in forty-three communities in North America and five communities in England, Australia, South Africa, and Hong Kong.

Lessons for Today

1. A strong organization is built on good communication and the honest, dependable relationships it makes possible. People prefer to do business with others whom they trust, from whom they benefit, and whose company they enjoy.

2. Professional learning strengthens a school by nurturing the growth of every individual that is part of it. It can occur formally in conferences and workshops, or informally through collegial conversations in the hall or around a lunch table.

3. A successful learning experience frequently involves the creation of a learning community, students who learn together, share experiences, and support each other.

4. Create a structure for expanding and perpetuating an institution or program including a way to become as close to self-sustaining as possible. Total dependency on philanthropic funds weakens the chance for long-term success.

5. Share the responsibility. A national organization must develop local partnerships that buy into the idea and take responsibility for success and longevity. An institution must earn the commitment and loyalty of its partners.

6. Assure that everything does not depend on one or two individuals, not only in terms of implementation and funding, but also in terms of sustaining the effort.

7. Plan for succession of professional and volunteer leadership. Expand ownership of the project beyond its present boundaries.

Chapter VIII

Scaffolding

Support for Jews
Who Choose to Learn

Make a fence around the Torah — Pirke Avot 1:1

No story of an organization would be complete without noting outside influences that shape it. Much was happening in the broader world of Jewish education that contributed to the success of the Florence Melton Adult Mini-School; at the same time, certain community dynamics challenged the very context of the school. In the 1980s, the time was ripe for innovation. Concern for the continuation of a strong Jewish community in North America led to demands for vibrant adult education. At the same time, innovations in adult learning benefitted from a surge in philanthropy and from new research about education. Competition among nationwide educational programs added to knowledge of education, raised educational standards, and increased the pressure for excellence.

Philanthropy and Leadership

The priorities of Jewish philanthropists have had far-reaching effects on the Jewish community. Federations allocate funds based on perceptions of the most important needs of the community. During the time that "continuity" and "renaissance" of Jewish life were the major topics of discussion among federations, adult learning ranked high on their priority lists. Federations, directly and indirectly, funded Florence Melton Adult Mini-Schools in the great majority of the communities where they were adopted.

Because of the positive results of the Mini-Schools, some federations made funds for adult learning a fixed line in their budgets. Although Mini-Schools are frequently funded by federations' contributions to Jewish community centers or central agencies, some federations, particularly in smaller communities, sponsor the Mini-School directly. In Sarasota, Florida, for instance, since the mid-1990s, the federation has taken advantage of all that the Mini-School has had to offer. Besides the two-year Mini-School and graduate courses, the Sarasota Federation funded classes for leadership and the Parent Education Program. In the successful Mini-Schools in such smaller cities, the participation of Jewish adults relative to the eligible population exceeds that in larger communities. This confirms research that shows that, when given the opportunity, Jews in less densely-populated areas participate in adult learning more than Jews in larger cities. Learning is perceived as an expression of Jewish identity where it is more difficult to maintain and Jews in smaller locales feel a strong commitment to their Jewish institutions.

Funding local educational needs became a priority beginning in the 1990s and into the twenty-first century. Awareness of the shrinking Jewish population documented in Jewish population studies was only the beginning of concerns. Fundraisers could no longer rely on emotions aroused by the Holocaust or the creation of Israel to motivate giving. Younger donors, in particular, did not have memories of the miraculous creation of the Jewish state. Anti-Semitism had decreased; personal contact with Holocaust survivors was lessening. Vast sums were no longer necessary to save the Jews of Yemen, the Soviet Union, or Ethiopia. These compelling issues were no longer the moral and spiritual magnets for attracting donors. Would the importance of funding education and culture, as opposed to rescuing Jews in distress, maintain the motivation for giving?

In addition, major contributors to federations were turning over responsibility for allocation of family resources to members of younger generations. Embodying more universalistic tendencies, these adults in their mid-forties or younger were giving less to Jewish causes than their parents and grandparents. Another factor was influencing those generations—the growing rate of intermarriage. Twenty-seven percent of intermarried children gave to Jewish causes, with 13 percent of their contributions going to federations. By contrast, 74 percent of their parents gave to Jewish causes, with 59 percent of their contributions going to federations.

Those working in adult learning have been faced with an additional challenge. Funds for education overwhelmingly go to children's education. This continues a long-existing pattern in American philanthropy. Those communities with a specific budget line for adult learning have challenged the practice of giving exclusively to children's education. These funders realize that children's education—without the reinforcement of a Jewish home and parents who model lifelong learning—has greater potential for failure.

Jewish leaders have had to confront another dilemma. With less money going to centralized philanthropic institutions, leaders in many communities have not only had to choose between educating children and educating adults but also between education and social services. Feeding the hungry, caring for the homeless, providing care to the elderly all take priority in a time of need, such as in our recent financial crisis. Although Jewish tradition recognizes learning as a value as precious as food, clothing or shelter, it is difficult to maintain this model in today's challenging reality. In considering this ideal, some communities have turned to donors for additional funds, while some are committed to restoring funds for learning projects as soon as possible. Others, sadly, have chosen to end funding of adult education.

Family foundations provide some of the strongest examples of philanthropy directed to adult learning. Their generosity and guidance have created new initiatives and expanded successful ones. Besides the example of the generosity of the Sam and Florence Melton, Gordon Zacks and Donald Katz families who have made the Florence Melton Adult Mini-School possible, the Norton Wasserman family, The Covenant Foundation, Cummings Foundation, Meyerhoff Foundation, and Avi Chai Foundation all provided funding and encouragement that led to specialized Melton programs: graduate classes and courses that teach Jewish literacy to supplementary and day school teachers and to parents of young children. One Covenant grant supported Mini-Schools in small Jewish communities.

There is a downside to all of this. If organizations do not carefully evaluate the acceptance and use of funding initiated by funders, they can be distracted from accomplishing their priority goals. If the expectations of funders include preparing the project for replication outside of the funded organization, this requires knowledge, skills, and time an organization may not readily have available. If organizations do not anticipate the ending of foundation funding by creating sources of income to continue their work, projects—even successful projects—collapse when funding ends. A philanthropist can lose interest in an initiative, decide it is not accomplishing enough, or conclude that it has done all it can do. When critique is justified, an innovation should come to an end. When it is not, closing down can be avoided by alternative means of funding.

Private foundations have not always given directly to education. The trend began in the 1960s when a Columbus, Ohio, businessman, Sam Mendel Melton, frustrated with education standards in synagogues, funded the Samuel Mendel Melton Center at the Jewish Theological Seminary. The Seminary's best scholars and educators created curriculum and provided teacher training for the study of Torah, and, later, holidays and prayer in Conservative congregations and camps. The Samuel Mendel Melton Department of Judaic Studies at Ohio State University was founded several years later as well as the Samuel Mendel Melton Centre for Jewish Education in the Diaspora at the Hebrew University in Jerusalem. Sam Melton's efforts were continued by his Columbus family, Florence Zacks Melton, Gordon Zacks, and Donald Katz. The Melton family's support for Jewish education improved the quality of learning and provides a model that continues to inspire other philanthropists.

Ohio's unique, philanthropic Jewish community followed Sam Melton's example. By now, it has influenced Jewish education around the world. Art Scroll Publishers revolutionized the Jewish publishing business when the Shottenstein family made Jewish texts available in English translation. Leslie Wexner's foundation has shaped Jewish leadership and learning through the Wexner Heritage Program and the Wexner Israel Fellowship Program. Morton Mandel's commitment to learning transformed teacher education in North America and Israel for almost a decade.

Elsewhere in the country, Chicago's Crown family (through its Covenant Foundation) and the Nathan Cummings Foundation recognized Jewish educators and supported projects that moved education into the twenty-first century. They, along with many other foundations like the James Joseph Foundation, Harold Grinspoon Foundation, Charles and Lynn Schusterman Foundation, Steinhardt Foundation, and Andrea and Charles Bronfmann Foundation have recognized the importance of Jewish education and contributed not only financial support but some of the most creative educational ideas over the past fifty years. All of these have believed in the importance of adult education and have shown what can be accomplished through partnerships between philanthropists and competent educators. It would be difficult to imagine in what condition Jewish education might be if not for the generosity of such individuals and foundations. Judging from the giving patterns of many in the younger generation, it may be necessary to face that possiobility.

Research: Examining Accomplishments and Failures

In a paper written for her master's degree from the School of Education at the Jewish Theological Seminary, Kate O'Brien conducted interviews with five directors and staff of the Mini-School. Asked to describe "ideal" Melton Mini-School graduates, the most common responses were that they:

❧ Realize there are more questions than answers.

❧ Ask questions, express ideas, engage their teachers, and are not being passive students.

❧ Are committed to continuing their Jewish learning and *Torah liShemah*, "learning for the sake of learning."

❧ Can open a Jewish text and locate what they are seeking.

❧ Appreciate a wide variety of Jews and of ways of being Jewish.

❧ Develop a new appreciation for the depth of meaning of *klal Yisrael*, "the unity of the people of Israel."

❧ Think deeply about their Jewish practice and commitments and, ideally, serve the community to the best of their abilities.

Much research has focused on how the Mini-School affects individuals—the accomplishments of local programs and the impact of the national project. Some research is quantitative. It measures numbers of students enrolled, retention through the two-year program, and specific results of learning in the Mini-School. More recently, however, different methods of research have produced a different kind of information. Qualitative studies allow researchers to gather information based on personal responses to Jewish learning experiences through interviews and classroom observations. This approach provides practical insights and personalized information that can be used to guide other inquiries as well as professional decision-making.

In 2004, the Jewish Theological Seminary of America published *A Journey of Heart and Mind: Transformative Jewish Learning in Adulthood* by Lisa D. Grant, Diane Tickton Schuster, Meredith Woocher, and Steven M. Cohen. Their research was based on interviews with Mini-School staff, students, teachers, and school directors. Examining teaching materials and documents, observing classes, and conducting surveys of graduates uncovered the nature of the school's students, how participation in learning was affecting their lives, and the challenges of adult learning that still need to be addressed. The study identified seven ways Melton students were being changed:

✹ Making new meaning of pre-existing Jewish activity.

✹ Expanding involvement in Jewish learning.

✹ Connecting ethics with everyday life.

✹ Developing appreciation for traditional Judaism.

✹ Encountering God and spirituality.

✹ Transmitting meaning to others.

✹ Building a sense of belonging through Jewish networks and community involvement.

Although these lists are informative, the best way to illustrate the Mini-School's impact is through the stories of its students, directors, and teachers:

Making New Meaning of Pre-Existing Jewish Activity

Michael observed the laws of *kashruth* because that was how he was raised. When he married, he and his wife also had a *kosher* kitchen. The two of them enrolled in the Mini-School. A class in "The Rhythms of Jewish Living" that discusses laws of *kashruth* was their first opportunity to explore why these laws and traditions are observed. They were grateful that they had been given this perspective and were able to move beyond keeping *kosher* simply because their parents had.

Expanding Involvement in Jewish Learning

Paula—an intelligent, articulate woman who raised important questions and listened carefully to her Mini-School classmates—was hired as a director of a FMAMS Parent Education Program when she completed the two-year Melton curriculum. Soon, she learned about a program at Spertus Institute in Chicago where she could earn a Masters of Arts in Jewish Professional Studies. She has completed that program and is making valuable contributions to the Jewish education community.

Connecting Ethics with Everyday Life

The Baltimore Jewish Times (April, 2001) ran the following story about the local Florence Melton Adult Mini-School: Phyllis Friedman, an area attorney and Melton graduate, listened carefully as her client, a homeowner who had hired a carpenter explained his dilemma. The construction worker demanded his week's pay for the entire week though the project for which he had been contracted was not finished. If he was paid, the homeowner had doubts he would return on Monday to finish the job. Couldn't he just be paid upon completion? Attorney Friedman didn't hesitate. "I remembered the Torah portion that we learned that says you should not withhold pay until after the sunset. I said to my client, 'We're going to pay him.' And we did." Withholding pay until after a weekend, like not paying the worker in the talmudic passage until after sunset, can cause the worker hardship. The worker must be trusted to finish his work. "I knew it was the right answer," said Friedman, "and it was an easy answer because I knew it was right."

Developing Understanding of Traditional Judaism

Marti and Jim enrolled in the Mini-School to understand more about Judaism and make it a greater part of their lives. They had always celebrated Hanukkah, but now they started bringing their family together for a Passover *seder*. They also began to observe Shabbat on Friday evenings. "We started with *kiddush*, the blessing of the wine, and the blessing on the challah," Marti said. "We've already added blessing the children and Jim recites a modern version of 'A Woman of Valor.' Now, we are starting to keep *kosher* on Shabbat."

Encountering God and Spirituality

An articulate, confident Mini-School student who had been raised as a secular Israeli now belongs to a Humanist congregation. At first, as a Melton student, she had frequently expressed her lack of belief in God and pointed to inconsistencies or inexplicable statements in Jewish texts. Some students agreed with her, some disagreed politely, some admitting that she was forcing them to think deeply about their own beliefs. One of the goals of the Melton school is to allow the ideas from texts that are studied to speak for themselves. As the year progressed, she maintained her original position, but influenced by comments from classmates and their debates and discussions triggered by the texts, she admitted that she now understood why Jews over the centuries—and those in her class—have affirmed the existence of a higher power.

Transmitting Meaning to Others

Gwen, a Melton student in Florida, had two children of *bar* and *bat mitzvah* age. "I had been looking for a class like this since I got married," she said,

> when I knew that I wanted my children to grow up being more Jewish than I had been in my own youth. The Mini-School helped me understand Jewish ways of life as well as the holidays. I was able to learn with my children and answer their questions and share in the meaning and feeling of being Jewish.

Building a Sense of Belonging through Jewish Networks and Community Involvement

A student in Pittsburgh said,

> I felt before that my involvement in Jewish organizations was almost a function of being a lawyer, of being out and about in the community: this was just something you did. I still feel that, but I also feel that doing it because I am part of the Jewish community is just as important .... Now I don't look at it just from the perspective of getting my name out into the community, I also see it as something that is important to others and to me as well. I don't know if my attitude would have changed if I hadn't enrolled in the Mini-School two years ago.

Comfort in Studying Jewish Texts

The most frequently-reported change in Melton students was their growing comfort in studying Jewish texts. Ninety-two percent said they now were either "somewhat" or "greatly" more comfortable studying Jewish texts in English. In a graduation speech from a Mini-School in Calgary, Alberta, Canada, one student said:

> Sources studied in any particular lesson include Torah as well as commentary such as Mishnah, Talmud, *The Code of Jewish Law*, ancient and modern religious philosophers from every imaginable stream of Judaism, prayer

books, poetry, and song. The conversation is always great—and we usually remember to keep ourselves grounded in the literature. Those words, after all, are the wellspring that brings us together—though they do not, necessarily, take us to the same conclusions. It's okay: in keeping with the tradition of Hillel and Shammai. And, if you don't know who they are, drop everything and register immediately for the next Melton session coming this fall to a classroom near you!

Information gathered through research shapes the Mini-School. From 1990 when Gaby Horencyk published the first research on the Florence Melton Adult Mini-School, practitioners have examined the studies carefully. At times it reinforced earlier decisions on curriculum, marketing, and teaching. Other times, it changed the organization. One important use of this knowledge was in determining what is discussed in Melton's teacher development sessions. Knowing why students come to study and what happens to them while they are enrolled influence what texts teachers teach, how they present information, and what questions they raise in their classes. It helps teachers think differently about how changes occur in students and how a teacher's style affects them. A teacher who asks good questions rather than providing answers through lecturing is prodding a student to think. A teacher who gives students a variety of Jewish texts that contain a variety of perspectives helps students see the richness of Judaism and realize the choices that they have before them.

Such research also generated many other intense discussions among the North American staff members. An example of a question still important today is why fewer men than women attend Jewish adult learning programs in the non-Orthodox community. Only 20 percent of Mini-School students are men. The vast majority of these are over the age of fifty-five. Many attend at the request of their wives or for intellectual enrichment now that they are retired. An understanding of this pattern emerges from notes on a staff discussion of the research.

❧ Men below retirement age have less discretionary time than many women and other activities compete for their time.

❧ In spite of changes in the roles of men and women in recent decades, creating a Jewish home and enrolling children in Jewish schools remain primarily a woman's responsibility.

❧ As a basic survey of Judaism, the Mini-School has attracted beginning and intermediate level learners. Men, however, prefer the challenge of high-level learning—perhaps because of the status that such a program has in their eyes or because a less rigorous curriculum suggests a lack of knowledge. A greater percentage of men enroll in CLAL and Wexner leadership programs that determine enrollment based on applications and interviews and offer higher-level learning.

Another major discussion on who was—and was not—learning in the Mini-School began with findings from research conducted by JLearn, a project of the Federation of Long Island. Initially, it was hoped that the Mini-School would attract unaffiliated Jews who reside along the periphery of Jewish life. This did not happen. However, much could be learned about those who did attend.

When the Long Island Federation created its adult education initiative, it simultaneously funded a study of the impact of the Mini-School as well as that of the Me'ah program affiliated with Boston Hebrew College and several short-term programs focused on observing Jewish traditions. (More about Me'ah follows.) The study revealed that people who enrolled in any of these learning experiences were already on some kind of Jewish journey. They were "highly engaged" in Jewish life. Most belonged to synagogues and their children were in synagogue schools or day schools. The majority were dedicated learners who were looking for serious learning opportunities. Compared to other Jews, they were more ritually observant, belonged to various Jewish organizations, and had greater involvement in Jewish communal activities. They were also drawn to studying Jewish texts over an extended period of time and to learning about Judaism from multiple perspectives. The study concluded that Melton students could eventually be recruited for leadership roles throughout Long Island and, ideally, could affect cultural change in their communities.

The study addressed a second group of learners—those "somewhat engaged in Jewish life." For them, learning was primarily about gaining knowledge about Judaism to enrich their own Jewish experience. This group was attracted to learning for specific reasons: to learn how to celebrate Shabbat, how to observe the holidays, how to read the prayer book. Although some members of this group were stimulated by the intellectual excitement of studying texts, most were attracted to a more experiential type of study that was tied to the Jewish calendar and life cycle events.

In 2011, Jack Wertheimer compiled *The New Jewish Leaders: Reshaping the American Jewish Landscape*. Based on surveys, website exploration, and interviews it describes the new generation of Jewish leaders and the world they guide. Understanding that world and the younger and older adults in it, explains much about adult learning as it exists today. It also provides essential information that can shape adult learning in the next decade.

There had never been so much knowledge available on adult Jewish learning. One of the ideals in Jewish education is the weaving of research, evaluation, scholarship, and practice. Research in adult learning increased respect for the field. Besides influencing the Florence Melton Adult Mini-School practice, research and scholarship became the basis of courses in Jewish adult learning in a growing number of Jewish academic settings. When adult learning is taught to present and future teachers, rabbis, and organization leaders as a formal course of study, the quality of adult education grows, its impact increases, and it can become a higher priority of Jewish organizations.

Competition: Me'ah and Rohr Jewish Learning Institute

Boston is one example of a community that has made an outstanding commitment to adult Jewish education. Boston Hebrew College (supported by the Boston Combined Jewish Federation or CJF) made adult learning a high priority for over twenty years. The result was a program called Me'ah which offers classes taught by the best instructors in a city known for its outstanding academics. The Boston Jewish community enjoys a three-way partnership among CJF, synagogues, and institutions of higher learning like the Hebrew College and Brandeis University. After gaining momentum in the Boston area, Me'ah offered classes in such East Coast regions as New York, New Jersey, Washington, D.C., Maryland and Virginia. Many of its 3,500 graduates continue to learn in high-level courses in their synagogues and at Hebrew College. In 2011, responding to financial pressures, the Me'ah program outside of Boston became ConText, a project of the Jewish Theological Seminary.

One way Me'ah differs from Melton is its requirement that all faculty have advanced degrees in an aspect of Jewish studies. The faculty also determines the specifics of what to teach within broad guidelines of Me'ah's two-year, one hundred-hour, program (the word *me'ah* means "one hundred"). Its courses are organized according to Jewish history. Most classes are held in synagogues. Me'ah's self-description reveals its similarities—and its differences with the Mini-School. In 2010, its website stated that Me'ah is intended to answer questions like

> Who am I? What is my history? How did the Jewish religion and culture develop and what does it mean to me? Me'ah answers these questions with substance, from multiple perspectives; enabling you to find your place in the continuum of Jewish life .... You'll be immersed in reading core Jewish texts, grappling with concepts representing the historical, cultural, and political movements from four eras—biblical, rabbinic, medieval, and modern.

Me'ah's success and growing competition stimulated self-evaluation in the Mini-School. It increased learning for local and national Mini-School staff and strengthened its marketing efforts. Jewish communities around the country sometimes compare the two programs and choose between them. Both have served American Jews well, stimulating interest in adult learning and provoking discussions about what makes for quality adult education.

Other Voices

David Starr, Bronfmann Fellow, Brandeis University, former director of Me'ah.

A few weeks ago my alarm woke me with a radio report of a new edition of *The Adventures of Huckleberry Finn.* Why a new edition? Someone decided to take out the N-word, and in its place, substitute the bland and utterly decontextualized, "slave." You may ask, what's wrong with a bit of sensitivity, if it drives a hateful term a little further into obscurity? Nothing, other than that it robs the reader of the context in which Twain's story not only takes place, but makes meaning, *i.e.*, the omnipresent race-based reality of the nineteenth-century American South, a society that relied upon humiliating words wreaking far more domination and dehumanization than the dry legal term "slave." Put a little more broadly, well-meaning but misguided attempts to clean up difficult texts and histories shield readers and end up inhibiting a struggle that is the essence of learning, the struggle with strange words and worlds that forces us to think by wrenching us out of our comfort zone.

Every person, every educator, has to ask themselves two simple questions: is there a question that you wouldn't ask? Is there anywhere you wouldn't go to answer your question? Me'ah rests upon the commitment to context and to strangeness. In other words, learning is mostly about the questions that teachers bring (and the students, too) to the classroom, the reaction of the learners to those questions, and the questions that stick with one after one's encounter with Jewish texts, ideas, and history. The necessary and essential imparting of information takes shape through the creation of context, a medium to help students think things through. The program's historical approach tells students that to understand something requires placing it in time, grasping how it came to be, changed, helped bring other things into being. For instance, the world of ancient Israel gave way to other new forms of Judaism out of which came the rabbinic form that prevailed and left us the sources through which we attempt to reconstruct our past; a once-normative Judaism of the Middle Ages eventually morphed into a variety of modern and regularly contradictory Jewish cultures. Getting a handle on these processes entails grasping the distance between here and there, then and now. Change means strange.

This emphasis on questions is not merely a matter of pedagogy or epistemology but carries ethical and spiritual weight. Questioning—when carried out in an honest quest and not as an exercise in free-floating skepticism—reinforces the autonomy of the self and one's subject. Student and the object of study stand alone as necessary units, but they remain insufficient in some sense until the other demands and inquires of them.

A kind of covenant binds teacher, student, and subject. Each exists independently with a force and dignity that must be respected by the other parties. They meet in the middle, in the questions that suggest the need of each of these parties for the others. I acknowledge the radicalism of this approach in the context of Jewish education, which traditionally focuses upon on the self-sufficiency of the text and the Tradition it embodies.

The Melton Mini-School and Me'ah, respectful rivals in the quest to build an educated Jewish adult public, in effect have posed their own questions of each other over the years. Each asks what the best way of teaching adult Jews is, and what a proper vision of the Jewish adult is. Mindful of this philosophical and educational conversation, here I offer two short vignettes of Me'ah questions, problems that likely remained with learners, teachers, and the tradition, hopefully goading them to more learning and growth.

From the world of ideas, I remember a poignant example of a student's reaction to learning. At a year-end social gathering to reflect on the year spent studying the Bible through a critical lens, one student lamented to his Bible teacher, "You took my God away." His perplexity came with greater knowledge and greater investment in his learning. Or maybe this little story slights others for whom such encounters plunged them into crisis. Questions that matter can endanger one's equilibrium. How could it be otherwise?

Finally, from the world of history, a teacher of medieval Jewish history greeted students returning for the second year of study by connecting the world of the Talmud with the Jewish Middle Ages. After teaching a strange talmudic text in tractate *Avodah Zarah* about the primordial leviathan, the teacher explained the strange case of the Talmud's cultural standing as a somewhat dysfunctional canonical text, yet one that nevertheless became the binding text for medieval Jewry. To which one student then asked, "Why didn't the medievals (aside from Maimonides) create another canonical text to supplant or replace the Talmud, similar to how the Mishnah functioned *vis a vis* the bible?" The instructor smiled and said, "That's one of the great unanswered questions of Jewish cultural history."

In the end it comes down to treating adults like adults. Not talking down to them, but talking to them, teaching them, listening to them, hearing the gaps between life's questions and the tradition's answers, the spaces between the tradition's own questions and answers. A *Tosafot* in tractate *Kiddushin* denounces converts as a scab on Israel, enumerating various ways in which they cause problems for Judaism and the Jewish people. At a Me'ah faculty seminar one instructor ventured that she would avoid teaching such a text in class, for fear that someone—a convert, a spouse, whomever—would take offense. To which another teacher responded: "You think that converts don't know that this is what many Jews say about them?"

This exchange leaves me with a question of my own. I began this essay lamenting the fear of history's messiness that sometimes tempts us to impose too much order on life's chaos. Yet it remains fair to question the one asking the question. Do we ask solely for the fun of it, because we can, because we train our minds to be acute and so we enjoy flexing our mental muscles, without caring whom our question might hurt? In the story above the ethical dimension of teaching and learning insists that we question because out of our raw honesty with the convert we hope and believe that a new dialogue may emerge, in effect a new relationship between Self, Teacher, and Tradition.

The Rohr Jewish Learning Institute (JLI) also educates Jewish adults. Since opening in sixteen locations in 1997-1998, Chabad-affiliated JLI has developed twenty-eight courses. Written by rabbis and academics, these address a wide variety of subjects, from Kabbalah and the Holocaust to models of leadership and "Life, Death, and Beyond." JLI incorporates teacher orientation and development as an essential part of its work and its use of technology to enhance the experience of faculty and students in achieving its goals is outstanding.

JLI courses are taught in 325 locations in North America and abroad. In its first ten years, 181,217 adults attended these classes. Sixty-two percent of these adults are still associated with JLI and/or the Chabad congregations that sponsor it. There are advanced classes based on study of a Jewish text, a yearly national retreat, and an educational tour of Israel. Over eight hundred participants attended the August 2011 national retreat in Old Greenwich, CT.

One of JLI's greatest strengths is the system through which it has expanded around the world. Its classes are held in Chabad congregations. They are taught by the rabbis of these synagogues. Curriculum consists of short-term classes. In 2011, their website listed thirty-five of these courses. Entering JLI students have more choices about what to study, and the length of its courses attracts more students whose crowded schedules prevent them from making a long-term commitment to study. Many eventually enroll in year-long advanced study.

Although Melton, Me'ah, and JLI all focus on studying texts, JLI includes more Orthodox-based texts in contrast to FMAMS's effort to expose students to texts with a variety of denominational perspectives. While both Melton and Me'ah are dedicated to educating Jews so they can make informed choices that shape their Jewish lives, Chabad encourages informed choice while steering students into a long-term relationship with the Orthodox community.

Other Voices

Rabbi Efraim Mintz, Executive Director of the Rohr Jewish Learning Institute, Brooklyn, NY.

Our teachers are the rabbis of the sponsoring congregations. JLI now has about three hundred and sixty instructors. They attend a training institute before they start teaching and a yearly institute every year they teach. Overseas teachers attend a training institute every other year. In addition, there is extensive marketing and instructional support for them from the national office. All classes follow the same time schedule with five model lessons online the week before a lesson is taught as well as a Message Board where teachers can discuss their teaching with each other. Each model lesson gets about one hundred hits a week.

At the training institute, teachers are taught about how adults learn. They discuss the various modalities of learning: analytical learning through lecturing, exploratory learning based on text study and peer learning, procedural learning through learning activities, and emotional learning by applying what is learned to life.

Participation in JLI is maintained because the teachers—the rabbis—develop strong relationships with their students. This forms a community that the students can be part of, a community that encourages continued learning in JLI classes. There is also an array of programs at *shuls* that the students can attend. These include social activities, holiday celebrations, and Shabbat prayer—not only learning.

Because of differences between JLI and the Florence Melton Adult Mini-School, they rarely compete directly with each other for students or funding. It does not prevent them from learning from the other's strengths and successes. From JLI, Melton can learn about the effective use of the internet—particularly in the areas of marketing and recruitment, faculty education, and lesson enrichment. The value of short-term courses as entry-points for students is evident. From Melton, JLI can learn about the benefits of university-based research and evaluation and about advantages of knowledge of diverse Jewish perspectives. While the paths of these Jewish organizations rarely cross, learning from each other increases the effectiveness of both.

Lessons for Today

1. Jewish philanthropists have a far-reaching impact upon the quality and priorities in Jewish education but total dependence on philanthropy for sustaining an initiative may limit its longevity.

2. If learning is the sole mission of the organization, an adult education program is more likely to be sustained there than in an organization that has competing priorities.

3. (Again.) Children's education without reinforcement of a Jewish home and parents involved in Jewish learning and culture will be more likely to fail.

4. Research provides insights into the nature and impact of education and knowledge of research shapes teachers' choices of what and how to teach.

5. To increase participation of men in adult learning, changes need to be made in accessibility, timing, and level of course offerings.

6. The great majority of learners who attend long term classes are already on a Jewish journey. We have not yet met the challenge of attracting those who are on the periphery of the Jewish community.

7. Competition among institutions that offer adult learning can stimulate self-evaluation, increased effort to achieve excellence, and strength-

ened marketing. Coordination and collaboration can allow us to serve more learners in more ways.

8. Success of an excellent learning experience comes not from being the best at what you do but from being the only one doing it.

Chapter IX

Teachers

Learning in Order to Teach

Rabbi Yehuda Nesiah sent Rabbi Hiyya and Rabbi Ammi and Rabbi Assi out to survey whether or not the Jewish communities of the Land of Israel had appropriate teachers of Written Torah and Oral Torah. When they came to a certain community and found no such teachers, they said to the members of the local Jewish community, "Bring us the guardians of the city." The members of the community brought them the city police officers. They said, "These are not the guardians of the city. Rather, they are the destroyers of the city." The local Jews then asked, "And who, then, are the guardians of the city?" They [the Rabbis] said to them, "The teachers of the Written Torah and the Oral Torah, as the verse states, 'If God does not build the city, the workers have labored in vain' (Psalm 127:1)." — Talmud Yerushalmi, Hagiga 1:7

One dimension of adult education that is sometimes overlooked—because of the tendency to place it in its own separate category—is the education of teachers. As the ones who largely determine the quality of children's learning, it is essential that teachers know Judaism, know pedagogy, and know the children they teach. By definition, they should be lifelong Jewish learners. Whether talking about teachers in synagogue schools, community centers, or day schools, more and more of them are American-born. Rather than depending on Eastern European immigrants or Israelis, as schools had done earlier in the twentieth century, a survey of educators in Jewish schools in 2008 showed that more than 85 percent of teachers who responded to the survey were raised in the United States. As the numbers of American-born teachers have increased, on-the-job education has become a greater priority.

The 2009 School Opening Institute was a three-hour seminar for synagogue school directors and teachers. It was sponsored by Chicago's Community Foundation for Jewish Education. An inspiring keynote address introduced the theme of the conference, "Keeping the Flame Alive: Renewing Judaism in Every Classroom." It was based on traditional sources that assign teachers the responsibility to show students they are an irreplaceable link in the growth and development of Torah. As the invitation to the Institute stated, the conference would challenge teachers

> to make the Jewish classroom a dynamic, searching environment where students are taught to be not only "consumers" of Judaism but also its interpreters .... Students are to create Judaism, accepting what was done in the past and shaping Judaism for the future .... Students' quest for Jewish meaning informs and transforms their lives and their identities.

The invitation described the high ideals of synagogue education, but it is questionable whether a teacher can learn what is necessary to accomplish all this in a three-hour conference. The teachers for whom this conference was planned manage Jewish classrooms where 70 percent of American children receiving a Jewish education are enrolled. Their success—or failure—influences the overall quality of future American Jewish life. Concerns about the knowledge and skills of Jewish teachers in synagogue schools are widespread. Unless the importance of teacher education is recognized by leaders and funders and made part of job expectations, there is little chance that the quality of education in synagogues will improve, especially when the hours devoted to this Jewish education are shrinking and when attendance is in competition with public school activities. This is one of the most serious problems in Jewish education today.

Many Jewish parents are not invested in the Jewish future. They ask only that their children's Jewish education be good enough to prepare them for *bar* or *bat mitzvah*. They do not demand excellence that could lead to higher standards for teachers. It becomes obvious to children that Jewish learning is not a priority when so many other pursuits are given greater priority and there is little relationship between what they learn and the life they lead outside the synagogue walls. To paraphrase an observation by Franz Rosensweig, when Jewish education sits in a safe, quiet, little corner, life flows past it unconcerned.

Teachers as the Guarantors of Success:
Kohl Jewish Teacher Center

It is nine o'clock in the morning when Bryna, a member of the education staff, opens the door of the Kohl Jewish Teacher Center in Wilmette, Illinois, and greets a school principal who frequently stops at the Kohl Center on his way to work. He has come to meet with teachers and principals from other schools to plan activities and materials for a citywide celebration of Israel Independence Day. Soon, everyone is engaged in a lively brainstorming session.

One teacher previews a video about Passover she plans to use in her classroom. Another gathers books and educational materials on teaching about Jewish life in Poland before World War II. Four teachers travel four hundred miles from Cincinnati so they can browse through the Center, taking notes on displays and resources and making sketches of the materials they see. These materials and ideas from the Kohl Center became a starting point for a similar center in Cincinnati. The visitors pause at the Teachers' Store noting the items for sale, some published by the Kohl Center, others commercially published such as stick-on Hebrew letters that help teachers create their own classroom materials.

Soon it is one o'clock, and in comes a visiting third-grade day school class. Their materials are waiting for them. The teacher, who had visited the Center earlier in the week to plan what to do, leads them in a discussion of Purim and helps them design books with their own illustrations of the Purim story. They will use these to tell the story of Esther, Mordecai, and Haman to their families. Students who finish early play learning games until everyone is done. Two students slip into the cardboard puppet theater and put on a show for themselves. Another flops down on a pile of *aleph-bet* pillows and reads a book written by a child about her family's coming to America in the 1920's. A teacher doing research in the library ends up joining some students on the floor for a lively game of Hebrew vocabulary pick-up-sticks. When it is time to put everything away, someone is missing. Jeremy, it turns out, is sitting in a cardboard study center flipping through a learning packet on the *Shema*. He doesn't want to leave, but then neither did anyone else who came to the Center.

Neither did I. I worked at the Kohl Jewish Teacher Center from its beginning in 1975 through 1981. The center model was conceived by Dolores Kohl, who was especially adept at adapting ideas for Jewish education that had been successful in public education. Dolores' staff modified the philosophy and structure of the public school teacher center, learned what professionals in the Jewish community wanted, and came up with the first Jewish teacher center in the world.

From its beginning, the center focused on the guarantor of success in Jewish education. By observing Jewish schools in action and reading research about teachers in public schools, we documented how much a child's success in school depends on teachers. Involving teachers in activities that would improve what they do in classrooms was a particular challenge because of changes then occurring in Jewish education. In the 1970s, agencies like Chicago's Board of Jewish Education were convening community-wide conferences and classes, conducting large-scale curriculum development projects, and collecting educational guides, media, and texts. They were not, however, concerned with meeting specific needs of individual teachers.

There were other changes that affected what took place in the classroom. Consolidated community schools over which a central agency could exert some control had yielded to multiple independent schools based in congregations. The eight- to ten-hour school week was replaced by the five-, six-, or even two-hour-a-week school. Full-time teachers in synagogue schools were rare. Typical teachers were pursuing another career, attending college, or were homemakers and were teaching only a few hours a week. To meet the needs of those teachers, support had to fit their schedule and be immediately applicable to their teaching.

Until the teacher center opened, little was done to individualize professional learning. Supervisors' contact with teachers was commonly limited to classroom visits and brief meetings in which the teacher's work was evaluated. Classroom curriculum, where it existed, was written by scholars and central agency staff who were not involved in the day-to-day work in schools. The curriculum would be handed to a teacher, sometimes with a teacher's guide. Training sessions tied to the curriculum were rate. As Ruth Shane, the first director of Chicago's Jewish Teacher Center, wrote, "Teachers came with their questions, interests, and concerns and built with us their solutions, their new knowledge, their new tools to use for their teaching." This contrasted with other approaches that were premised on the belief "that knowledge is something passed from the expert to the learner. We saw the learner as the source of generating and expanding their own knowledge."

The Kohl Teacher Center was intended to help teachers create materials that would match their style of teaching and their students' needs. In the spirit of *havurah*-style, do-it-yourself Judaism, the teacher center stimulated creation of a personal, tailored-made classroom. Now, more than thirty years later, the important issues are how to encourage teachers to devote time to planning and preparation, provide them with support, and encourage them to grow beyond their immediate needs. A larger question is how to consistently build professionalism, increase Jewish knowledge, and enhance teachers' pride in work that is so essential to the Jewish community.

This teacher-centered type of professional education in public schools was encouraged by government-funded research. Its findings are applicable to Jewish schools, too. One report described the negative consequences of handing teachers packages of materials to teach which, to overcome their alleged weaknesses, were "teacher-proof." In such situations, teachers do not feel responsible for the success—or failure—of their classrooms. They see what takes place as a result of what others have accomplished—not their ability and efforts. Teachers are intelligent and thoughtful individuals. They are mature, smart, savvy professionals capable of analyzing subject matter, making decisions about their students, and teaching accordingly. They are not technicians who simply do as they are told—funnels into which curriculum and textbook information are poured.

The teacher-centered approach is now a major theory of teacher development. Teacher growth is based on thoughtful reflection on what occurs in classrooms, on comments from students, on learning with other teachers. It can take the form of collegial discussion groups, viewing videos of teaching in action, analyzing case studies, sharing journals about teaching. Today, this is called "reflective practice." Originally, it was called "teacher center practice."

Building on these ideas, the Kohl Center was created to support, inform, and encourage teachers. It would be a place where they could share accomplishments, doubts, questions, and inspiration. The center's message was that Jewish education could be exciting and colorful and speak positively to children—even in the days of the 5x8 blue-and-black *mahberet*, a notebook for practicing Hebrew writing that had a solemn-bearded portrait of Maimonides on its cover.

Teachers and principals were instantly attracted to the Center. By 1980, an average of one hundred educators per month was visiting it. Participation was enriched by the diversity of people contributing to what the Center had to offer. They came from day schools, synagogue schools, Sunday schools. They were Orthodox, Conservative, Reform, Reconstructionist; primary, intermediate, and high school teachers; as well as student teachers and teachers with decades of experience.

In summer of 1975, forty teachers from across North America gathered at the center for an intense, hectic six weeks of creativity. The overall purpose was to talk about the greatest needs in Jewish education and to create models to fill those needs. The teachers brainstormed, created, and evaluated materials. There were Hebrew grammar and vocabulary games; teaching aids on the Bible, the *shtetl*, and *tzedakah*; and materials for teaching about Israel. There were discussions of what a center should contain and what services it should offer, examinations of Jewish and pedagogic philosophy, and analysis about how to develop new materials. Everyone had the opportunity to talk about basics like teaching approaches, learning styles, and classroom management. By the end of the summer, the Kohl Center had a clearer view of its objectives, the beginning of an inventory of games, materials, and resources and a calendar filled with workshops, seminars, "make 'n take" sessions, and discussion groups.

After an initial introduction to the nationwide community of educational leaders at the 1976 National Educators' Assembly—a conference for North American Conservative educational leaders—the Center's staff conducted a series of out-of-town workshops for teachers on creating teaching materials. Suitcases of exciting colorful models developed in the Center were taken from New York to Omaha from Toronto to Los Angeles and many cities in between. Workshops, focused on materials that teachers could adapt to their individual classrooms, motivated teachers and school directors to create centers in their communities and schools. As an article written in 1978, "The Teacher Center: An Idea Whose Time Has Come," concluded:

> The Jewish Teacher Center has much to offer Jewish education. Its potential as an in-service and pre-service teacher training center, as a workshop for the creation of carefully thought-out, tastefully-executed materials, and as a comfortable place for teachers to meet, share, and grow has barely been tapped. It does not claim to solve all the problems of Jewish education nor to set the world on fire, but with its boldness and its imagina-

tion, the Jewish Teacher Center has kindled a light that can be seen in the sparkle of the eye of many a teacher and in the glimmer of optimism in the mind of many involved in Jewish education.

When I recently reread this article, I re-experienced some of the excitement and exhilaration that comes from building something new. Nothing can match meeting old challenges in new ways. Those first years—the constant innovation, the inventive experimentation, the creative chaos were enormously fulfilling.

Much has happened since then, and much did not happen. The success of the Kohl Jewish Teacher Center led to its replication in at least thirty Jewish communities in North America. It expanded to the extent that people spoke of the Jewish Teacher Center *movement*. Two centers opened in Israel. Centers flourished. Then slowly, things changed.

As publishers began to release attractive, smart teaching materials and games, teachers did not have to devote as much time creating their own materials. But that meant they did not consider the unique needs of their students nor distinctive approaches to the subject matter that reflected students' skills and their interests. While the new materials were more polished and professional, something was lost in the process.

Children's activity centers and interactive children's museums were created in community centers and synagogues. Here, teachers taught classes and parents learned with their children. They were filled with colorful materials and entertaining educational exercises. Learning was more interactive and personalized. But something was lost.

Conversations among teachers about the best ways to teach still take place. Ideas are shared in well-planned workshops and seminars that, in some settings, are continued throughout the year. But something was lost.

Jewish teacher centers have become media centers and resource centers and computer centers. Schools and some communities have teacher resource rooms. Only in a handful of settings, such as the Board of Jewish Education's Marshall Jewish Learning Center in Chicago where concern for each teacher has been maintained, has something not been lost. Overall, few institutions exist that systematically work to develop creativity and professional self-esteem in the individual Jewish school teacher.

A warm, respectful bond still exists among those of us who met while working in teacher centers. We often tell each other, "You can take people out of a teacher center, but you can't take the teacher center out of people." As individuals, we still focus on building competence and self-esteem in Jewish educators, but community-wide institutions that made this a priority are less common. On a national level, the Covenant Foundation and the Grinspoon Foundation honor excellent educators with monetary rewards presented at an annual ceremony. These grants encourage creativity and commitment and have spurred innovations that other teachers have adopted. The recognition raises the status of teachers throughout the Jewish community. Hopefully, those who receive recognition inspire others.

By educating those who train teachers, the Mandel Teacher Educator Institute has contributed to teacher quality and status. But do enough local organizations now convey the message that Jewish teaching is exciting, that Jewish teachers are capable and important? Jewish tradition, research and logic all tell us that teachers are the strongest influence in determining the success of learning. They are, as Talmud Yerushalmi, *Hagiga*, tells us, "the guardians of the city." But is enough being done for them?

Other Voices

Rolly Cohen, Director, Marshall Jewish Learning Center at the Board of Jewish Education of Metropolitan Chicago.

The Jewish teacher center model is alive and well at Chicago's Marshall Jewish Learning Center (MJLC). Every day, we inspire and assist one teacher at a time. We give teachers a chance to share ideas and to "talk teaching."

The first time I visited the MJLC, I was like a kid in a candy shop! I pored over boxes filled with games, worksheets, and holiday stories, and spent hours coloring pictures and cutting out words to make an interactive poster that taught vocabulary, matching, and sequencing. My ideas about what I could do in a classroom expanded as I talked with the staff about using video clips. I designed a unit on *tzedakah* ("charity"). I continued to grow by enrolling in classes at the center. I also made a commitment to be a lifelong Jewish learner.

That was eighteen years ago. In fact, I never left the center. I worked there as a creative consultant, developing new models of games and posters. Then as family educator, I found innovative ways to incorporate materials for educating children and their parents. For the past ten years, I have been the director of the center. Now, I try to inspire my staff and teachers—one at a time—to follow their own Jewish journey.

Competence, Community and Congregations

Teacher education was not my primary responsibility during the sixteen years I worked in family and adult education and as a consultant to the Reform Movement at the Board of Jewish Education. However, I worked closely with Sarah Shapiro, the BJE's Director of Professional Education, who helped educate hundreds of teachers and school directors. A testimony to Sarah's accomplishments was the relationship the BJE developed with rabbis, community leaders, school directors, and teachers as well as with Chicago's broader academic community. Collaboration, cooperation, and mutual respect permeated our work. Programs like the Beginning Teachers Institute, the Master Teachers Institute, the Mentor-Teachers Program, and the Principals Center drastically changed Jewish education in Chicago in the 1980s and 1990s. Hundreds of educators attended the Summer Institute held shortly before the opening of school in the fall, the Winter Conference held in January or February, and various teacher retreats and workshops throughout the year.

I met Sandy Robbins when I led the Beginning Teachers Institute in 1986. The Institute was designed for people with Jewish knowledge and/or teaching experience, but with little or no experience teaching in a Jewish setting. They studied with the BJE's staff, principals, and master teachers; put into practice what they had learned; and talked about the results with each other. Sandy also participated in the Institute for the Training of Master Teachers. This extended and expanded her skills using a new technology—videotaping—which allowed teachers to observe themselves and other teachers in action.

Other Voices

Sandy Robbins, Director of Education at B'nai Jehoshua Beth Elohim in Deerfield, Illinois, and board member of the National Association of Temple Educators

I started my twenty-sixth year at BJBE in July, 2010. I was hired originally to teach third grade by Bernice Waitsman, a wonderful woman and mentor. Bernice was a proponent of the programs offered by the Board of Jewish Education, and she thought the Beginning Teachers Institute would be a perfect place for a new teacher like me to get training. I remember the class well. We brought in lessons we had taught, looked them over together, talked about how the class had gone and how we could improve it. This was very helpful. The BJE's teachers cared about us. Everything was done with integrity and quality and was worth my time.

I became part of one of the first Master Teacher Programs run by Sarah Shapiro. She flew in scholars from all over the country—for us. It was incredibly empowering to realize she took us seriously enough to bring in these wonderful minds to help us do our jobs better. The classes gave me a sense of professionalism. Frankly, if you are teaching two hours a week at your synagogue, it's hard to make it a priority in your life. But the classes made my teaching and learning more important.

As a result of these experiences, I realize how important teacher training is in a Jewish supplemental religious school. I started a teenage teacher program in my school. Our students, after studying for an intensive semester during seventh grade, can teach in the school. Over seventy teenagers assist in both religious school and Hebrew school each year. Often, they go on to teach Sunday school in towns where they attend college, and some are now returning to BJBE as young adults, applying for jobs on our staff.

Many of us who were in the Master Teachers class went on to bigger and better jobs in the profession. Certainly one of the significant reasons for this was the support and encouragement of the BJE.

Each year, the Board of Jewish Education sponsored institutes for all the school directors and teachers in the community. Three-day institutes adopted themes that were woven through a variety of sessions. Teachers studied Torah or wrote curriculum or attended workshops focusing on teaching skills. Rather than starting with the specific needs of classroom teachers as was done at the Kohl Center, BJE's curriculum work began with theory and led to the classroom.

Effective curriculum must consider both theory and practice, sound theoretical knowledge and the experiences of teachers. It involves teachers translating written materials to fit specific settings. Curriculum is necessary to good learning in a particular school because it focuses teachers on specific school-determined goals and enables the coordination of learning from one grade to another. It also provides teachers with variable amounts of support, depending on their educational background, teaching experience, and the time they devote to planning.

My thinking about curriculum was strongly influenced by a philosopher of education from the University of Chicago, Joseph J. Schwab. I first met Schwab at a Camp Ramah staff meeting at the New York Jewish Theological Seminary where he spoke of "curriculum" as the total experience of a camper, the path that he or she would travel during the eight weeks of his summer experience. Planning took into consideration a camper's entire life—his physical, intellectual, spiritual, aesthetic, and emotional experiences. Schwab taught that each camper responds to different components of Judaism, and that camp was a setting where all of them could be encountered—text study, prayer, music, dance, art, social justice, and Shabbat observance. Camp becomes a place where the threads of Jewish life are woven together. Unlike most of their experiences at synagogue schools, camp learning is accompanied by living knowledge, by practice.

Joseph Schwab used the word "commonplaces" to describe the five dimensions of an educational plan: (1) subject matter; (2) learners, be they campers or students; (3) milieu or surroundings; (4) counselors or teachers; and (5) the process of constructing a curriculum. Proper planning required collaboration by "experts" in these areas. Most experts are knowledgeable in two or three areas, but a team of curriculum writers more often leads to overall success.

In his later writings, Schwab observed that the ultimate success of a curriculum lies with whoever is teaching it. How a teacher translates a printed page into the reality of a classroom determines how students will respond to it. Even the best curriculum is theoretical until it is taught. Therefore, it is incomplete. In addition, teachers' evaluations of the curriculum must be considered before curriculum writing is complete. Although no curriculum is ever "finished," revisions improve it and increase the chances that teachers will use it.

While at the Board of Jewish Education, I interacted with individual congregation faculty. This became a highlight of my work, although I was pretty shaky at first. During my first week on the job, I met with the faculty of a synagogue school on Chicago's North Side. This was intimidating. These teachers were experienced and successful. I was a new, young "hotshot" from the Board of Jewish Education. But I believed in supporting teachers' experimentation and growth. After introducing myself to the eight people around the table, I spoke about lifelong learning in the Jewish tradition and the need to keep up with innovations in education and changes in the Jewish community. I then asked them to talk about one aspect of their teaching they would like to explore and improve. The teacher to my right frowned and said, "There is nothing I can think of that I want to change. I have taught here for thirty years. I am teaching the same subjects that I taught last year. Why would I want to do anything differently?" Taking her lead, the man next to her said, "I am teaching the same Torah course I've taught the last twelve years. It works." The next teacher shrugged and said, "I haven't been teaching as long as they have, but my teaching is okay, too."

What did I learn from this? For some teachers, changing and growing means imperfection. It means they are doing something wrong. My experiences at the Kohl Center should have taught me to start with the positive, with recognizing a teacher's accomplishments. Better to start with a question about their greatest success the past year or about advice they would offer a novice (like me) in Jewish education. At my first meeting in another congregation, I did exactly that. The response was positive.

An extended project that I led with several congregations was based on what Jerome Bruner called "spiral curriculum." At the time, one of the challenges in synagogue schools was its repetitive curriculum. In most grades, it was based on approaching holidays and supplemented by studying Shabbat, prayer, and Torah. I had learned about creating a spiral curriculum project at the Kohl Jewish Teacher Center. Several teachers from the same school would visit the center at different times looking for materials for teaching Shabbat. Although we knew what they read in the resource room and what they selected for their classroom, they did not know each other's work. At one point, we contacted their school director and suggested they meet together to share what each had designed for their classes to see if there was repetition from year to year or if curriculum recognized students' growing sophistication and changing interests. The result was the creation of a school-wide spiral curriculum. "Spiral" meant returning to a subject in a more advanced way as students progressed through the grades.

In a Reform congregation, a spiral curriculum resulted from a faculty discussion about coordinating teaching about Israel. The entire school staff participated in the project. It required teachers to collaborate to determine what to teach and how to teach it at each grade level. The faculty's subsequent discussions touched on all of Joseph Schwab's "commonplaces": goals for teaching about Israel (subject);

the interests and strengths of students in each grade (learners); the variety of strategies that could be used (teachers); and the perspectives of families, the school, the congregation, and the community in relation to Israel (the milieu). Teachers evaluated available curriculum, then discussed with each other the goals for their grade level. The school's director guided the process. What resulted was a curriculum that explored symbols in the youngest grades; Israeli heroes, history, and geography in the middle grades; and ideas shaping modern Israeli government, society, and politics in the upper grades. The curriculum was used successfully for many years.

Samuel Schaffler, the Superintendent of the Board of Jewish Education, and Sarah Shapiro excelled at building relationships between Jewish educators and Jewish academics in colleges and universities. The February 1986 issue of *Highlights*, a newsletter published by the Board of Jewish Education, describes a midwinter conference on the theme of "Nurturing Faith." Participants included Professor Samuel Heilman, a sociology professor at Queens College who discussed his ethnographic study of Jewish schools; Dr. Mayer Gruber of Ben-Gurion University, who led a seminar on "Fifteen Centuries of Faith: Bible, Midrash, and the Commentaries"; Dr. Larry Nucci of the University of Illinois, who described developmental stages in acquiring faith; and Zanvel Klein, a University of Chicago professor who presented "Stories that Nurture Faith."

The same issue of *Highlights* describes a course offered by Spertus College of Judaica and the BJE High School of Jewish Studies on "The Jewish-Christian Encounter in History and Ideas," a four-session course by Dr. Gruber for day school teachers; "An Interdisciplinary Approach to Bible"; and a seminar on Holocaust Studies conducted by Yad Vashem and the Melton Centre for Jewish Education of the Hebrew University. Laying out a path my career would be following, that same issue of *Highlights* contained an announcement that the Board of Jewish Education and the Jewish Community Centers of Chicago were partnering with the Hebrew University in Jerusalem to pilot a specially-designed curriculum for adults developed by the Melton Centre for Jewish Education.

This sort of involvement of scholars and universities with agencies and schools improves teaching and learning and changes lives. Scholars add depth of knowledge, keep the community up-to-date on advances in psychology, education, and contemporary society, and act as advisors in creating new curriculum and programs. All this motivates teachers and school directors and increases the credibility of Jewish education and respect for Jewish teachers.

Two multi-day teacher seminars a year, participation in educational planning and curriculum development, classroom observations and seminars within congregations served to raise the quality of synagogue and day school education. The story of Jewish teacher education today is a very different one. Bureaus of Jewish education around the country are merging with other organizations and shrinking hours of teacher employment inhibit the demands that can be made on teachers and temper their responses. The ending of face-to-face activities of the Mandel Teacher Educator Institute and the Jewish Early Childhood Education Initiative reflect the lack of interest and commitment on the part of funders in sustaining two important national teacher education organizations. Although resources for teachers exist within congregations and day schools and remaining centers for teacher learning continue to offer professional growth opportunities, participation relies on the motivation of the individual teacher. Unless this changes, the future of Jewish education is bleak.

A Pilgrimage of Renewal

One of the most moving moments in my career took place in 1988 at the Thirteenth Conference on Alternatives in Jewish Education, which was held in Jerusalem. This *bar/bat mitzvah* year of CAJE (the Coalition for Alternatives in Jewish Education, later known as the Coalition for the Advancement of Jewish Education) coincided with Israel's fortieth anniversary. A joint venture between American and Israeli educators was a fitting celebration.

The conference began with Shabbat services at Hebrew University's Mt. Scopus campus followed by text study sessions in the university's synagogue. Sunday was devoted to orientation sessions and exciting learning that embodied both tradition, such as a Mishnah class led by Dov Berkovits in the synagogue overlooking the Old City, and current challenges in Judaism, such as a symposium that addressed Israel's recent controversial decision to compel Soviet-Jewish émigrés to come directly to Israel from the USSR. That session was on my mind as I descended the stone stairs to the stage of the university amphitheater where the conference official opening was being held. Across the Judean desert in the distance, the sun was setting and shadows were lengthening. The auditorium would be filled in a few more minutes. My job was to greet educators from around the world. I knew I had to compose myself to welcome them, yet I was overwhelmed by emotion as I discovered I would be seated next to Joseph Begun.

In 1986, I had visited the Soviet Union to meet with Jewish teachers and the wives of prisoners of conscience —men imprisoned because of their "illegal" Jewish activities. A CAJE conference I had chaired the year before had been dedicated to Russian refusniks. Photographs of Joseph Begun and other prisoners of conscience were prominently displayed on the stage at that conference's opening session. On a trip to Moscow a few months later, I met Joseph's wife. She and I spoke of his heroic efforts and that of other Jewish teachers who had secretly taught Jewish children against the orders of the Soviet government. To teach one group of children, families had organized weekly "birthday parties." Dressed in party clothes and carrying gifts, children gathered at different houses each week to study Jewish holidays, history, and beliefs.

I had read with relief of Joseph's liberation from prison and his emigration to Israel. Now a smiling Joseph was greeting me. At that moment, I felt a deep connection with the Jewish people, appreciation for the State of Israel, and overwhelming gratitude for being a witness to Jewish resilience.

CAJE (originally conceived by the North American Jewish Students Network) had been organized by a group of mainly Boston-based, anti-establishment educators in 1973. Between 1976 and 2008, it held annual educational conferences. My first conference was at Rutgers University in 1979 where 1,000 teachers, principals, agency staff, counselors, students, lay leadership, and academics could choose from three hundred different sessions. The numbers of participants and sessions grew in the coming years. This was seen as an acknowledgement of the pivotal role Jewish education and Jewish teachers play in the Jewish community. Conferences eventually included a teacher center, media centers, computer centers, and exhibits of educational materials and art. Dialogues with educators from around the world, an Israel Pavilion, a program for teens, and evening programs that attracted top Jewish entertainers were standard. For educators, the conference was "a pilgrimage of renewal," to quote Seymour Rossel, a CAJE leader and its unofficial historian. For thirty-five years, CAJE served Jewish teachers, fought indifference and mediocrity in Jewish education, and kept quality Jewish education on the Jewish world's local and national agenda. For better and for worse, it evolved into a professionally-led organization lacking the oversight and insights of a traditional board of directors.

I was tremendously disappointed to hear of the cancellation of the 2009 CAJE Conference, then of the closing of its national office, then of its bankruptcy. With CAJE's demise, there would no longer be a national or international conference, an event designed specifically around the interests and needs of Jewish teachers. As former chairperson, Jerry Benjamin, wrote about what had occurred,

> CAJE was managed into financial destruction by a series of business decisions made by its professional leadership, and I assumed agreed to by its Board .... These decisions happened over a number of years. In no way was the collapse caused by the CAJE mission itself. CAJE was popular when it fell and remains popular.

With CAJE's demise, Jewish teachers and educators were deprived of the only pluralistic national setting designed specifically for their learning, for educational experimentation, for international dialogue, and for recognizing individuals committed to meeting the challenges of Jewish education. Former leaders of CAJE and young educators rapidly created NewCAJE in 2010. *Limmud*, an international gathering for Jewish learning, with the assistance of the Covenant Foundation has created new opportunities for teacher education at their conferences in three communities in North America in 2012 and 2013. It will be supplemented by on-line learning and discussions during the year. This is where the next generation of Jewish students and teachers can learn—and celebrate—Jewish education in the twenty-first century. Is either effort adequate? Regretfully, the best that can be said is that it is better than nothing.

Creating Compelling Jewish Education

When the Mandel Teacher Educator Institute (TEI, later MTEI) began in 1995, I joined with other teacher educators from around the country to study and design new strategies for teaching teachers. A 1991 report by the Commission on Jewish Education in North America, "A Time to Act," had stressed the need for such a program after recognizing—twenty years ago—the crisis in the Jewish community. Large numbers of Jews had lost interest in Jewish values, ideals, and behavior. They no longer believed that Judaism could play a role in their lives. "In our uniquely pluralistic society," the report stated,

> where there are so many philosophies and ideologies competing for attention, and where the pursuit of Judaism involves a conscious choice, the burden of preparation for such a decision resides with education. Jewish education must be compelling—emotionally, intellectually, and spiritually—so that Jews, young and old, will say to themselves: "I have decided to remain engaged, to continue to investigate and grapple with these ideas, and to choose an appropriate Jewish way of life." Jewish education must be sustained, expanded, and vastly improved if it is to achieve this objective.

The commission hoped to improve the professionalism of Jewish educators by creating an infrastructure that would recruit and train qualified personnel to educate Jewish teachers, mobilize community support for Jewish education, and place Jewish education at the top of the communal agenda. MTEI's purpose was to prepare teams of educators to be "the teachers of teachers" in communities across the United States and Canada.

I enrolled in MTEI with Judy Mars Kupchan, then the Director of the Marshall Jewish Learning Center at the Chicago Board of Jewish Education. MTEI included six four-day seminars over two years plus a meeting in Israel where we learned from Israeli colleagues. The faculty included some of the best scholars and teachers in Jewish and general education. The closing down of the MTEI seminars in 2010 is a serious loss to the Jewish community. Although MTEI graduates continue to motivate and guide teacher education in schools, and in community and in national organizations, the loss of the program will impact negatively on the quality of future Jewish education at a time when it cannot afford further disintegration.

Judy and I used what we learned at MTEI to create the Teacher Education Program (TEP) of the Florence Melton Adult Mini-School. We had seen the need for a high quality teacher education program that would incorporate not only pedagogy, curriculum design skills, and child development, but also knowledge of Judaism and the ability to closely observe and analyze teaching. The program was intended for both day school and synagogue school teachers.

It was crucial to involve teachers in synagogue schools. A 1998 analysis of the educational background of Jewish teachers in synagogue schools by the Council for Initiatives in Jewish Education (CIJE) reported that supplementary school classes were often taught by teachers who, although committed Jews, knew little about the subjects they teach .... A study of Jewish educators in three communities in the United States found that close to 80 percent of the teachers in supplementary schools have neither a degree in Jewish studies nor certification as Jewish educators. In preschools, 10 percent of the teachers are not Jewish. In one community the figure was as high as 21 percent.

Teachers participating in TEP studied Jewish content in the two-year Florence Melton Adult Mini-School courses. In addition, monthly sessions taught basic skills to new teachers and helped experienced teachers keep pace with the changes in the Jewish community and Jewish education. TEP provided opportunities to share classroom experiences and discuss situations that may or may not have been successful. From these discussions, we hoped teachers would acquire other qualities that cannot be taught—sensitivity to students, commitment to excellence, and confidence.

Recognizing that teachers were not required to attend, we took advantage of what we knew about adult learners and added incentives. Unfortunately, completion of the two-year program would rarely be recognized by salary raises or bonuses from schools where they taught, so Chicago's Shapiro Foundation subsidized tuition and a trip to Israel as the incentive to complete the course of study. On the other hand, those who attended—committed, passionate educators—realized the importance of what they were doing. They also loved to learn.

Principles of adult learning emphasize that all adults have a reservoir of experience and knowledge they can share with each other. We taught in a way that encouraged interaction—discussions, debates, open questioning, and *hevrutah*, text learning between two students or in small groups. Even the fifteen-minute break between classes, when students talk with each other and their teachers, is part of the learning experience. In professional education today, this concept has evolved into "communities of practice," defined as diverse groups of people engaged in the same work over a significant period of time. Through communities of practice, teachers refine ideas, solve problems, learn, and invent. In short, they collaboratively evolve a way of teaching that is highly skilled and highly creative.

Professional Development for Melton Faculty

A noteworthy community of practice consists of teachers in the Florence Melton Adult Mini-School. Unique in that it is designed for knowledgeable faculty with extensive experience teaching adults, it required reshaping teacher education. Important goals include conveying the distinctive principles and use of the curriculum of the Mini-School and describing the pluralistic, interactive approach to adult learning. In addition, local faculty meetings led by Melton staff, joined by Hebrew University faculty when conferences are held in Israel, include Jewish text study and discussions that allow for reflection, problem-solving, and applications of theory to Jewish education practice. More recently, faculty orientation to curriculum has taken place through conference calls and exchanges through a Facebook Faculty Club. There is also a faculty website filled with resources, model lessons, and bibliographies for further study.

Much needs to be accomplished in Jewish teacher education. True, there are pockets of success, but the recent merging of four central agencies that were responsible for educating teachers with other community-funded organizations and the shrinking of teacher education budgets in many synagogues and communities reflect the current low priority of these efforts. If lessons can be learned from the past, one of the most important is that, if communities will not properly support Jewish educators, children now growing up will be less involved—and less capable—members of those communities in the future.

Lessons for Today

1. Because of the seriousness of their role in shaping the next generation, teachers must be lifelong learners of Judaism, pedagogy, and child development.

2. Learners are both consumers and interpreters of Judaism. Successful classrooms support both.

3. Teachers' growth is predicated on acquiring knowledge and reflection on what occurs in the classroom.

4. Teachers learn from their experience, colleagues, students, and education theory.

5. Because of the scarcity of pre-service education for Jewish teachers, more must be done by community organizations, day schools, and synagogue schools to build competence, professionalism, and self-esteem.

6. A formal curriculum outline reflecting an institution's vision and goals is the starting point for teachers who will integrate it into their classrooms.

7. The collaboration of college and university scholars with local agencies and schools improves teaching and learning.

8. If communities do not properly support Jewish educators, children now growing up will be less involved—and less capable—members of those communities in the future.

Chapter X

Israel Education

Supporting the State and American Jewish Identity

I will maintain My covenant between Me and you; and your offspring to come, as an everlasting covenant throughout the ages .... I give the land you sojourn in to you and your offspring to come, all the land of Canaan, as an everlasting possession. I will be their God. — Genesis 17:7-8

The State of Israel will foster the development of the country for the benefit of all inhabitants; it will be based on freedom, justice, and peace as envisioned by the prophets of Israel; it will ensure complete equality of social and political rights to all its inhabitants irrespective of religion, race, or sex. — Israel's Declaration of Independence

*I*srael had a positive prominent place in American Jews' identity from the late 1940s through the 1970s. Zionism had achieved its goals. Israel seemed invincible. Its progress from a desert land to a flourishing modern nation was inspiring. Americans were proud of Israel. It was part of our genes because of our ancient textual and historical relationship with it. During the centuries when few Jews lived there, Israel existed in our prayers, our rituals, our literature, and our hearts. It became our privilege to identify with the realization of the Zionist dream, the creation of a state that would help assure security for the Jewish people worldwide. Surveys of Jewish education in the 1950s and 1960s show a dramatic increase in the number of schools that taught Israel as a discrete subject. The relationships of children and their parents to Israel were strengthened through learning about the country, celebrating Israel Independence Day, and collecting *tzedakah* for Israel.

165

Adult learning about Israel was conducted primarily by *shlihim* (literally, "messengers"), Israeli teachers and youth workers, who visited American congregations, camps, conferences, and community meetings. Israeli government officials and Jewish Agency leaders were prominent speakers around the country. Their message was clear: Celebrate Israel. Support Israel. Come for a visit and stay for a lifetime.

How things have changed! Since the Lebanese War in the late 1970s, telling Israel's story has become more difficult. The victories of the War for Independence, the Six-Day War, the Yom Kippur War, the successful integration of immigrants who outnumbered the resident population, the creation of a prosperous and democratic society, the blending of diverse cultural and religious expressions of Judaism, were no longer the primary messages that diaspora Jews were hearing. Newspapers and broadcasters and later the internet with its bloggers, Facebook groups, Twitter, and websites were all telling different stories. There was the infamy of the Sabra and Shatila incidents, the two intifadas, the assassination of Yitzhak Rabin, and the endless conflicts over Gaza, Palestinians, Israeli Arabs; and the debates over nuclear power. More recently, diaspora Jewry has had to confront growing dissonance created by increased power of the ultra-Orthodox in Israel.

Barry Chazan, Director of the Masters of Jewish Professional Studies program and the faculty member of Chicago's Spertus Institute of Jewish Studies, has identified three sources of the problems that are faced today when teaching about Israel. "First," he says, "the meaning of Israel for a Jewish life is still not clear." That Israel is phenomenally important is clear. The nature of that importance is far less clear. A second problem Chazan identifies is the fact that there is little precedent to refer to when one wants to teach about Israel. Both general education and traditional Jewish education are of little help since both involve totally different settings and starting points for learning about Israel. "Third," he concludes,

> the subject of Israel is intense and explosive. It's about the "big" issues of Jewish life and existence and, consequently, it arouses much passion and controversy.

Robbie Gringras, artist-in-residence for MAKOM Israel Engagement Network, provides a possible response to Chazen's concerns:

> We need to shift from hugging [Israel] to "wrestling [with it]." Just as its biblical echoes suggest, wrestling with Israel requires an effort, a fight, a

> struggle. It also demands an intimacy and a commitment. The time has
> come for us to wrestle with Israel in the dust, in the night, and, yes, some-
> times in our pain.

He writes of the importance of finding a way to "hug," to build a sense
of belonging through learning about our strong, deep connections with
Israel and to "wrestle," to confront problems and work as a partner
with Israel to solve its dilemmas and ills.

Changing adult education—classrooms, leadership forums, and
tours—to match Israel's new realities has been challenging. If it were
simply a matter of updating text books, designing more exciting curriculum, and creating new activities, this would be easier. When it was
a matter of explaining the meaning of Israel's miraculous birth, Jewish education excelled. Now that we must also teach that it is possible
to love a country that is imperfect, a country which embodies the miraculous and the controversial, some teachers feel afraid they will do
more harm than good. But while attempting to avoid the less attractive aspects of Israel—its urban problems, political corruption, attitudes toward minorities, Arabs, and Palestinians—teachers appear
dishonest. Their adult students are well aware of what is occurring in
the Middle East and anyone traveling to Israel discovers it soon after
arriving. One tour educator, Judith Wasserman Rosenberg, recalled
what the principal of an American Jewish school said after her first
trip to Israel.

> She couldn't believe what she was seeing. "My teachers lied to me," she
> said. "How can you tell me this is a beautiful country when citizens don't
> even clean up after themselves?" Another person on one of my tours could
> not believe that people in Jerusalem had to lock their doors—that there
> was crime in Israel.

Recent studies about American Jews' identification with Israel
reach diverse conclusions. In 2007, Dr. Steven M. Cohen and Ari
Kelman reported that Jewish attachment to Israel has been eroding
steadily since the 1990s. A 2011 study of young Jewish leaders reported
increasing distance from Israel and criticism of its policies concerning
Palestinians and the settlements. On the other hand, Theodore Sasoon
and Leonard Saxe from Brandeis University take similar results and interpret them differently. They concluded in 2008 that Jewish attachment to Israel was fairly steady between 1994 and 2007. They observed
that any differences were related to the ages of those surveyed rather
than different experiences of successive generations. Their theory is

that we become more emotionally attached to Israel as we age. Looking at the Jewish community overall, there is some loss and some gain. They conclude, commitment to Israel is essentially stable.

Sasoon and Saxe also report that negative attitudes of young liberals toward Israel partly derive from what they hear from Israel's own opposition parties. Because of the internet and international television, diaspora Jews are now privy to Israel's own internal debates over the Middle East. The attitudes of these young adults reflect their knowledge of the dissention among Israelis as much as the varying opinions around the world.

Regardless of which of these studies is correct, we cannot take American Jews' commitment to Israel for granted. Just as diaspora Jews are asking, "Why be Jewish?" they are also asking, "Why should I care about Israel?" Jewish educators must not only answer that question, but assure that it is asked. An indicator of the change in perception of Israel—from the beloved Jewish national homeland to Israel as a modern state fraught with internal and external challenges—will be reflected in what is taught to children and adults. The past decades have witnessed a transition in the nature of Zionism and the relationship American Jews have with Israel. The educational experiences that shape that relationship must also change. This transition is still in progress.

Building New Foundations

Like many others in my generation, I remember where I was in June 1967. As the school year was winding down at North Suburban Synagogue Beth El, the principal called a special assembly to tell students and teachers what was occurring in the Middle East. This was around the middle of the Six-Day War. Its outcome was still unknown. We read a poem in Hebrew by Hayyim Nahman Bialik. We said a prayer for Israel and another for its soldiers. We sang *HaTikvah*.

Israel's victory was a cause for celebration, a celebration that extended through the Yom Kippur War six years later and throughout much of the 1970s. Israel, the underdog, was overcoming gigantic obstacles. We were still celebrating Israel's victories when I worked at the Kohl Jewish Teacher Center. One wall in the teacher center was dedicated to a life-size photo of a portion of the Western Wall in Jerusalem. Adjacent to it was a bulletin board with recent articles about Israel and a mail box where visitors could write notes containing thoughts and prayers that would be delivered to the Western Wall and placed in the crevices like those visible in the photograph.

The Kohl Center was one of several successful collaborations between Israel and American educators. The teacher center was designed with the help of a staff member of Jerusalem's Israel Museum. Inspiration also traveled in the other direction. Dolores Kohl established additional teacher centers in Jerusalem and Beersheba. These evolved into a children's museum in Beersheba for Jews and Arabs.

In the 1980s, a project of the Melton Centre for Jewish Education in the Diaspora that lasted over three summers produced a new curriculum for Jewish schools, "Israel: A Course of Study." Teams of Israeli and American educators established goals, themes, and activities for an eight-year learning experience, first grade through junior high school. Its lessons reflected the changing conditions in Israel. The curriculum writers captured the wonder of the founding of the state and the evolving Jewish nation but, depending on the age of the learners, there was recognition that a different side of Israeli life existed. A component of the curriculum, "One People Many Faces," taught about immigration to Israel and how the nation absorbed people from diverse birthplaces, cultures, languages, and religious beliefs. It addressed the difficulties of integrating them into society and it questioned the "melting pot" philosophy. The existing practice of absorbing immigrants into the dominant Western European culture did not recognize potential contributions new immigrant cultures could make to the character of the country. Another component, "Jerusalem—Here and Now," taught about the complexities of a city that was holy and mundane, old and new, a symbol and a reality. Emblematic of this was the Abu Tor neighborhood in Jerusalem. At first after 1948, Abu Tor was divided from Israeli Jerusalem by barbed wire. After 1967, it became a community where Arabs and Jews lived peacefully side by side. In 1987, it was a neighborhood scarred by the intifada. While younger students studied the symbols of Israel and the celebration of Israel's Independence Day, older students learned about the complicated relations between Israel and the Diaspora and its social and political implications.

Some of the American and Israeli educators who created this curriculum also contributed to a 1997 initiative sponsored by the CRB Foundation, the Joint Authority for Jewish Zionist Education Department, and the Charles Bronfman Centre for the Israel Experience. The project, *Israel in Our Lives*, resulted in a series of booklets with theoretical and practical information about teaching Israel in various settings. These subjects included face-to-face meetings between Americans and Israelis and tours of Israel. On this occasion, Israeli experts were not writing curriculum as they had in past projects; they were articulating philosophical guidelines, issues, and educational principles while admitting that the challenges they faced were different from those of teachers in previous decades. The introduction to the project reads:

> As we enter the new millennium, two educational challenges call out to us. The first challenge is to make Israel a dynamic and living force in the personal life of every modern Jew. While there is little doubt that Israel has become a major factor in the life of the Jewish people as a whole, it is less clear that enough Jews are personally touched and moved by the miracle called Israel. Consequently, great energy needs to be invested in making Israel "speak" to every Jew in a very personal and compelling way …. The second challenge is to significantly increase the number of Jews—particularly young Jews—who visit Israel.

When Yonatan Mirvis and I wrote the "Israel in Adult Education" booklet which is part of the *Israel in Our Lives* series, we were specific about changes in America and Israel. Adults were living longer and having more productive lives with more time for leisure and learning. Jewish adults who had graduated from day schools, studied on campuses offering Judaic studies, and enjoyed Jewish camping and travel were eager to continue learning. On the other hand, Israel as a place of refuge had lost its urgency and it was no longer the poor relative which needed our financial support. The purpose of learning about Israel was now to gain a new deeper understanding of the country, to explore its place in our Jewish identity, and ultimately to strengthen bonds between American and Israeli Jewish communities. We wrote that "effective education could foster perception of Israel as central to Judaism, as a sustaining force in Jewish identity, and as a partner in a shared vision of what Judaism can be in the coming decades." Remaining unexplained was the content of that "new deeper understanding" and what was necessary to make Israel part of personal Jewish identity.

Israel in the Adult Mini-School

The core curriculum of the Florence Melton Adult Mini-School was developed in the 1980s. The subject of this collaboration was broader than others described so far. Israeli scholars and teachers created a curriculum that addressed key areas of Jewish literacy. This was not just a curriculum on Israel. As a matter of fact, the university professors who created a document describing what a literate Jew should know did not recommend a separate course devoted to Israel. Dr. Michael Swersky took this document and guided the process that turned it into the courses of the Florence Melton Adult Mini-School. Israel was included as part of celebrations—*Yom HaAtzmaut*, Israel Independence Day; our belief system—Israel as part of the covenant between God and the Jewish people; and our history—biblical Israel and the various expressions of Zionism in 1948. However, studying Israel in Melton did not include its role in Jewish identity and the bonds that exist between diaspora Jewry—Melton students—and the modern state.

More recently, courses that are part of the Rachel Wasserman Scholars Curriculum for graduates of the Mini-School reflect a growing awareness of the need to address contemporary Israel and its challenges. "Israel through Modern Hebrew Literature" and "Beyond Borders: the Arab-Israeli Conflict" discuss Israel on an honest and mature level. In addition, the Foundations of Jewish Family Living course written for parents contains a lesson, "Birth of a Nation," that includes a contemporary text about moving to Israel.

When the student seminars in Israel were instituted under Haim Aronovitz's direction in the mid-1990s, they became a popular addition to the Mini-School experience. The seminar helps the timeline of Jewish life become tangible. Two years of study are placed into a context of time and place, and Jerusalem becomes a true blending of the past and the present, linking our heritage with life today. Like all Melton efforts, the primary goal of this experience is to convey Jewish literacy. It incorporates the great beauty and deep spirituality of Israel along with the complexity of Israeli life today.

Other Voices

Haim Aronovitz, Director of Israel Seminars for the Florence Melton Adult Mini-School.

Jerusalem is the prominent symbol of Israel for Melton Israel Seminar participants. Judaism—meaning "religion"—is a major dimension of life since it is part of the lives of so many Israelis. An early experience for Melton students after arriving in Israel is a session that takes place on the Haas Promenade, a park overlooking the city of Jerusalem. When we go there at the beginning of the trip, we get off the buses and face north and west. The view is stunning: the City of David, the Old City walls, the Temple Mount, the Arab village of Silwan and the Jerusalem forest. Beyond all this is the modern city of Jerusalem.

At the end of our ten days in Israel, we return to the western end of the Promenade and face primarily north and east. At the beginning of our trip, I say the story that will unfold will connect us to the land that goes back to Abraham and the Foundation stone on the Temple Mount. As the trip progresses, Israel becomes complex, an experience with more layers. At the end of the trip, more of the contemporary tensions are visible—the walls, the fences, the boundaries. We have to face the reality of the Israel of today. At the end, we close the loop of old meeting new, of Jew meeting Arab.

Defining the Dilemma for Teachers

For decades, there have been numerous successful collaborative efforts in teacher education between Israel and North America. Travel to Israel is, by far, the most effective collaboration. Whether the goal is to provide travelers with a context for their learning, to create a sense of connection and belonging, to inspire with stories and experiences that become part of Jewish identity, or to provide teachers with knowledge and motivation so they can teach others, a trip to Israel is the most powerful educational experience. Many organizations like the Community Foundation for Jewish Education and the Board of Jewish Education of Metropolitan Chicago, the Rohr Jewish Learning Institute, Me'ah, and the Florence Melton Adult Mini-School have brought educators to Israel to learn about the land, to travel its length and breadth, and to meet with Israeli educators and citizens. These journeys were always informative and inspirational. They allow learners to integrate Israel into their knowledge and their identity. They prepare teachers to teach about Israel as no book can.

Other Voices

Zohar Raviv, Director of Education, Taglit Birthright Israel, Jerusalem.

Since the first line of Israel's Declaration of Independence makes a connection between the land and the state, one way to study Israel is to study the role of the land. One may render this Israel a "constitutional/covenantal landscape." What does it mean to have a land as part of your constitution/covenant? And how does it affect life in the State of Israel? These questions are arguably unique in the history of the world; no other examples of such complexity of identification exist among other nations.

A second way is to study Israel in the context of the country today. You can come to terms—or, at least, you can wrestle—with the many forms of relation between the state and its people, from the radical religious to the secular atheists. Third, Israeli studies can't come to fruition without experiencing the landscape itself. This provides a dimension of education that cannot be duplicated in a classroom setting. American Jews have become aware of Israel as a corresponding environment for the Jewish narrative. They understand Israel as a landscape that is committed to both memory and commemoration. The State of Israel is a lived landscape brushed against the backdrop of the land which itself is a mythical, imagined landscape. Everything in Israel, in fact, speaks to Jewish memory—its language, the names of its streets, its monuments, national symbols, flag, music, even the most vehemently anti-religious, atheist, secular Israeli. When Israelis reject Judaism, they still do this in Hebrew. In other words, there is a Jewish existence that transcends choice that is embedded into the very fabric of daily life. It is simply there.

So, Israel itself, as a land, is a primary educational setting for Israel education. It sounds so obvious, but it is not necessarily so. The land has its own vocabulary. It tells a story that can't be grasped anywhere else and it stimulates sensitivities in ways that go beyond the intellectual, beyond words, beyond what can be assessed and measured in the mind alone. The landscape does not necessarily address the mind. I have seen its power many times in people whose Jewish identity has been transformed because of a passing encounter with someone on the street, by a small gesture by an Arab in the market in Jerusalem. You just go to a site and absorb its meaning.

The problem is that we are really in a Catch-22. The stranger will not understand the potential impact of travel to Israel. Unless you are in Israel, you cannot understand why you should go there. And when you are there, you get it. That is profoundly difficult to make people understand .... You must take a leap of Jewish faith. You must go to Israel and allow yourself to be touched. You can return home with greater criticism of the place, but at least your criticism will be more intelligent and more informed than before. It will be based on experience. It will be grounded—grounded quite literally. Experiencing Israel is at the top of our goals for adult learning.

American teachers have life-changing experiences in Israel. But when they return home, they face a dilemma. They want to create a bond between their students and Israel, but as much as they want to teach about Israel in all its wonder and excitement, this must be accompanied by learning about the "real Israel" with its imperfections. Israeli tour educators who work with these teachers talk with them about the challenge.

Other Voices

Steve Israel, Israeli tour educator, Jerusalem.

I believe very strongly in presenting Israel as a fascinating and extremely complex society. Israel is not perfect; my students are not stupid (I work principally with adults over the age of eighteen) and should not be patronized by the presentation of a mythic reality which is not connected with the difficult reality of this most difficult of states. The educator's duty is to present an accessible picture of the society as it is—vibrant, complex, conflicted, and deeply troubled.

Some people complain that this will alienate diaspora Jews and make them care little for a society afflicted by the same ills that afflict their own societies. They argue: Why should diaspora Jews know about an Israel where there is racism (Jew against Arab, Jew against Jew), family violence, trafficking in women, drug addiction, and abuse etc.? They get that at home. We must present a picture of Israel as an alternative, a different kind of society attacked from the outside but suffused by a golden glow from the inside. Only in this way will we get them to care. So goes the argument.

I don't buy it. I believe that it is ineffective and ultimately counterproductive. You cannot and should not educate through lies. I believe that from the bottom of my educational soul.

The View from Israel: 2010 Vision

In early 2010, I spent a month interviewing academics, educators, tour educators, and leaders in Israel about current collaborations between Israel and America to educate American Jewish adults. What I observed was the increasing role Israel educators play in creating new ways to make Israel part of American Jewish identity.

Israeli educators are taking responsibility for teaching massive numbers of young adults, now over 300,000, coming to Israel through such new programs as Birthright Israel and MASA. MASA is a Jewish Agency program consisting of internships and learning for young professionals. No longer content with writing curriculum, publishing guidelines, and training teachers, Israelis are providing crucial experiences and expertise. Avram Infeld, Senior Consultant for the NADAV

Foundation in Israel, believes that, for many years, Israelis operated according to a misconception of Jewish peoplehood—the belief that Jews' role is to support Israel. But Israel forgot its initial role: to support the Jewish people. Israel is now doing that through adult educational experiences.

The innovations in travel to Israel made possible by generous American philanthropists and federations are evident. Taglit Birthright Israel is the most successful educational endeavor linking American Jews and Israel since the state was founded. The program offers a free ten-day trip to Israel for any American Jew between the ages of eighteen and twenty-six. Website registration for a new cohort of Birthright Israel opened on February 22, 2010. By February 24, 40,000 young adults had registered. One year later, January 2011, Prime Minister Benjamin Netanyahu announced that the Israeli government would give Birthright $100 million over the next three years to help alleviate its massive waiting list. With assistance from other major American funders, the number of participants could reach as many as 51,000 per year. Taglit Birthright Israel and MASA are thriving beyond expectations. Participants surveyed following the experience attest to it being "life-changing" and creating the desire to reconnect with their Jewish identity. Books are being written on what makes it work—most recently Saul Kelner's *Tours That Bind: Diaspora, Pilgrimage, and Israeli Birthright Tourism*.

But does it work? What happens when these young adults return home with their new lives and interest in Jewish identity? Where Birthright has not succeeded yet is in its follow up. Most young adults return home with new relationships, knowledge, and an emotional attachment to Israel. It is not long, however, before they lose sight of the gifts they received. A major shortcoming of Taglit Birthright funding—and subsequently planning—is the belief that a trip to Israel would do "it." Ten days in Israel is an inoculation, a one-time experience that would change Jewish lives. If it were only so! For many participants, Birthright serves as a potential entry-point into the Jewish community. It is an opportunity that funders, planners, and educators have not exploited. What was missing from the beginning was, at least, a vision of what could occur when inspired, motivated young adults return to the bubbling pot of American life. In accordance with the temperament and preferences of the Millennials, there would have to be a variety of choices, a multiplicity of models with which they could experiment. Just that is emerging—slowly—and long overdue. After eleven years of the existence of Taglit Birthright, Birthright Next, one formal follow-up to the journey, is getting off the ground. In partnership with campus organizations, Birthright Next focuses on follow-up experiences like Shabbat dinners, Hebrew language study, linking Jews around the world on the internet, Israel education and further travel in Israel. While research is being conducted on long-term effects of Taglit Birthright, including correlation between in-marriage and participation in this "life-changing" experience, it is very rare that a one-time experience can effectively and on its own alter lives in the long run.

New Audience, New Strategies, New Results

Israelis are committed to developing new ways to educate and engage young diaspora adults. They know that this group will eventually determine the future of American-Israel relations. These Jewish Gen-Xers and Millennials are different from earlier generations, but so is the current generation of Israel educators. People I spoke to on my most recent trip to Israel recognize the differences. They see them as new opportunities since:

❧ Younger Jewish Americans are "losing memory." They do not remember the Holocaust and Israel's role in saving the Jews who survived World War II. They are more concerned with contemporary issues in Israel. Memory, for them, exists on the computer and can be accessed—or deleted—as necessary. History is on the History Channel. Young adults must be brought back to the past in order to secure the future.

❧ Younger Jewish adults who are walking away from religious institutions are finding community through Jewish cultural events, learning centers, social justice activities, or spiritual pursuits. They still want to be part of something larger than themselves. They still want to belong.

❧ Younger Jewish Americans, claimed one Israeli academic, are not deep thinkers. Action-oriented, they are not interested in intellectual or philosophical discussion. They can become directly involved in improving Israeli society. The personal, intense experience that engages young adults in problem solving in Israel is a key to building a lasting relationship.

❧ Organized religion is only part of the Judaism of many young adults in spite of its emphasis in America. Exposure to Israeli art, music, literature, drama, film, and pop culture allows Americans and Israelis to share cultural accomplishments. It encourages creativity and increases the integration of Israel into their Jewish life.

MAKOM is an Israeli education network concerned with renewing the importance of Israel in American Jewish life. Supported by the Jewish Agency and the New York Federation, its programs reach young Jewish professionals in thirteen North American communities. MAKOM's teachers use specific educational strategies that bring Americans into debates that characterize Israel today, such as questions like "Who is a Jew?" and the political future of Jerusalem. Essential to dispelling the inconsistencies between what American Jews were previously taught about Israel and what actually exists is being frank about all the facts about Israel. This allows for exploration of ways to solve problems that now seem intractable. Such conversations, along with text learning and experiencing the positive realities of Israel, account for some of the success of Birthright. MAKOM teachers and leaders engage the spirit, intellect, and emotions of young adults and in doing so begin to build commitment to the future of Israel.

Other Voices

Jonathan Ariel, MAKOM Executive Director, Jerusalem.

We work with rabbis, educators, people in cultural arts, informal educators and bring them into the discussions that take place every day among Israelis. This is liberating for them. They didn't know they could talk with Israelis about what they see as negative. They feared that if they did this, they would compromise their loyalty to Israel. They did not want to disturb the existing consensus between Americans and Israelis. The discussions legitimatize the fact that there is no consensus. It is not good to avoid facts.

We have met difficulties, a pushback from those who don't want to criticize Israel out of the fear of losing support. But this attitude has led to a lack of knowledge about Israel, settling for meaningless slogans that don't add up to "Israel," "Zionism," and "peoplehood." Other people are not afraid to struggle with these issues. Through this process, they encounter other voices and consider them. They can see beyond themselves. This allows them to appreciate what they have, what they stand for, what they know. In the process, we delve into Jewish civilization and other Jews in other eras who confronted similar problems. We become aware of Jewish history; what has happened before. And what we did then. We learned what others have said about this. Through all this, participants in MAKOM can offer intelligent responses to what is occurring now.

Another major educational initiative pursued by MAKOM is the promotion of "peoplehood." This links individual Israelis and diaspora Jews by teaching and applying principles we share. "Peoplehood" is not a new word for Jews. Mordecai Kaplan used it to replace "nationhood" which implied a connection to individual countries rather than a worldwide community. Israelis are still seeking a way to translate "peoplehood" into Hebrew so it does not have the religious connotations of *k'lal Yisrael*. MAKOM intends that discussions and activities centered on "peoplehood" will replace the faltering conversations about Zionism and the centrality of Israel in the world Jewish community. Under the rubric of "peoplehood," Jews learn and participate in such social action projects as preserving the environment, expanding literacy, and improving living conditions all over the world. This is a way to unite Jews, to make us aware of belonging to a people unlimited by boundaries. It has become a new pathway to strengthen Jewish identity.

The Next Stage of Zionism

It was easier to feel an emotional bond with Israel when the State was struggling to come into existence; when it was working to free the Jews of Yemen, the Soviet Union and Ethiopia; and when it was memorializing the victims of the *Shoah*. It has successfully accomplished all that. These efforts are now part of its history. What now becomes the mission of Zionism?

Other Voices

Michael Swersky, Education consultant, Jerusalem.

The Zionist project succeeded in establishing the State of Israel. Its goal was to normalize the Jewish people. With Israel's creation, we became like other people: a nation like all other nations with institutions, borders, organizations, government—and with problems. But Zionism should not end with the establishment of the state. To resort to a paradox, our normalization is not like the normalization of others. Our "normalization" must be "unique." That singularity has defined us through the ages: our history, our heritage, our Jewish texts, our language. We have a homeland, but what furnishes that home is what Jewish people have brought into it. It is not simple. There are serious differences among those who live here. We reject one another. There is animosity rather than an effort to understand or, at least, tolerate our differences. We are a blended family trying to live together. In addition, Jews all over the world need to understand or, at least, tolerate, each other. Education must encourage being open to diversity and celebrating it. At minimum, it must encourage respecting our differences.

Michael Swersky believes that what is now taking place is the second phase of Zionism. New goals of Zionism will strengthen the Jewish dimension of Israel and build strong relationships with Jews around the world. It will emphasize similarities between Jews in Israel and those in America. Among the similarities are the problems that educators address in relation to Jewish identity. Being a citizen in Israel—like living in America—should not take the place of a Jewish identity. An Israeli's national identity includes living according to a Jewish calendar and being surrounded by Jewish history, but this is not sufficient when forging relationships with Jews beyond Israel. Similarly, identifying as an American who values freedom, equality, pluralism, and respect for the individual—all good Jewish values—is not sufficient to link American Jews with Jews in Israel and around the world. Shaping a vibrant, multi-cultural Jewish community in the context of a freedom-loving country is a challenge for both Israel and America. We are both asking how to make Judaism compelling to individuals living in an open and fluid society.

Israel Education for Those Who Stay Behind and Those Who Return

My stay in Israel in 2010 left me confident that education for young adults who meet with scholars, educators, and young Israelis has accomplished much. Other American Jewish adults who travel to Israel as part of educational seminars run by federations, congregations, and national education programs like the Florence Melton Adult Mini-School and the Rohr Jewish Learning Institute also return home more knowledgeable, inspired, and emotionally connected to the Jewish state. Likewise, congregation trips and tours, some arranged around b'nai mitzvah, create relationships between individuals and Israel. An unanswered challenge to all of these, however, is finding the most effective ways to follow-up on these experiences. Avrum Infeld believes that effective Jewish education is a series of moments—not a curriculum. As with Taglit Birthright Israel, all these experiences, moments of excitement and Jewish growth, are only the beginning stage of a relationship. American educators are responsible for what happens next. They are responsible for turning a moment into a lifetime of meaningful

Jewish experiences. The ICenter in Chicago, Illinois, a new initiative funded by The Charles and Lynn Schusterman Family Foundation and the Jim Joseph Foundation, provides resources on Israel education to day school, supplementary school, and high school teachers. It offers educators an online catalogue of educational resources plus training sessions. Although directed to the education of children, the ideas it develops can inform those who work with adults. If successful, the ICenter will make the teaching of Israel a specialty among Jewish teachers in North America.

Successful educators of American adults present their students with the wonders of Israel's past as an exciting and valuable foundation for what exists today. And although Israel's vital importance to Jews—as a people and as individuals—can be obscured by politics and international crises, effective education can engage students in the life of that country. The questions, criticism, and multitude of opinions about Israel will not conceal the role it plays in the destiny of the Jews and in the enrichment of individual Jewish lives. Commitments and connections to it grow from knowledge of the past, engagement in the present, and a vision of the future.

Lessons for Today

1. When teaching adults about Israel, the obvious tensions and divisions cannot be ignored. They must be confronted and discussed openly. At the same time, we must continue to teach about the vital role Israel played in our past and will continue to play in our future.

2. It is essential to address the question: "Why care about Israel?"

3. Travel to Israel, being in the land, and meeting its citizens, is the most effective and meaningful way to know Israel and realize its importance.

4. Through the efforts and ability of Israeli educators, tour guides, and *shlihim*, Israel is providing support to the Jewish people and Judaism around the world.

5. Very rarely can one experience—even one like Taglit Birthright Israel—be life changing in the long run. A series of experiences reinforce one another and are more likely to lead to transformation.

6. There are multiple aspects of teaching Israel: *Eretz Yisrael*—the land of Israel; *Medinat Yisrael*—the nation-state of Israel; *Dat Yis-*

rael—the religious life of the state and the Jewish people; *Am Yisrael*—the people of Israel.

7. A relationship with Israel is part of American Jewish identity.

Chapter XI

A Vision for 2020

The Role of Adult Jewish Learning in the Next Decade

I am made from remnants of flesh and blood and leftovers of philosophies. — Yehuda Amichai

We now have an historic opportunity to focus the great human energy of the Jewish people to create a golden age of Jewish learning, culture and spiritual engagement that will revitalize Jewish life today for ourselves and insure a vibrant future for generations to come. -- Barry Schrage

Groundwork for Barry Schrage's statement had been laid in the decades leading up to 1998, and the human energy, philanthropic support and programs that followed did revitalize Jewish learning, culture, and spiritual engagement. Today we are harvesting the benefits of this effort. Jewish texts are translated into English, on-line learning and other opportunities for learning are expanding, and teaching adults has become a recognized profession. Funding for education in synagogues and on the community level supports adult, as well as children's, learning. Since the 1980's, over 250,000 adults have enrolled in such long-term learning experiences as the Florence Melton Adult Mini-School, Me'ah (ConText outside of Boston) Wexner Heritage Program, and the Jewish Learning Institute. Forty percent of American Jews have visited Israel. A study published in July 2011 in Chicago reports that 50 percent of the Chicago Jewish community has traveled to Israel. Adult Jewish learning was reinvented.

The prime question lies in how this trend will continue and how adult Jewish learning can continue to contribute to strengthening the Jewish community in the future. The financial downturn that began in 2008 was an obstacle to continued growth, but it also provided an opportunity to introduce change. The weakened economy destabilized some educational institutions while others adapted in positive ways. Many organizations that had a clear mission continued their work uninterrupted, while some institutions supported by a funding agency with multiple goals became victims of competing community priorities.

An environment that requires change in existing institutions invites innovation. Building upon commitment to strengthening the Jewish community and responding to the needs and preferences of emerging Jewish adults, a new generation of leaders has entered the adult learning scene. Enthusiastic and passionate, they are committed to solving problems relevant to their future. Because each generation tends to support what it has created—the Talmud teaches that people prefer fruits that are homegrown to those that are bought in the market—existing organizations and practices in adult learning face what these young adults call "a revolution" in education. Will these young revolutionaries adapt and build upon what earlier generations created? Will they reject their past? Or do both?

In 2010, a blog by David Bryfman, Director of the New Center for Collaborative Leadership at the Board of Jewish Education in New York, described the forms of education that appeal to the younger adult generation. They, Bryfman said, reject much that has characterized the past forty years: the leadership and authority of knowledgeable, trained Jewish professionals; Jewish text and commentaries on texts written by well-educated and well-informed experts; adults' affiliation and membership in Jewish organizations and institutions. At the same time, Bryfman wrote positively of building new educational structures that reflect trends in globalization, peoplehood, and technology.

Whether intended to be provocative in its extreme or an honest assessment of what is needed to strengthen the American Jewish community, there are wise insights as well as dangerous assumptions in his essay. The blog presented me with a model of the new leader for whom I could summarize some of the most important lessons learned about adult Jewish education during the past four decades. They can serve as a guide for innovation or as a foil for revolution.

Serving Veterans and
Attracting New Learners

As a result of the growth of adult and family education over the past four decades, many adult Jews have committed themselves to lifelong learning, to seeking stimulating quality educational experiences. The growth of enrollment in day schools, Israel experiences, camping, and departments of Judaic Studies has increased the potential audience for high level adult learning. At the same time, those whose education was limited to training for a *bar* or *bat mitzvah* and those who had no Jewish education at all, may be ready to claim their Jewish identity.

Bryfman's recommendations appeal to many young adults seeking purpose, fulfillment, and comfort in a newly designed Jewish community. They are a call to action. At the same time, they offer professionals possible answers to complicated questions of how to attract those in their twenties and thirties to Jewish life. Steven M. Cohen's research in 2011 comparing establishment with non-establishment leaders shows that when it comes to text learning and Torah study differences between the groups are small. We must not overlook growing numbers of individuals who are seeking continuing learning experiences. Social service projects, concerts, and holiday dances are fine for bringing young people into the community, but high-level challenging learning is attractive to many young Jews and is necessary to support the goals of those already involved. Even for those new to Jewish learning, beginning at a high level can be appealing. The inherent challenge will arouse their interest, and there is a chance they will want to continue to learn in order to fill in blanks in their knowledge that they now know exist. Curiosity will drive them forward.

Enhancing Congregation Education

Few congregations have exploited the opportunities that exist. The times call for a new, more systematic approach to learning in synagogues that will increase involvement in lifelong Jewish education. This means creating ways to guide individuals along a continuous sequence of learning experiences—building upon the ideals of long-term membership and the close relationships that can form among teachers and friends. Encouraging entry into adult learning can be as simple as asking members how they want to continue to grow as Jews and allowing their answers to guide congregation programming. New members of synagogue are provided with information on payment of dues and building funds. They can also participate in discussions on how they want to grow as Jews. Options range from basic literacy classes to pursuing congregants' interests, text study, Hebrew language and literature, culture, history, modern Israel, Jewish practice, or philosophy. They can build on personal interests like learning that is tied to their professions—to law, medicine, accounting, business, and so on; their hobbies, whether cooking, creative arts, or literature; their families—teaching children or grandchildren about Judaism or creating a Jewish home.

As members become involved in congregation life, preparation for work on a congregation's education committee or even teaching in the school can be motivation for mastering basic Jewish literacy. Assuming a volunteer position on the board, ritual committee, or education committee is an opportunity to study Jewish ethics and decision-making, models of leadership, and the varied population groups that make up the synagogue community.

Existing institutions must also grapple with whether they are fulfilling their mission by serving only the core of the Jewish community, people who are choosing to affiliate. To reach beyond that group, congregations must adapt what they do—in terms of learning activities and marketing efforts—to attract more members. In financially challenging time, being responsive to those who cannot or will not pay full yearly membership dues has to be a subject of discussion. More and more congregations are inviting nonmembers to attend one-time educational events. Some are establishing multiple ways in which to be part of synagogue life including joining specific groups within the congregation like becoming part of a synagogue's school for adults, a grandparents' club, an artists' group, the sisterhood, or a social service club. It can extend to support groups, for example those for the bereaved, the unemployed, or people with chronic illness. These specialized forms of affiliation can be an entry point into broader synagogue affiliation. A description of synagogue life in the 1950s highlighted—even then—membership in the Sisterhood as a gateway to synagogue affiliation.

Knowledgeable synagogue volunteers can participate in a community outreach initiative. It can include activities for unaffiliated Jews who want to learn skills related to holiday celebrations, social action projects, and cultural experiences. They can help organize a *shiva minyan*, demonstrate Jewish cooking, and even organize trips to Israel for the unaffiliated, many of whom may be former participants in Birthright.

The thinking of leaders of institutions must respond to the changing Jewish community. Redefining synagogue life in these and other ways may be necessary if the synagogue is to remain the center of American Judaism.

Included in the Bryfman blog was a correct—and indispensable—recommendation to Jewish institutions including but not exclusively directed to synagogues. Jewish experiences should be welcoming to as many participants as possible rather than fracturing the community by creating boundaries. Boundaries are constructed not only by high membership dues but also by policies that limit affiliation based on explicit or implicit rejection of individuals because of religious, cultural, or social behavior. Singles, gay and lesbian individuals and couples, intermarried Jews all may feel unwelcomed in our Jewish community.

Institutions vary as to the extent to which non-Jewish spouses can participate in synagogue life. Discussions in synagogues focus primarily on participation in rituals—*aliyot*, burial ceremonies, and *b'nai mitzvot*. More and more congregations are being more welcoming to non-Jewish spouses of members. Reform congregations recite a blessing found on the Union for Reform Judaism website for non-Jewish spouses thanking them for their support and contributions to the Jewish life of their families—be it driving children to religious school, keeping a *kosher* home, or learning to make *latkes* and *kugels*. Some Conservative communities have Keruv Committees or Interfaith Initiatives. Their purpose according to one website is:

> to welcome people whose lives are touched by, or who are involved in, interfaith relationships. Our goal is to make them feel a part of, rather than apart from, the synagogue. This includes both existing and potential synagogue members.

Congregations that want to expand affiliation and remain relevant in a changing world need to consider these factors. If options are not created in existing Jewish institutions, new institutions will undoubtedly be created by the unaffiliated to serve those who want to be Jewish in their own unique way.

Finally, congregations do not have to do everything on their own. Territorialism is not uncommon. After all, in urban and suburban areas where many Jews live, congregations regardless of denomination,

compete for members. However, programs in consortia of congregations can be entry points to affiliation where there are more and more
unaffiliated Jews.

Educating the Unaffiliated

And what about the Jewish learning of the unaffiliated? Although
participation in adult learning expanded over the past forty years, the
majority of adults who were attracted to learning were already affiliated with the Jewish community. Programs in synagogues and those
sponsored by national/international organizations like Melton and
Me'ah rarely reached people who were not already participating in
Jewish life. If the goal is to ensure that every Jew has the opportunity
to become a participating member of the Jewish community, then we
have failed. Growing numbers of Jews exist on the periphery of Jewish
life. There are those whose indifference takes them beyond its borders.
But as research on young Jewish adults has shown, many individuals
on the borders are reachable. Apathy and ignorance—not rejection or
antagonism—is the challenge.

The universalistic tendencies that characterize the young adults
who remain unaffiliated provide one opportunity for involvement.
Universalism does not have to replace Judaism. Program planners,
curriculum writers, and teachers can and should emphasize the universal dimensions of Judaism bringing in examples of these "Western"
principles from Jewish experiences and Jewish texts. Judaism is basic
to Western ethics and values. Although many have forgotten the role
it plays in shaping the world we live in, what is called "universalism"—the sacredness of life, the dignity of the individual, freedom,
justice, and mercy—has roots in Judaism. Reviving that memory can
remind Jews, build pride and self-respect, and, perhaps, motivate
participation.

I am continually inspired by Franz Rosensweig, the creator of the
Freies Juedisches Lehrhaus in Frankfort in 1920. Its purpose was to attract intelligent young Jews to Jewish learning and participation in
the Jewish community. He sought out the intellectual leaders, the
greatest teachers, who would share Judaism's riches and stimulate the
minds of young adults. Unless we accept the judgment that young
Jewish adults avoid intellectual and spiritual challenge, that they are,
in the words of some Israeli colleagues, "shallow and lazy," we cannot
compromise, we cannot "dumb down" our heritage. We need to at-

tract more students to a twenty-first century *Lehrhaus* where Jewish learning can be the entry point to the Jewish community. We need to adopt what has helped preserve us through the centuries and adapt it to the times in which we live.

Studying Texts: Shaping the Individual and the Future

One of the most important developments of the past fifty years is the proliferation of translated Jewish texts. Once accessible only to those who could read Hebrew, Yiddish, or Aramaic, classical texts now can be studied by all English-speaking Jews. Adult learning provides Jewish adults—perhaps more than ever before—the opportunity to read texts, to interpret them, and to grapple with their meanings. The distinct Jewish way of life as well as the ideas and ideals of Western civilization are accessible. As a Mini-School student said, "Jewish learning is a banquet, and I now have a place at the table." Through translations, adult learners can examine the sources of Jewish and universal thinking and living and participate in a discussion whose history goes back to the Bible.

The challenge today, in light of "wisdom" easily accessed through Google, Facebook, Twitter and blogging, is how to motivate intellectually-capable adults to immerse themselves in text learning. How do we convince young adults satisfied with fast answers to life's questions that treasures are waiting for them in Jewish texts? How do we convince them that the act of studying and interpreting is a reward in itself? We can turn to Google to find an answer to a question; but by studying Jewish texts, we discover the questions, the process for examining these questions, and multiple answers for us to consider.

Respectful questioning and challenging ideas is a time-honored Jewish pastime. It should be encouraged in every setting for learning. For example, an important question that learners frequently raise is about the truth of our sources. Did the events of the Bible really happen? Recognizing different perspectives does not diminish the value of the text. Jewish belief and practice have met the challenges of the documentary hypothesis that identifies human authors of the Torah. In addition, there is an ever-retreating point at which what is unproven in Torah meets discoveries of archeologists. The lack of archeological evidence for the existence of Abraham does not diminish the lessons learned from his life. Archeology contributes to both sides of the argu-

ment. Most biblical narratives, including those that are unsupported
by archeological evidence, establish moral sensitivities—like childhood experiences that leave an indelible mark on our soul. We may
question the historical truth of the conquest of Canaan by Joshua,
while a shard of pottery has been unearthed that could support the existence of the House of David. The biblical narrative has captivated
humankind for centuries and will continue to do so. Regardless of its
historical truth, the Bible teaches morality, ethics, and values that are
relevant today and that teach about ancient society. Questioning
whether these events actually occurred does not weaken the truths
they contain and their importance to Judaism's survival throughout
history. Passing it from one generation to the next to question and
interpret its meaning for each generation has been a source of vitality
in Jewish life.

Many young adults reportedly shy away from text study. Some
responsibility for their avoiding this intellectual challenge lies with
those who provided their earlier education experiences. If not alien-
ated by synagogue education, they are not motivated to continue
learning nor do they have the skills that would make them feel competent studying Jewish texts as adults. Public school education does not
help. Its success is measured by whether students pass tests and get
into college. Less is done to encourage problem solving, analysis, and
critical thinking. While acknowledging that day school education and
educational camps have improved the situation, some of the younger
generation, the new consumers and producers of knowledge, believe,
as David Bryfman wrote, that

> the textual canon of Jewish life is merely one sliver of that which should be
> regarded as essential to contributing to Jewish life today and tomorrow
> .... Combined with a general societal milieu that dictates that all voices
> should be valued and respected, the centrality of the Jewish canon in the
> life of Jews is at the very least being questioned and possibly even being
> disregarded.

Arguments are frequently advanced in favor of text study. Observant Jews believe that learning is a _mitzvah_, a religious obligation.
Here are ten additional reasons for studying Jewish texts:

1. Texts reflect the great literature of a great people. Studying Judaism is like studying great people or great writing—the Greeks
   and Romans, Homer or Shakespeare, Descartes or Plato. The
   beauty and wisdom in the writing have enriched all of civiliza-

tion. Studying this literature is intellectually challenging. There is joy in discovering its meaning. Yet, Torah is different from Shakespeare: it is the text of the Jewish people. These great texts reveal a collective story—as well as a personal one. Jewish history, the collective memory of the Jewish people, conveys knowledge and a way of life that we have inherited and that, ideally, we are passing on to our children and our students.

2. Jewish survival has been based on Jewish learning. Since Sinai, universal literacy is a Jewish value. All Jews received the Torah—not just a narrow and elite segment of the community. Literacy has helped sustain the Jewish people. After the destruction of Temple, the role of the teacher grew in importance. Teachers then—and now—assure that Jews tell their stories and count days, months, and years of the calendar that define a unique, unifying Jewish rhythm of life. Other people cannot do this for us. Individuals, families, communities have to take responsibility for knowing, remembering, and commemorating distinctive moments in life. When the Temple was destroyed, Yohanan Ben Zakkai asked the Roman General Vespasian to allow him to go to Yavne and establish a school. Through the learning that took place in Yavne and other schools like it, the Jews endured.

3. Through text, Jews learn about their distinctive past and feel that they are part of an historic community. Studying is a way to become acquainted with ancestors. What did they think about? How did they understand life and its rewards and challenges? What was valued? What was preserved? How did Judaism become what it is today? Learning is a way to claim our shared memory and its evolution.

4. Studying text creates a Jewish community of shared knowledge and shared intellectual accomplishments. One scenario that illustrates this is the celebration of the completion of a tractate of the Talmud that occurs in Madison Square Garden and is televised all over the world. Thousands of Jews participate in Daf Yomi— studying one page of Talmud page each day. Another scenario is one in which a Florence Melton Adult Mini-School student is walking along a beach in Mexico, spots a woman reading a book she recognizes from the Melton Mini-School's curriculum. She introduces herself, and they discover they are enrolled in Melton

classes on opposite coasts. They spend the rest of the hour together talking about the Melton experience. A final illustration is
at an international Jewish education research conference. In one
session, participants representing four different countries share
an anecdote based on knowledge of a fragment of text from the
Torah. All participants have, at some time, studied this Jewish
source and its commentaries and are immediately drawn into a
debate based on the varied commentaries they have studied and
that they support.

5. Someone who is learning text becomes part of an intimate community that shares basic knowledge, language, skills, and discussions about the big questions in life. Classmates agree, disagree,
debate, find consensus. Or not. They discover unifying beliefs and
commitments and share stories, jokes, holiday celebrations, and
life-cycle events. Their commitment and concern for each other
can become intense. A mother schedules car pools so she will not
miss classes. Weddings and honeymoons are timed according to
the school calendar. Learners share joy and sadness—baby nam-
ings and *shiva*. Something very powerful occurs when people
study life and its meaning together.

6. Through text study, learners discover what Jews do, and they
find meaning in the rituals and traditions they have chosen to observe. They discover the sources of commandments, customs, and
traditions. They learn to accommodate alternate beliefs and behaviors—understanding each another even as they disagree.

7. Texts are pathways to the spiritual dimension of life. For some,
this emerges from the power of what is learned. Other people are
inspired by prophets, matriarchs, and ordinary human beings
who have been touched by God. Others discover that God speaks
to them through the words they study. Regardless of what is considered to be the source of these great works and regardless of
what some see as contradictions within them, texts contain an element of something beyond our worldly existence. Abraham
Joshua Heschel points out that people speak to God when they
pray and God speaks to us when we study. (Someone added: that
is why we pray fast and study slowly.)

8. Text study can soothe and create order in life. Learners find
strength in stories and sustenance in immersing themselves in

their lessons. There are no recipes, no simple answers. But there are pathways to follow and companions in seeking answers to important questions that we wrestle with in life.

9. To all adults: It is never too late to begin studying of Jewish text. A commentary on Deuteronomy says it eloquently:

> "When Moses charged us with the teaching as the heritage of the congregation of Jacob ..." (Deuteronomy 3:22). This shows that the Torah is the heritage of Israel. To what may this be compared? To a king's son who when small was taken away into captivity to a country across the sea. If he wants to return, even after a hundred years, he will not be embarrassed to do so because he can say, "I am returning to my inheritance."

10. Texts provide all adults—but particularly teachers and parents— an opportunity to study so they can teach and model learning for others. In acquiring their own experience with texts, they assure that their children are aware of the opportunities Jews have had throughout generations. It would be a mistake for one generation to deprive future generations of this option. Young people today want to fashion their own Jewish life. It should be done intelligently. Choice is important but informed choice is more important. If Jewish life is to be ignored or rejected, it should be done knowledgeably—not out of ignorance. And if experience is a teacher, knowledge of Judaism on an adult level is a proven first step into the Jewish community.

New Models of Leadership

Who will lead us in these new directions? There are voices questioning the validity of leadership as it has been understood in the past. This questioning is a consequence of an open society, the individualistic tendencies of youth, and perceptions of a rigid, self-serving leadership. Some young adults conclude that they no longer require, in the words of Bryfman, "age-old standard bearers of Jewish power and knowledge to determine or even guide their agendas."

The growing strength of individualism, the "sovereign self" in the words of Arnold Eisen and Steven Cohen, creates resistance to being led. Effective leadership takes this into consideration and creates experiences that work. Maintenance and growth of valuable existing institutions and creation of new ones result from the hard work and inspiration of strong leaders.

There is a place for leaderless organization but exclusive pursuit of them inhibits the potential of good work already being accomplished. Rejecting forms of stable political, moral, and spiritual leadership weakens a community. Little binds Jews together that does not require some form of leadership, and little threatens Jewish existence more than the loss of community. With the absence of influence, inspiration, and momentum that comes from community, the ability to have an impact is lost. The impermanence of leaderless groups that come and go weakens the potential to make a meaningful sustained difference in the world. An uncoordinated series of individual leaders may be able to fulfill immediate expectations but only in rare instances can they affect a broader group for a longer period of time. In addition, a unified community advocating for what is good has plausibility and will be more likely to influence change. Under ordinary circumstances, multiple voices speaking together are more believable than one voice alone.

Leadership that might be acceptable to those rejecting its traditional forms must be responsive to personal agency and foster individuality. That form of leadership succeeds by providing continuity, direction, and constructive challenge while sharing power and remaining flexible. Individuals can organize a transient, one-time gathering like a cultural event or a lecture but it is difficult to nurture relationships with participants, sustain relationships among them, and stimulate continued involvement under these circumstances. Exodus and Sinai have bequeathed to us the lesson that community is a basic component of Judaism. Our communities have sustained us. What makes prayer Jewish is community. What makes learning Jewish is community. What makes social service Jewish is community. What makes spirituality Jewish is community. Without community and the leaders who create and sustain it, an activity may continue, but Judaism will not. Without emotional bonds and commitment, it is even questionable that the individual activity will continue.

There are untapped sources of leadership that would match the needs and expectations of those who reject power-based influences. One option is groups—learning communities, social action teams. and *minyanim* ("prayer communities") that are guided by shared leadership. Collaboration and cooperation sustain them. Decisions are made through dialogue and consensus. Authority is shared.

There is another untapped source of leadership that is worth considering. It should not be surprising that among our best Jewish educators and teachers, we can find leaders who know how to build relationships, motivate involvement, and empower individuals. Teachers can be leaders outside as well as inside classrooms. Many sustained learning experiences include the formation of a micro-society not characterized by authority and power. In the classroom and the community, teachers lead others through modeling, building relationships, and their style of making knowledge accessible. Teachers share responsibility for learning with students. They transform a room of individuals into a community by transferring authority to students who become teachers of each other. It is a form of leadership based on knowledge, humility, and respect. All contemporary leaders would benefit by studying models of education that are built on this form of leadership.

Much of our present Jewish education system does not take advantage of the potential to develop teachers into leaders possessing the qualities respected by young adults. Good professional education for teachers can encourage their independent thinking and motivate their contributions beyond their classroom. Strengthening communication skills provides the confidence and competence to relate effectively to parents, as well as students, and to contribute to community decision-making. Teachers' natural leadership style is subtle but strong, based on facilitation skills rather than control. Its goal is to strengthen and inspire others—students, parents, and colleagues. As some of the other voices in this book testify, classroom teachers can become leaders who influence positive change in schools and in the broader community.

The challenge introduced in Chapter Ten is that teacher education in most synagogue schools is weak. Part-time employment creates limits on additional demands that can be made on teachers' time, including time devoted to professional development. Recently effort has been made to vary the synagogue school schedule adding informal activities for students and alternating teaching assignments to allow for "released time" for teacher learning. In some schools, introduction of new learning experiences and new curriculum prompt teacher professional development.

In addition, addressing the challenge of inadequately trained teachers may require rethinking sponsorship of synagogue schools. Synagogues that can overcome fear of competition can collaborate in building regional schools. This provides excellent professionals with an opportunity to be professional—more hours of work, adequate compensation, benefits, and the funds and programs for teacher education. Incentives like certification with salary increases, or bonuses, or subsidized travel to Israel motivate and reward participation. What self-respecting profession does not provide opportunities and rewards for growth? Professional education incorporating learning Jewish content and pedagogy will provide knowledge, skills, and attitudes that transform teachers into the kind of teachers and leaders being sought in the Jewish community.

Unifying a Divided Jewish World through Education

Teaching about Israel as an irrevocable part of American Jewish identity has become more difficult in the last four decades. The unique powerful role Israel played in past generations—first as a dream, then as a miracle—was an essential part of the Jewish spirit. Children and adults from the 1970s on, however, have seen the miracle merge with reality—the dream of the Jewish state blending with the challenges facing a modern nation. As the loudest voice that represents Jews throughout the world, what Israel says and does affects us all.

Consequently, Israel education during this same period has become more vital. It is important not only to maintain support of a Jewish State—regardless of its temporary problems, but it is important to support Israel because of what it does for American Judaism. The idea of all Jews going to live in Israel is passé. Americans travel periodically to Israel but live here, admiring or criticizing Israel at a distance. Regardless of where they live, however, knowledge and identification with Israel defines and deepens Jewish identity. When assimilation threatens, Israel is an important element in expressing what it means to be Jewish.

There is no question that teaching about Israel is becoming more thoughtful, more careful, and, consequently, more effective. Participation in Birthright Israel has exceeded expectations. One of the outcomes of being in Israel, meeting Israelis, and participating in conversations and debates on what is occurring there, connects some young adults to

Israel in spite of the current vicissitudes of its image. Here institutions like the ICenter provide excellent resources and bring together teachers and educational leaders who focus on contemporary challenges.

While taking advantage of new resources, teacher creativity, and technology, Israel education must be honest. As described in Chapter X, teachers and tour educators have always been "honest" when it comes to the richness of the Israel landscape, the expertise of archeologists and biblical scholars, the wonderful kaleidoscope of neighborhoods and communities, the talent of musicians and artists. They have generated high level intellectual, emotional, and spiritual experiences for travelers and learners. They are "honest" about what Israel's contributions are to science, technology, education, defense, and agriculture. Today, however, honesty and humility must also be part of discussions about Israel's political and military situation and its domestic shortcomings. Adults of all ages have access as never before to current news and opinions in editorials and blogs, petitions, Twitter, Facebook YouTube and Podcasts. There are few secrets in the age of technology.

The Israel-Diaspora relationship is only one aspect of the problem of divisions within the Jewish world. Within North America, the walls that exist among Jews are stauncher than they have ever been. We have entered a period of time when differences are increasing. Effort to live with each other must also increase learning in order that we may understand one another and tolerate, if not affirm, those whose lives embody different beliefs and practices. In spite of differences, Jewish professionals and individuals must find ways to share knowledge and resources, to collaborate on community activities, and to work together to solve common problems. Territorialism, intolerance, and antagonism harm Jewish life regardless of how it is defined.

Whether dealing with relationships between Jews in Israel and the diaspora or those within a North American community, Jews share concerns that we all need to address together. We need the knowledge and insights of every one of us to move toward a positive future. Our texts, our history, provide insights into the dilemmas we face today. Meeting together to study can be the basis of our discussion, our debates, and our disagreements. If tradition holds true, respectful disagreement can lead to insight and progress. Common challenges include:

❧ Combating assimilation and loss of religious Jewish identity.

༈ Teaching "Judaisms" that can compete in a world of multiple identities.

༈ Finding the best way to teach the Holocaust to generations who will never know a survivor. How can we utilize museums and memorials to teach the lessons of that painful history?

༈ Strengthening the world Jewish community at a time when many adults do not look far beyond their own personal borders. How do we convey a knowledge and appreciation of Jews around the world and within a community? How do we create relationships based on knowledge, respect, and concern for fellow Jews?

༈ Creating shared celebrations—not only *Yom HaAtzmaut* and *Yom Yerushalyim* but also the birthdays of significant Jewish leaders. In American Jewish settings, we can commemorate the birthday of the first prime minister of Israel just as we celebrate George Washington's birthday each year. In the same way, we honor Martin Luther King, Jr., who had a dream, we can celebrate Theodor Herzl.

༈ Maintaining the spiritual dimension of life amidst political corruption, religious dissention, and economic or political threats to individual security and peace of mind.

༈ Creating more entryways into Jewish learning, particularly text study, that can become a beginning of Jewish identity and a relationship to the Jewish community.

༈ Finding new ways to bring a divided Jewish community together both within Israel and North America and between the two major Jewish communities in the world.

The challenges are great. Through learning together, Jews can become united advocates for change, participate in solving problems of mutual concern, and become members of a world Jewish community that shares the pain, the progress, the mistakes, and the victories.

Expanding our Expertise in Adult Learning: Areas for Investigation

Advances in adult Jewish learning have created courses for Jewish professionals in Jewish colleges, universities, and seminaries. Knowledge of Judaism can be conveyed more effectively when a teacher knows adult development, sociology, psychology, and andragogy. Working with Jewish adults in all kinds of settings is a subject for examination and discussion. Professional education programs are conducting studies and research that increase the quality of experiences of Jewish adults whether it be at Hillel, on Birthright Israel, in Jewish classes, in teacher training settings, or at camp. More refined skills and tools for analyzing formal and informal education settings are being developed. Questions are being raised that merit investigation and whose answers will expand and enrich adult Jewish learning. Some of them are:

❧ While research in general adult development and learning contributes to adult Jewish learning, it is important to examine adult development and learning theories through a Jewish prism. Is Jewish development the same as other human development patterns? Do adult bar/bat mitzvah and Israel travel affect development uniquely? Do classroom interactions among Jews differ from those in a multi-cultural group? How does teaching vary when addressing Jewish leaders, teachers, and other professionals?

❧ What are the best contexts and the best content for adult Jewish learning that conveys the universal values underlying Western civilization? What Jewish texts are the basis of principles such as freedom, individual dignity, justice and compassion, the significance of human life, and ethical decision making? Where can they be taught?

❧ Who are the best teachers? What makes them good teachers?

❧ How can formal and experiential education be blended effectively. Although this book predominantly addresses formal adult learning, it also describes the informal interaction that occurs in classrooms and the relationships that develop among learners. Long-term classes provide opportunities for learning through modeling, life-stories, and practical problem solving. Field trips to Jewish institutions, experiencing and then discussing religious services and other observances are models of experiential learning that can be integrated with formal education.

❧ Does teaching Bible to adults differ from teaching Jewish history? How? Why? What are the specific skills needed by a teacher of Talmud? Scholars today refer to this as a teacher's pedagogic content knowledge.

❧ How today can we best use traditional Jewish learning strategies like those used in the b'tai midrash and yeshivot? How would we adapt them to the changing nature of the Jewish learner?

❧ What is the role of Hebrew language? We have translated texts, but should translations only be a temporary resource for lifelong learners? What are the goals and, therefore, the content of teaching the Hebrew language? Should Hebrew be taught as a tool for learning Jewish text or should modern Hebrew as spoken in Israel and expressed in modern Hebrew literature be the subject? And how important is it to learn to write in Hebrew?

There are so many opportunities and responsibilities for those involved in adult Jewish education! A final wish for those who will determine what lies ahead in this vital field is for each of us to continue learning. The more we study, the better teachers we will be and the better Jews we will be—however defined. The more we make learning part of our lives, the more it will enrich our lives and the lives of others. As John Dewey wrote, "Education is not preparation for life. Education is life," a contemporary expression of *Talmud Torah k'neged kulum*, "Learning is part of everything."

Bibliography

Ackerman, Walter. Ari Ackerman, Hanan Alexander, Brenda Bacon, David Golinkin, eds. 2008. *Jewish Education—for What? And Other Essays.* Haifa, Israel: Ben-Gurion University; Schechter Institute of Jewish Studies, Tel Aviv University, University of Haifa.

Adult Jewish Learning Development Committee. 1993. *Adult Jewish Learning Reader.* New York: Jewish Education Services of North America.

Ament, Jonathan. 2004. "The Union for Traditional Judaism: A Case Study of Contemporary Challenges to a New Religious Movement," Unpublished dissertation, Brandeis University.

Apter, Terri. 2001. *The Myth of Maturity: What Teenagers Need from Parents to Become Adults.* New York: W.W. Norton.

Arnett, Jeffrey J. 2004. *Emerging Adulthood: The Winding Road from the Late Teens through the Twenties.* Oxford, England: Oxford Press.

Bee, Helen and B.R. Bjorkland. 2004. *The Journey of Adulthood.* 5th ed. Englewood Cliffs, NJ: Prentice Hall.

Belenky, M.F., B.M. Clinchy, N.R. Goldberger, J.M. Tarule. 1986. *Women's Way of Knowing: The Development of Self, Voice, and Mind.* New York: Basic Books.

Brookfield, Stephen D. 1987. *Understanding and Facilitating Adult Learning.* San Francisco: Jossey-Bass.

_____. 1990. *The Skillful Teacher: On Technique, Trust, and Responsiveness in the Classroom.* San Francisco: Jossey-Bass.

Brooks, David. October 9, 2007. "The Odyssey Years," *The New York Times.*

Bruner, Jerome Seymour. 1962. *The Process of Education.* Cambridge, MA: Harvard University Press.

Bryfman, David, May 26, 2010. "The Revolution Before Our Eyes." *www.eJewishPhilanthropy.com.*

Chazan, Barry. 2004. "Schechter's Lament: Israel and Jewish Education Once Again." Jewish Education Service of North America.

Cohen, Elliot E. November 1945. "An Act of Affirmation," *Commentary* I

Cohen, Samuel. 1967. "History of Adult Education in Four National Jewish Organizations." Unpublished dissertation, Yeshiva University.

Cohen, Steven M. and Aryeh Davidson. 2001. "Adult Jewish Learning in America: Current Patterns and Prospects for Growth." New York: Florence Heller/JCC Association Research Center.

Cohen, Steven M. and Arnold Eisen, 2000. *The Jew Within: Self, Family and Community in America*. Bloomington, IN.: Indiana University Press.

Cohen, Steven M. and Ari Kelman. 2007. "The Continuity of Discontinuity: How Young Jews are Connecting, Creating, and Organizing Their Own Jewish Lives." Andrea and Charles Bronfman Philanthropies, Wagner, NY: Berman Jewish Policy Archives (NYU).

Commission on Jewish Education in North America. November 1990. *A Time to Act*. New York: University Press of America.

Dashefsky, Arnold and Ira Sheskin. 2011. *Jewish Demography Project*. Miami, FL: Miami University Press.

Freedman, Samuel G. 2000. *Jew vs. Jew: The Struggle for the Soul of American Jewry*. New York: Simon and Schuster.

Freire, Paulo. 1981. *Pedagogy of the Oppressed*. New York: Continuum.

Glatzer, Nahum N. 1953. *Franz Rosenzweig: His Life and Thought*. New York: Schocken.

Goldfarb, Bob. July 6, 2010. "The American Jewish Scene: Shifting Paradigms." *eJewishPhilanthropy.com* (The Jewish Philanthropy Blog).

Goldman, Israel M. 1975. *Life-Long Learning among Jews: Adult Education in Judaism from Biblical Times to the Twentieth Century*. New York: Ktav.

Goodman, Roberta and Betsy Dolgin Katz. 2003. *The Adult Jewish Education Handbook*. Denver, CO: ARE Publishing, Inc.

Graff, Gil. 2008. *And You Shall Teach Them Diligently: A Concise History of Jewish Education in the United States 1776-2000*. New York: The Jewish Theological Seminary of America.

Grant, Lisa, Diane Tickton Schuster, Meredith Woocher, Steven M. Cohen. 2004. *A Journey of Heart and Mind: Transformative Jewish Learning in Adulthood*. New York: The Jewish Theological Seminary of America.

Gringras, Robbie. 2006. "Wrestling and Hugging." Makom: Israel Engagement Network. www.makomisrael.net

Haase, Linda S. July 2011. "Chicago's Jewish Community Is Growing, Committed and Connected." Chicago: *JUF News: 2011-2012 Guide to Jewish Living in Chicago*. 41:8.

Hawkins, David. 1974. "I, Thou and It." *The Informed Vision: Essays on Learning and Human Nature*. New York: Agathon.

Hertzberg, Arthur. 1989. *The Jews in America: Four Centuries of an Uneasy Encounter: A History*. New York: Simon and Schuster.

Holtz, Barry. 1992. *Back to the Sources: Reading the Classic Jewish Texts*. New York: Simon & Schuster.

_____. 2004. *Textual Knowledge: Teaching the Bible in Theory and Practice*. New York: The Jewish Theological Seminary of America.

Horenczyk, G. August 1990. "Research on Adult Jewish Education," *Beinei-nu, Newsletter of the Florence Melton Adult Mini-School*, II:1.
Horowitz, Bethamie. 2003. "Connections and Journeys." New York: UJA/Federation.
Hutchins, Robert M. 1968. *The Learning Society*. New York: Frederick A. Praeger.
Janowsky, Oscar. 1965. "Adult Jewish Education—Analysis of a Survey," *Jewish Education*, 36:1.
Kail, Robert V. and John C. Cavanaugh. 2010. *Human Development: A Life-Span View*, 5th ed. Belmont, CA: Wadsworth Cengage Learning.
Kaplan, Mordecai M. 1948. *The Future of the American Jew*. New York: Random House.
Katz, Betsy Dolgin. Summer 1999. "Adult Jewish Learning—Ten Years of Returning: 1989-1999," *Agenda: Jewish Education*. JESNA, Issue 12.
_____. 2001. "Andragogy—The Art and Science of Transformative Adult Education in Congregations," *Proceedings of the 2001 Convention*.
_____. Spring 1990. "Diversity in Adult Jewish Education," *Pedagogic Reporter*, 41:2.
_____. November 1978. "The Jewish Teacher Center: An Idea Whose Time Has Come," *Compass*.
Katz, B.D. and J. Mirvis. 1997. *Israel in Adult Education*. Jerusalem: Hebrew University Press.
Kelner, Shaul. 2010. *Tours that Bind: Diaspora, Pilgrimage and Israeli Birthright Tourism*. New York: New York University Press.
Keeney, Lorraine and Heidi Watts. July 2006. "Aged Wine for New Bottles: Teachers' Centers for the Twenty-First Century," Unpublished, Dolores Kohl Education Foundation.
Knowles, Malcolm. 1980. *Modern Practice of Adult Education: From Pedagogy to Andragogy*. Chicago, IL: Follett Publishing Company.
_____. 1984. *The Adult Learner: A Neglected Species*. Houston, TX: Gulf
_____, Elwood Holton III, Richard A. Swanson. 2005. *The Adult Learner*, 6th ed. London: Taylor and Francis.
Kozol, Jonathan. 1985. *Illiterate America*. New York: Random House.
Krasner, Jonathan D. 2011. *The Benderly Boys and American Jewish Education*. Boston: Brandeis University.
Lamm, Norman in Joseph Talushkin. 2006. *You Shall Be Holy: A Code of Jewish Ethics*. New York: Bell Tower.
Marcus, Jacob Rader. 1993. *United States Jewry, 1776-1985*, Vol. IV. Detroit, MI: Wayne State University Press.
McLoughlin, William. 1982. "Revivals, Awakenings and Reform," *Journal of American History* 69.
Mendelsohn, Martin 2004. *The Guide to Franchising*, 7th ed. London: Thomson Learning.

Merriam, Sharan B., Rosemary S. Caffarella, Lisa M. Baumgartner. 2007. *Learning in Adulthood*. San Francisco: John Wiley & Sons, Inc.

Mezirow, Jack. 1990. *Fostering Critical Reflection in Adulthood: A Guide to Transformative and Emancipatory Learning*. San Francisco: Jossey-Bass.

National Center for Research on Teacher Learning, Director: Mary Kennedy. 1992. "Findings on Learning to Teach." East Lansing, MI: Michigan State University Press.

National Conference on Jewish Women and Men Report. 1974. Jewish Women's Archives. www.jwa.org/feminism

National Jewish Population Survey, 2000-2001. 2003. New York: NJPS.

O'Brien, Kate. 2008. "The Florence Melton Adult Mini-School: Communicating Mission, Vision, and Culture in a Global Jewish Educational System." Unpublished. Davidson School, The Jewish Theological Seminary of America.

Palmer, Parker. 2007. *The Courage to Teach*. San Francisco: Jossey-Bass.

Pedagogic Reporter. January 1990. Jewish Education Services of North America.

Pilch, Judah, ed. 1969. *A History of Jewish Education in America*. New York: American Association of Jewish Education.

Pratt, Daniel. 1998. *Five Perspectives on Teaching in Adult and Higher Education*. Malabar, FL: Krieger.

Root, Wade Clark. 1993. *Generation of Seekers*. San Francisco: Harper.

Rosen, Mark I. 2006. "Jewish Engagement from Birth: A Blueprint for Outreach to First Time Parents." Waltham, MA: Maurice and Marilyn Cohen Center for Modern Jewish Studies.

Rosenzweig, Franz. 1955. *On Jewish Learning*. Madison, WI: University of Wisconsin Press.

Sarna, Jonathan D. 1995. *A Great Awakening*. New York: Council for Initiatives in Jewish Education.

———. 2004. *American Judaism*. New Haven: Yale University Press.

Schrage, B. 1998. "Working Paper for a national commission on Jewish Renaissance." Unpublished, Combined Jewish Philanthropies of Greater Boston.

Schuster, Diane Tickton. 2003. *Jewish Lives, Jewish Learning: Adult Jewish Learning in Theory and Practice*. New York: UAHC Press.

Schwab, Joseph J. August 1973. "The Practical 3: Translation into Curriculum." *School Review*. 81:4.

Shapiro, Edward S. 1992. *A Time for Healing: American Jewry Since World War II (The Jewish People in America Series*, Vol. 5). Baltimore: Johns Hopkins University Press.

Shulman, Lee S. February 1987. "Knowledge and Teaching: Foundations of the New Reform." *Harvard Educational Review*, 57:1.

Siegel, Richard, Michael Strassfeld, and Sharon Strassfeld. 1973. *The Jewish Catalogue*. Philadelphia: Jewish Publication Society.

Silberman, Charles. 1986. *A Certain People: American Jews And Their Lives Today*. New York: Simon and Schuster.

Singer B. 1974. "The Future-Focused Role-Image" in Alvin Toffler, *Learning for Tomorrow, The Role of the Future in Education*. New York: Random House.

Sklare, Marshall. 1972. *Conservative Judaism: An American Religious Movement*. New York: Schocken Books.

Starkman, Sandy. 2010. "Final Report: Lifelong Learning Task Force." Unpublished. Highland Park, IL: North Suburban Synagogue Beth El.

Taylor, Kathleen. 2000. *Learning as Transformation: Critical Perspectives on a Theory in Progress*. San Francisco: Jossey-Bass.

Wenger, Etienne, Richard McDermott, William M. Snyder. 2002. *Cultivating Communities of Practice*. Boston: Harvard Business School Press.

Wertheimer, J. 2008. *A Census of Jewish Supplementary Schools in the United States*. New York: Avi Chai Foundation.

_____, ed. 2011. *The New Jewish Leaders: Reshaping the American Jewish Landscape*. Waltham, MA: Brandeis University Press.

CPSIA information can be obtained at www.ICGtesting.com
Printed in the USA
BVOW010542230312

285894BV00001B/8/P